FIRST WORLD WAR UNIFORMS

Lives, Logistics, and Legacy in
British Army Uniform Production
1914–1918

Catherine Price-Rowe

PEN & SWORD
ARCHAEOLOGY

First published in Great Britain in 2018 by
Pen & Sword Archaeology
An imprint of
Pen & Sword Books Ltd
Yorkshire - Philadelphia

ISBN 978 1 47383 389 0

Typeset by Aura Technology and Software Services, India
Printed and bound in India
By Replika Press Pvt. Ltd.

Pen & Sword Books Ltd incorporates the Imprints of Pen & Sword Books Archaeology, Atlas, Aviation, Battleground, Discovery, Family History, History, Maritime, Military, Naval, Politics, Railways, Select, Transport, True Crime, Fiction, Frontline Books, Leo Cooper, Praetorian Press, Seaforth Publishing, Wharncliffe and White Owl.

For a complete list of Pen & Sword titles please contact
PEN & SWORD BOOKS LIMITED
47 Church Street, Barnsley, South Yorkshire, S70 2AS, England
E-mail: enquiries@pen-and-sword.co.uk
Website: www.pen-and-sword.co.uk

or

PEN AND SWORD BOOKS
1950 Lawrence Rd, Havertown, PA 19083, USA
E-mail: uspen-and-sword@casematepublishers.com
Website: www.penandswordbooks.com

Contents

Acknowledgements

I would like to firstly thank my editor, Professor Nick Saunders, who saw the potential in telling the story of uniform production. Giving me much needed advice and guidance, his encouragement and belief enabled me to write my first book. To tell a story is one thing, to write a book is quite another! At Pen and Sword, I would like to thank both Eloise Hanson and Heather Williams for their support and patience whilst writing the manuscript.

In undertaking the research for the book many thanks must go to all those who have contributed in bringing the story of uniform from an idea to realisation, both at home as well as in France and Belgium: Armley Mills Industrial Museum; Peter Tilley, Curator, Gieves and Hawkes Archives; The Stroudwater Textile Trust; Coldharbour Mill Museum; Richard Osgood; Barry Baxter; Veterans Affairs Canada; Bertin Deniverier, Trustee of Talbot House; Christine Pécourt, L' Amartinierre Courcelles-au-Bois; Guy Depootr, Behind the Lines Museum, Johan Regheere, Local Historian, Dominiek Dendooven, In-Flanders Field Museum; Royal Logistics Corps Museum, Deepcut Barracks; Keith Nickless; Ben Dorrington; Soren Hawkes, Passchendaele Prints; Commonwealth War Graves Commission; Dirk and Barbara Cardoen, Varlet Farm; Queens Own Royal West Kent Regiment Living History Group; Ashley Bellingham, Nicola Nash, Joint Casualty and Compassionate Centre; Coldharbour Mill Museum; and Gill Rushton, AW Hainsworth Ltd & Sons Ltd. If I have forgotten anyone from this list then I most sincerely apologise as I have endeavoured to acknowledge all the sources of my data, and have made every effort to trace all copyright information.

Special thanks must also go to our friend Nick Fear, 'Nick In Time', who unlocked the door to George's records by finding his second service number, without which we would never had known his story; Charles Booth, Soldiers Corner Historian Arnos Vale Cemetery, whose information and guidance helped find George's final resting place; and Rodney, Simon, Ben and Joseph Ulrich, friends and members of The Garrison Artillery Volunteers, who not only supported and encouraged me in my research, but also allowed Phil and I to 'gate-crash' their family holiday to France and Belgium (sorry Sarah and Wendy!).

To my husband Phil, whose never-ending support and encouragement has given me belief in my abilities. It was your passion for conflict archaeology that convinced me that my initial research into George and uniform construction would make a great story. Without your love, friendship, and patience I would never have finished this book – though by ending this book there is now NO excuse not to do the ironing!

Two very special people to me, my mum and dad, Ruth, and John Price. Dad I know you are no longer with us, but your passion, enthusiasm and knowledge of history continues in me. You always wanted to visit the battlefields of France and Belgium, and although we never physically went together, somehow it felt you were there by my side during my research trips. Mum, your skills, talent, and knowledge for sewing not only provided my sister and I with clothing when we were younger, but you also passed those skills on to me, enabling me to forge a business in which your guidance is still greatly appreciated. But most of all you have also allowed me to tell the story of your mother and grandfather and for that I am most grateful.

Lastly, to the lady who planted the seed in my mind some 20 years ago, Grandma Alice, we now know George's story; and finally, to George, I dedicate this book to you – I am proud to be your Great Granddaughter.

British Military Abbreviations & Acronyms

1902 PSD (ORs) – 1902 Pattern Service Dress (Other Ranks).

1907 PSD (ORs) – 1907 Pattern Service Dress (Other Ranks).

1908 PWIE – 1908 Pattern Web Infantry Equipment.

ADMS – Assistant Director of Medical Services.

AG – Assistant General.

AIF – Australian Imperial Force.

AMO – Army Medal Office.

AOD – Army Ordnance Department.

ASC – Army Service Corps.

BEF – British Expeditionary Force.

BCE – Before Christian Era.

BSO – Brigade Supply Officer.

BSSO – Brigade Senior Supply Officer.

COO – Chief Ordnance Officer.

COM – Controllers of Mines.

CWGC – Commonwealth War Graves Commission.

DAC – Director of Army Contracts.

DADOS – Deputy Assistant Director of Supplies.

DDOS – Deputy Director Ordnance Services.

DGAC – Director General of Army Clothing.

DGO – Director General of Ordnance.

DMS – Direct Moulded Sole.

DNA – Deoxyribonucleic Acid.

DOC – Director of Clothing.

DORM – Directorate of Raw Materials.

DOS – Director of Supplies.

DOST – Director of Sea Transport.

DOWTP – Directorate of Wool Textiles Production.

DPM – Disruptive Pattern Material.

DSO – Divisional Supply Officer.

EFC – Expeditionary Force Canteens.

FANY – First Aid Nursing Yeomanry.

GHQ – General Headquarters.

GS – General Service.

HRH – His Royal Highness.

IGC – Inspector General of Communications.

IOM – Inspector of Mines.

IWGC – Imperial War Graves Commission.

JCCC – Joint Casualty and Compassionate Centre.

KCB – Knight Commander of the Most Honourable Order of the Bath.

LG – Lewis Gunner.

L.of C – Line of Communication.

M1905 SD Cap – 1905 Pattern Service Dress Cap.

M1915 Winter Trench Cap – 1915 Pattern Winter Trench Cap or the '*Gor Blimey*'.

M1916 SD Trench Cap – 1916 Pattern Service Dress Trench Cap.

MFD – Military Forwarding Department.

MLO – Military Landing Officer.

MOM – Ministry of Munitions.

MM – Military Medal.

MTP – Multi–Terrain Pattern.

NCO – Non–Commissioned Officer.

OGL – Open Government Licence.

ORs – Other Ranks.

PSD – Pattern Service Dress.

PTSD – Post Traumatic Stress Disorder.

QAIMNS – Queen Alexandra's Imperial Military Nursing Service.

QMAAC – Queens Mary's Army Auxiliary Corps.

QM – Quartermaster.

QMG – Quartermaster General.

RACD – Royal Army Clothing Department.

RACF – Royal Army Clothing Factory.

RAF – Royal Air Force.

RAMC – Royal Army Medical Corps.

RFC – Royal Flying Corps.

RE – Royal Engineers.

RND – Royal Naval Division.

RSO – Railway Supply Officer.

RTO – Railway Transport Officer.

SBR – Small Box Respirator.

SD – Service Dress.

SGS – Surveyor General of Supplies.

SO – Supply Officer.

SS – Steam Ship.

SSO – Senior Supply Officer.

SWB – Silver War Badge.

UKNIWM – United Kingdom National Inventory of War Memorials.

VAD – Voluntary Aid Detachment.

WAAC – Women's Auxiliary Army Corps.

YMCA – Young Men's Christian Association.

Modern Conflict Archaeology

THE SERIES

Modern Conflict Archaeology is a new and interdisciplinary approach to the study of twentieth and twenty-first century conflicts. It focuses on the innumerable ways in which humans interact with, and are changed by the intense material realities of war. These can be traditional wars between nation states, civil wars, religious and ethnic conflicts, terrorism, and even proxy wars where hostilities have not been declared yet nevertheless exist. The material realities can be as small as a machine-gun, as intermediate as a war memorial or an aeroplane, or as large as a whole battle-zone landscape. As well as technologies, they can be more intimately personal – conflict-related photographs and diaries, films, uniforms, the war-maimed and 'the missing'. All are the consequences of conflict, as none would exist without it.

Modern Conflict Archaeology (MCA) is a handy title, but is really shorthand for a more powerful and hybrid agenda. It draws not only on modern scientific archaeology, but on the anthropology of material culture, landscape, and identity, as well as aspects of military and cultural history, geography, and museum, heritage, and tourism studies. All or some of these can inform different aspects of research, but none are overly privileged. The challenge posed by modern conflict demands a coherent, integrated, sensitized yet muscular response in order to capture as many different kinds of information and insight as possible by exploring the 'social lives' of war objects through the changing values and attitudes attached to them over time.

This series originates in this new engagement with modern conflict, and seeks to bring the extraordinary range of latest research to a passionate and informed general readership. The aim is to investigate and understand arguably the most powerful force to have shaped our world during the last century – modern industrialized conflict in its myriad shapes and guises, and in its enduring and volatile legacies.

THIS BOOK

It is rare that a subject concerning every soldier who fought in the First World War has so little presence in the vast literature of that conflict. The making, moving, wearing and repair of British Army uniforms is one of these subjects, and the focus of this extraordinary book by professional dressmaker Catherine Price-Rowe. It is a story driven by intellectual curiosity concerning her own profession (including making replica First World War uniforms), and evocatively focused by a search for her own great grandfather George Henry Ball who fought in the war. Appropriately, it skilfully interweaves decades of knowledge and insight into how cloth is made and tailored, with original research in Britain, Belgium and France concerning how uniforms travelled from factory to front, were repaired and recycled, and ultimately could cause mortal infection but also help retrieve the identities of 'the missing'.

This book is not about the symbolism of wearing clothing, but is rather what might be called a historical anthropology of making and distributing millions of uniforms for millions of men who had been gathered together from around the world to fight along the Western Front of France and Belgium between 1914 and 1918. In a philosophical sense, it is a book which goes to the heart of what material culture is in modern industrialised conflict – its relationships with technology, technique, and gendered bodies, and how it moves through geographical, social, and cultural space.

This was a war unlike any other before it, and required hitherto unimaginable quantities of uniforms and equipment to be made and transported as quickly, efficiently, and economically as possible. The challenges were unique. Not only were the numbers of items vast, but some, such as the gas mask, were unknown before the war, and had to be invented then refined, then refined again until they offered sufficient protection against a recently-developed and horrific weapon of mass destruction. The same was true for the steel helmet whose replacement of the soft cap was an urgent innovation to protect against shrapnel and high-explosive fragments and debris which fell from the sky in previously undreamt-of quantities.

Ironically for a battlefront characterised by trenches and stationary armies, it was the creation and perfection of behind-the-lines movement of supplies that was the real achievement of the Line-of-Communication system that Catherine so expertly describes and analyses in this book. Like veins in the body, an integrated series of roads, canals, rivers, and standard gauge and narrow gauge (Decauville) railways spread out from English Channel ports to connect with armies, hospitals, airfields, local industries, and the towns and cities of France and Belgium (and beyond) to keep the war going. Modern armies, like their predecessor's march on their stomachs, but require an ever-longer tail of supply. How this logistical marvel was forged from a standing start in August 1914 is just one of the remarkable stories told here.

One of the most astonishing inventions chronicled here is that of a system of salvage which helped the destruction of war pay for yet more destruction through the collection and recycling of old, damaged, abandoned, and lost clothing, armaments, and equipment. Even the useless had a use, every rag had a value, and every empty artillery shell could be refilled and used again. In a war of monumental wastage, very little was ultimately wasted.

By exploring these industrial sinews of war, Catherine allows us to see clearly for arguably the first time what has been invisible in plain view for a century – how the war worked on a daily basis, around the clock, and often to a meticulous timetable. She does so by drawing on her own experience, visiting obscure archives, rediscovering long-forgotten connections and insights, and conducting personal interviews. In this way, one of the Great War's least-known achievements is brought back to life, and given the prominence it deserves.

This is not a military history, but it is a history of how the British government, its people, and its military got to grips with waging a modern and unpredictable war. It complements the well-known stories of men and their regiments, their battles, their suffering, and their ultimate victory through its detailed account of how they obtained what they wore, what they carried, and what they lost and occasionally regained. It is a book which tells a century old story with a very modern message at its heart.

Nicholas J. Saunders, University of Bristol, March 2018

Introduction

Where It All Begins

When this story of this awful war comes to be written it will be found that women factory workers – as well as – men have done their bit. If they have not actually gone to the front and fought in the trenches, they have bravely and unselfishly helped to supply the sinews of war in the shape of uniform for the soldier's, without which no army could fight.[1]

This is a strange story, which begins at the end. I was always fascinated by my grandmother Alice's stories of 'make do and mend'. In some ways, this was not surprising, as sewing had been a commonplace in my family for at least five generations. It was natural therefore that dressmaking became a way to make a living. Alice also told me stories of her father, George Henry Ball's First World War experiences and this in turn led to family history becoming another of my life's passions. Combining sewing with a love of history, it seemed only a matter of time before I was creating replica uniforms, clothing, and costumes.

While examining an original First World War Service Dress (SD) Tunic (Jacket) belonging to my husband's Grandfather, I noted how cleverly it had been constructed and cut. Using it to reverse engineer a sewing pattern, I was astounded to see that although moth-eaten and worn, the body of the jacket had survived 100 years with pockets intact, all buttons and stripes attached, and none of the seams showing signs of wear and tear. It is rare to find a uniform dating to the First World War as many found in museum collections were made as sample garments and not battlefield wear.[2] I was intrigued by its construction: how did my great grandfather George receive his uniform? In four years of fighting where would he obtain a new one? Who made the uniform and who produced the cloth? How did the uniform get to the front? And where did George serve on the Western Front? Armed only with a copy of a family photograph of George in uniform, these questions and more began a journey of discovery – of family history, identity, and military clothing as a unique kind of twentieth century *matériel culture*.

Nearly nine million men and women served between 1914 and 1919,[3] and each one needed clothing. Total war creates a demand for uniforms, with civilians recruited now having to be clothed.[4] From 4 August 1914 to 31 March 1919 over 31 million SD Jackets, 28 million SD Trousers and 46 million pairs of boots were produced for the British Army alone.[5] Photographs of 'Tommy' emphasise the man, not the uniform which he wears. Few people today would consider how

George Henry Ball, stood on left, in uniform with two unidentified soldiers (Author's Collection).

and where that uniform was made – it seems invisible in plain view. Yet, over five million men in total served on the Western Front,[6] with tens of millions of items of kit issued here throughout the war. When this is multiplied by the number of other fronts, the total figure for items of soldiers' kit becomes astronomical. While innumerable books and television programmes chronicle the sheer scale of the First World War as the first globalised industrial conflict, there is a hidden history, a story which has not been told for a hundred years. This book is a chronicle of the extraordinary history of wartime production of uniforms and everything they represented for the women who made them, the men who wore them, and the industries they supported.

Worn by all ranks of men in the British Army, Royal Naval Division (RND) and Royal Flying Corps (RFC),[7] uniforms created an identity for the fighting forces, distinguished friend from foe and gave enlisted men respect and admiration from friends, family and society. At the same time as bestowing a sense of unity, a uniform also stripped away a soldier's personal identity and replaced it with a designated rank, and thereby turned a civilian into a fighting soldier. How ironic therefore that a century later the same uniform can now help bring the missing back to their families. In 2008, an archaeological team at St Yvon, Belgium, found the remains of an Australian infantry soldier, identified by remnants of his post-1915 British Empire webbing and khaki uniform.[8] Similarly, in 2009, archaeological excavations recovered 250 First World War servicemen and their associated artefacts from Fromelles, in northern France.[9] With the clear majority of the remains holding an intimate relationship with associated artefacts including uniforms, boots, buttons, buckles and badges, the combination of artefact analysis and ultimately DNA[10] has helped give a name to 144 of the 250.

Today DNA can help identify the missing, but during battlefield clearances and reburials of the inter-war years' identification relied solely on uniform, identity discs (if present), personal items of kit (inscribed with name or service number) or personal papers. The colour of cloth or type of hob nail in a boot could identify nationality, a shoulder title, and a button or badge might reveal regiment and/or rank. However, the hope was always that inside a jacket pocket was a diary, letter or article bearing the soldier's personal details. The khaki uniform that initially stripped men of their individuality while alive, ironically helps to re-establish their identity a hundred years after their death.

Given the right environment, cloth, and leather can stand the test of time, whether housed in a museum,[11] or wrapped and stored in a loft or garage. Fabric can also survive in extraordinary conditions, in some cases for thousands of years, such as the Tarkhan Dress, confirmed in 2016 as the world's oldest woven garment dating to the late fourth-millennium BCE.[12] Similarly, fragments of wool, silk and leather recovered from the Tudor warship Mary Rose have survived since 1545, buried deep in silt underwater in the Solent[13]. The mechanical processes of weaving cloth and sewing clothes are timeless, with only advances in technology speeding up the process - the method is identical. Cloth is tangible and tactile. The 'damp dog' smell of wet wool is the same today as it was in the trenches of the First World War. Buttons, stripes, badges and uniforms have sometimes survived, passed down in families as treasured or accidental heirlooms.

'Matériel Culture'

> The objects of war represent memories, ideals and emotions for the people who created them, for those family members or museums who inherit them, and for the archaeologists who excavate them. These objects recall the First World War in separate ways – they are inescapably real, and can be touched, handled, and sometimes smelt. They can transport us back some 90 years in an instant, and in a personal way more than any number of books about the war that we may read. These objects are three-dimensional memories of the war, fragments of a world long gone, yet from which our modern world is built.[14]

Described as 'matériel culture,' objects have meanings and evoke memories which may have nothing to do with their original design or purpose. Uniforms, however, while they are a definitive kind of war-related matériel culture, can become a means to discover the story behind the man in the photograph, the name in a diary, or the number in a service record. We all own an object treasured because of its associations, and its ability to link the past and present. Sewing machines are especially potent in this respect. While made of metal with cogs and gears and designed to do a specific job, when put on display they elicit very human stories from those who see them - people recount memories and tales of a favourite garment lovingly made by a long-departed family member. Many sewing machines are kept purely for sentimental reasons – in a sense for their ability to 'make' memories. The same can be said about the soldier's uniform, pieces of cloth sewn together with linen thread that has buttons to secure it – a singular item, but one of millions. Put it on a man however and both the man and the uniform can tell a story, from the cloth weavers, the garment sewers, and the tailors, to the soldier who lived, fought, died or survived while wearing it, leaving an imprint on history.

George Henry Ball MM

If a uniform is personal to the man, then it seems appropriate to tell this story through my great grandfather, Sergeant George Henry Ball MM. Anchoring the sprawling and anonymous story of uniform production, logistics and supply to an individual can't help but limit the focus of this book to, in this case, the infantry and Royal Engineers (RE). Nevertheless, in exploring the clothing of a British 'Tommy' Atkins we reveal the web of intriguing and long-forgotten stories that lie behind the production, distribution, and fate of the materials that made the British Army.

George and Lily Ball (Author's Collection).

Alice Ball, circa 1911-1912 (Author's Collection).

George was born in Bedminster, Bristol, in December 1884, and it was here that he met and married Lillian Ball (nee. Taylor) in 1906. They had three children Dora (b.1906), Alice (b.1908, my Grandmother) and Frank (b.1909). Bedminster was home to many trades and industries, the most prominent of which was coal mining, and this was George's occupation. 1911 turned George's life upside down, when, on Whit Monday and while playing with their children, Lillian collapsed and died – she was 24, and the children were 5 years, 3 years and 18 months old respectively. George struggled to cope on his own, and eventually Alice was taken in by friends,[15] Mr and Mrs Jones, whilst Dora and Frank stayed at home.

On 24 March 1913 George married Rosina Legg and moved to Pearl Street in Bedminster. Industrial unrest was commonplace, and the Bedminster coal miners faced uncertainty as 1913 rolled into 1914, and the area's mines began to close. George worked in South Liberty Lane Colliery but as European tensions rose throughout the summer a new world was being created – one that would change George's life forever.

Call to Arms – The Makeup of the British Army 1914 - 1915

Why George enlisted we shall never know. As a 30-year-old married man with children and as a Coal Face Examiner, both the War Office and the Bristol Citizens Recruiting Committee regarded him as exempt from joining up. That said, the regular army wage was probably better than the pay he received at the colliery, and besides which the mines were closing. George's four brothers were all miners and they may have decided to join up together as their patriotic duty. Whatever the reason, hundreds of thousands of men like George signed up and by the middle of September some 500,000 men had volunteered, increasing to 1,000,000 by February 1915.[16] Prior to Britain's declaration of war on 4 August 1914, the Infantry component of the British Army consisted of several different elements:

The Regulars: These men were full time professional soldiers who enlisted for a period of seven-years' service. They could be posted at home or overseas in various garrisons around the world. At the outbreak of war there were 247,432[17] Regulars in the British Army. The War Office was entirely responsible for providing their uniform, equipment, accommodation, and food.

The Territorials: These were part-time soldiers, men with full time civilian occupations. Created in 1908 the Territorials were made up from the old local Militia and Yeomanry. Recruitment stayed local and was controlled by the County Associations who were responsible for providing uniform, equipment and accommodation. Training on drill nights once or twice a week, regiments would come together and train in large annual summer camps. Becoming full-time soldiers in time of war, the Territorials could be posted anywhere in Britain on Home Defence, with overseas service optional. At the outbreak of war around 268,000 officers and men[18] were training in summer camps, with 17,000 having previously signed the 'Imperial Service' Obligation' for service overseas. Issued with a silver badge marked 'Imperial Service' denoting they had volunteered for overseas service, immediately prior to the outbreak of war many Territorial battalions were mobilised and sent overseas to relieve the regulars in various garrisons.

Army Reserve: These were regular soldiers who on completion of their service were placed on the Army Reserve list for five years. They could be called back to the Regulars in a state of national emergency and received a weekly payment in return for twelve days' refresher training each year.[19] All uniform and equipment would be provided by the battalions that called them up.

Special Reserve: These men joined for six years with an option to extend and consisted of individuals wanting to experience Army life without any commitment. After initial training of six months, a Special Reservist would return to his civilian occupation, undertaking four weeks training each year. There were one hundred of these battalions in August 1914 with around 64,000 men enlisted.[20]

National Reserve: These men had previous military experience but fell outside the Army Reserve obligation. They numbered around 215,000 in August 1914, and helped guard important locations and railways in Britain at the outbreak of war.[21]

Battalions of Regulars and Territorials made up a regiment or a corps and typically consisted of four battalions, 1st and 2nd comprising of regulars rotating between home and overseas service, the 3rd, a Reserve battalion, usually ran the administration, whilst the 4th was a Territorial battalion. At the outbreak of war Territorials and Reservist battalions were immediately mobilised and some sent overseas to relieve regulars posted in garrisons around the world. The remaining Regular, Territorial and Reservist battalions based in Britain became the British Expeditionary Force (BEF).

A single battalion consisted of around 29 officers and 977 other ranks[22] subdivided into four companies (A, B, C & D). Four battalions (from various regiments) combined to form a single brigade (5,000 men). Three brigades with support units, such as Army Service Corps (ASC), became a division of about 20,000 men with two divisions making a corps. Two corps and its support units became an army and it was two armies that made up the BEF sent to France and Belgium in August 1914. A Third Army was later formed in France on 31 August,[23] drawn from men who had enlisted into what very quickly became known as 'Kitchener's New Army'.[24]

Imperial 'Service' Battalions[25]*:* In Bristol, as with many cities across the country, a Citizen Recruiting Committee was formed to encourage enlistment. The response was huge and the existing Army Enlistment Centre became too small to accommodate the number of men wanting to join, so a larger venue was needed and the Colston Hall, a large city centre concert venue, was used as an alternative. Opened on 14 August, around this same time men such as Lord Derby[26] and Major General Sir Henry Rawlinson recognised that men would be prepared to fight if their work colleagues and friends could all stay together.

Soon battalions of men from workplaces and cities were formed, Bristol being no exception. As the number of men continued to grow they wanted to join a Bristol battalion and so on 27 August 1914 the War Office contacted the Bristol Citizens Recruiting Committee stating in the telegram received 'Lord Kitchener thanks you for your valuable help offered by Bristol. He sanctions your scheme of enrolment of names and formation of a battalion'.[27] In communicating with the General commanding the Southern Command area, Bristol's own 'Pals' or Locally Raised Service Battalions came into existence on 4 September 1914. From across the country these battalions would form part of the Fifth New Army (K5) on 10 December 1914.[28] To distinguish the local battalions from the service battalions of the new armies, an additional word identifying its city or area was included in its name. Following on in numerical order from the regimental number they were attached to, the War Office assigned the name and regimental number of 12th (Imperial Service) Battalion (Bristol) Gloucestershire Regiment.

More commonly shortened to 12th Service Battalion Gloucestershire Regiment, the battalion became fondly known as 'Bristol's Own' and needed around 1,000 men to come up to strength. Posters and adverts soon appeared in and around the city from the first day of Bristol's Own inception, detailing the following conditions of enlistment:

> To the Mercantile and Professional Young Men of the City of Bristol and Neighbourhood. Lord Kitchener has sanctioned the enrolment of names of single men of the City of Bristol and neighbourhood between the ages of 19 and 35, who are willing to join the Colours for the duration of the war. The intention is to form a battalion of Mercantile and Professional young men. Conditions… You agree to serve for the period the war lasts. You agree to serve at home or abroad as may be required. Kit to be found and payment made by the Government at the usual rate. The battalion is to be an Infantry one and will constitute a unit of the Regular Army, seven days' notice of calling up will be given.[29]

Within a fortnight of the Bristol Citizens Recruiting Committee appeal for volunteers, 500 men had enlisted, with one complete company (about 250 men) medically examined, attested, and enrolled within a week.[30] With the Colston Hall

The first parade of Bristol's Own at the Artillery Headquarters, Whiteladies Road,
Bristol (12th (Service) Battalion Gloucestershire Regiment "Bristol's Own"
Souvenir. *Anon: 1915 - Author's Collection).*

now doubling up as a temporary headquarters as well as recruiting centre, the
new recruits began their transformation into soldiers. Limiting the type of men
accepted to Mercantile and Professional could be perceived as an elitist notion,
but there was a sound reason behind it. An army will not succeed if the support
and supply for it is non-existent and Lord Kitchener knew this. Men working in
such industries as mining, engineering, manufacture, shipyard, and agriculture
(Bristol had them all), were essential workers compared with occupations
such as teachers, lawyers, shopkeepers, shop assistants, office workers and
bankers. A directive from the War Office had been issued to this effect and in
Bristol's case the committee took it literally. Despite the stipulations and to the
consternation of the recruiting committee, hundreds of men from the working
class ignored the conditions and signed up, and anyway a Recruiting Sergeant
was not going to turn anyone away.

The Lord Mayor of Bristol acknowledged the diversity of the men of the battalion
in a speech given at its first parade at the Colston Hall on 21 September 1914:

We are indebted to all classes of the community for the splendid response
to recruiting appeals. It is most encouraging to witness the labourer and the
working men, who made no special claims to birth or education, coming
forward and offering their lives for their country. In the Bristol battalion are

men drawn from the professional and commercial classes, men of education, and varied ability, whose services in this great cause will be invaluable.[31]

A patriotic fervour and a need for adventure may have driven some to enlist but not all'.[32] Reasons for enlisting can never wholly be answered, as in the case of George, but a closer look at an individual's circumstances can reveal more than just doing their bit. Britain saw prosperity during 1914 but it also saw discontented workers and strikes. Bristol had its share of both. The Army could be an attractive prospect, not only bringing the adventure and excitement missing from some lives, but providing clothing, food, accommodation, and a wage greater than could be earned in civilian life. For married men, a separation allowance, new scales of which had been introduced on 1 October 1914[33] would be paid to wives and children. However, for men across the country, persuasion, propaganda, peer pressure and friendship quite often made the decision easier, or the present of a white feather suggesting cowardice gave them no choice. After all no one could really foresee the war lasting four years.

Supply Pressures

Whether for financial security for his family or as a patriotic sense of duty, the true driving force behind George's enlistment is pure speculation. Like so many other family histories, the story will forever be incomplete. What is known however is that this extraordinary and unexpected response by the Nation's men created a huge logistical and supply problem as there was only a small reserve stock of uniform and equipment. This was compounded by administrative confusion, as responsibility for these supplies fell between the War Office, Territorial County Associations and locally raised battalions. Men in the Regulars, Kitchener's Army, and Reservists had their uniform provided by the War Office. The Territorial County Associations provided uniforms to both the Territorial and National Reserve battalions. Locally raised City, Pals, and Bantams battalions[34] had to raise money to buy their own uniform and equipment. They also needed to find suitable accommodation as well as feed and train the men until the War Office officially took charge, in many instances well into 1915.

With the Territorial County Associations, locally raised battalions, and the War Office now vying for the same goods, shortages were inevitable and competition in purchasing existing stocks locally, direct from manufacturers, or from middlemen drove up prices. Demand outstripped supply, and prices of raw materials, cloth and uniform continued to climb. A shipment of jerseys was bought by a firm of merchants at 3s.11d [£11.68[35]] and offered to the War Office at 4s.5d [£13.17]. The offer was refused as the price was too high, whereupon the jerseys were then sold to a provincial draper at 4s.11 [£14.67]. The draper then resold a sizable quantity of it to various Army Commands at 5s.10d [£17.40], with the remaining items sold to a firm of Army Contractors at 5s.9d [£17.15]. They in turn sold the jerseys to a Territorial Force Association for 6s.6d [£19.38],[36] on an overall mark-up of 2s.7d [£7.70].

Some of the men of Britain who had answered the call were now looking literally like a rag tag army. Men trained in civilian suits, old scarlet tunics familiar to a Victorian soldier, and Kitchener's Blues' - a stop gap uniform made from existing blue cloth. Uniform production had to increase and fast. Now it was time for the textile and clothing industries of Britain to answer the call to arms.

Chapter 1
Where's My Uniform?

For centuries soldiers had marched into battle in brightly coloured uniforms to help identify friend from foe. As the nineteenth century progressed, it became clear that camouflage was becoming an ever more crucial factor. In Peshawar in 1846 the Corps of Guards were ordered to take white cotton cloth to the river bank, soak it in water then rub with mud to blend in with the local plains landscape.[1] In 1848, Lieutenant William Hodson, Second in Command and Adjutant to the British Indian Army regiment the Corps of Guides requested a drab coloured uniform for the men to 'make them invisible in a land of dust'.[2] Khaki was born and its name was believed to come from the Hindu and Urdu word for something which was 'earth' or 'dust' coloured.[3] Made from cotton drill, the uniform was ideal for tropical conditions but unsuitable in other climates, as the Boer War of 1899 - 1902 highlighted. Its inadequacies in the cold nights encountered on the South African plains meant a thicker, warmer fabric was needed.

'Rank and File' Service Dress

At the start of the twentieth century, all aspects of the British Army needed to modernise and uniforms were no exception. A single camouflaging colour for a universal uniform was conceived from bringing together the diverse colours of regiments and corps. Made from dyed thick wool serge fabric, the new style uniform debuted in 1901, with the approved pattern (design) 'sealed'[4] a year later and known as the 1902 Pattern Service Dress (Other Ranks (ORs)).[5] Consisting of a tunic (jacket) and trousers, its manufacture was considered too expensive due to the coloured piping used to distinguish different regiments, corps, and services. The piping was removed and the revised design was approved and 'sealed' as the 1907 Pattern Service Dress (ORs).[6] The only regiments to retain any trace of colour in the new pattern SD were Scottish, where the kilt tartan of the regiment was worn in conjunction with a khaki tunic. No matter their rank, everyone in the British Army now wore khaki[7] in their daily work.

In 1914, the 1907 Pattern Service Dress was only seven years old and was supplied up to the outbreak of war. Although both 'rank and file' as well as officers wore khaki, the cloth was completely different, with the former made of a coarser wool that produced a strong, thick, durable cloth called 'serge', and the latter of a higher quality 'Merino' wool cloth called 'Barathea' that was a thinner and finer weave.

Other Ranks SD Tunic and Trousers (dismounted). Accurate Replica (Author's Collection).

Service Dress Tunic (ORs): These were worn by all non-commissioned ranks of the army regardless of regiment or corps, as a single-breasted jacket that fastened up to the neck, ending in a high collar which rolled back. Brass monogrammed buttons known as General Service (GS) buttons had the Kings Crown embossed on them and were 1½" (3.81cm) in diameter. Five of these secured the jacket with two hook and eyes at the collar to hold it together. Two pleated pockets were positioned on the chest, with smaller ¾" (1.90 cm) GS buttons securing the flaps to the pockets. These smaller buttons also secured the flaps on the larger pockets that were positioned on the lower section of the jacket below the waistline. To give a smart look to the jacket, the lower pockets were on the inside with the flaps on the outside. Inside on the front right side, a small pocket was created that was large enough to carry a soldier's field dressing.

Regimental brass shoulder titles were affixed to the shoulder epaulettes which were attached to the jacket with small GS buttons. Shoulder patches extended from the shoulder seam down the front ending just above the chest pockets, offering added protection against wear and tear when a rifle was used as well as webbing straps. The upper right sleeve between the elbow and shoulder bore the rank of the soldier, a Private wore nothing while chevrons made from cloth denoted non-commissioned officer (NCO) ranks. George was promoted several times throughout the war, first to Lance Corporal with a single chevron, then to Corporal with two chevrons before ending up as a Sergeant with three chevrons. For rank badges above that of Sergeant, there was a variety of crowns and laurels of which the highest non-commissioned rank was a Warrant Officer Class One. Furthermore, in some instances divisional insignia badges of cloth were worn on the sleeves above the rank; while on the left sleeve between the cuff and elbow, soldiers that had a specialist skilled job, such as a Farrier or Lewis Gunner, often wore a trade badge - in the case of a farrier a brass horseshoe and the Lewis gunner a brass 'LG' surrounded by a laurel wreath.

Later in 1916,[8] a two inch (5.08cm) vertical gold-colour metal 'wound stripe' was introduced for soldiers wounded since 4 August 1914, and worn on the left sleeve between cuff and elbow.[9] In addition, a Good Conduct Stripe was introduced as an inverted chevron for between two and four years 'good service' (i.e. no disciplinary record). In early 1918[10] 'Overseas Service' chevrons appeared and were worn on the right sleeve between the cuff and elbow. Consisting of small chevrons pointing towards the elbow, a red chevron indicated service on or before 31 December 1914, and a blue chevron for each full year (continuous or non-continuous) served overseas thereafter. Except for the wound stripe, all badges were made from a khaki cloth background embroidered with the design regardless of what they signified.

Service Dress Trousers (ORs): Sometimes described as dismounted trousers, SD Trousers were made from the same khaki serge cloth as the jacket and were designed to have a high waist with a V-shaped back which had changed little from the Victorian era.[11] They were fastened at the front by brass buttons in a concealed fly - the ½" (1.27cm) four-holed buttons punched from brass sheets, and usually had the manufacturers name embossed on the rim. Soldiers in mounted regiments, such as Royal Horse Artillery, wore beige-brown riding breeches made from a thick wool cloth known as 'Bedford Cord', with leather patches reinforcing the inside leg against wear on the saddle. Scottish kilted regiments wore kilts depicting their

'V' Shaped back of SD trousers with braces attached. Accurate Replica (Author's Collection).

regimental tartan, but instead of a standard khaki SD Tunic their jacket had the front hem edges cut back and rounded to allow for the wearing of a sporran. Operationally, khaki kilt covers were issued and worn over the kilt to provide camouflage.

Service Dress Cap: A stiff cap (SD Model 1905) was issued decorated with the soldier's brass regiment or corps badge in the centre above the peak and adjustable leather chin-strap. Made from khaki serge with a stiff peak and a crown held rigid by wire, the cap sat high on the head and gave little protection to the ears or back of the head in freezing weather.

During the winter of 1914 - 1915, a new cap was issued, to help alleviate manufacturing issues and protect against the cold. Made from flannel-lined khaki serge, but soft without a stiff peak or rigid crown, it was known as the Winter Trench Cap (Cap, Winter SD Model 1914),[12] and had side-flaps to cover the ears in cold weather, and was secured by an adjustable chin strap. In fine weather, when not required, the flaps were raised up and secured over the crown of the cap. An added strip of fabric at the back could be folded down to cover the neck during wintry weather. The cap was floppy and popular with the troops due to its relaxed look and functionality, though its unmilitary appearance was not universally welcome. It soon acquired the nickname *'Gor Blimey'*, an exclamation ('God Blind Me!) allegedly uttered by seasoned soldiers and sergeants upon seeing it.[13]

A 'soft' Trench Cap (Cap, Soft, SD Model 1916[14]) based on the original stiff-peaked SD cap was introduced in early 1916. Removal of the wire in the crown and the stiff peak made the cap softer and was easier and cheaper to manufacture than the original Model 1905 SD cap. In December 1917, the standard soft 'trench' cap was revised, being made this time from a waterproof cotton material (gabardine) (Cap, Soft, SD Model 1916 / 1917).[15]

Stiff Cap   **'Gor Blimey'**   **Soft Cap**

Cap SD Model 1905, Winter SD Model 1914 (commonly known as the 'Gor Blimey'), and Cap Soft SD Model 1916 (From Tradition to Protection – British Military Headgear in the First World War. Anon: 2015 - By kind permission of Philippe Oosterlinck Collection, In-Flanders Field Museum, Ypres).

Cap Badge / Shoulder Titles: The cap badge identified the regiment or corps[16] the soldier belonged too, and was worn in the centre of the headgear, with the shoulder titles mounted on the SD jacket epaulets. Predominately die struck (stamped or pressed out using a die), the cap badge was usually made of all brass, all nickel (white metal) or a combination of brass and nickel (bi-metal), whereas the shoulder titles were made of brass.

Cap badge and shoulder titles for the Gloucestershire Regiment and Royal Engineers (Author's Collection).

Shirt: Issued to soldiers since the mid-nineteenth century, the long-sleeved 'greyback' shirt was made from wool blue-grey flannel with a bib style buttoned half front that fastened to the neck in the same style of four-holed brass buttons as worn on the trouser. A 'grandad' collar[17] enabled the shirt to lay flat under the high collar of the jacket and a small cuff with a button placket secured the sleeve at the wrist. With a strip of white cotton affixed to the front for the soldier to write his service number on, it was cut long so that it would stay tucked into the trouser as the soldier carried out his daily duties.

When the shortage of uniform items took hold, the Army's Contracts Department was forced to buy civilian stocks of the same style of collarless shirt, making it common to see soldiers on parade in both military issued grey flannel as well as civilian white cotton pin stripe shirts.

Grey Flannel shirt. Accurate Replica (Author's Collection).

Puttees and B5 Ammunition Boot. Accurate Replica (Author's Collection).

Ammunition Boot and Puttees: These are stereotypical items of uniform depicted in most images of 'Tommy,' but there was a sound rationale behind the short boot and puttee. Worn with short ankle-high brown/black[18] B5 ammunition boots,[19] not only did the puttee cover the gap between the top of the boot and trouser, thus preventing dirt and stones from entering the boot, but it also gave valuable support to the calves and legs when marching long distances. However, puttees needed to be worn correctly. The technique was to wind them tight enough as to not slip down, but not so tight that they restricted circulation; a factor recollected by Fred Wood who recalled the attempts of his fellow soldiers to tie them neatly: 'Some chaps had them tied from ankles, others wound them round and round their calves like bandages. We were saved by an older man who had served in the Boer War, who showed us the trick…'[20]

The direction of the puttee wind varied too. Mounted regiments, such as the Royal Field Artillery, wound their puttees from knee to ankle with the knot of the binding tape on the outside of the leg, which prevented them from coming undone when rubbed against the saddle. Unmounted, such as infantry regiments, wound their puttees from ankle to knee, with the binding tape on the inside leg. This classic but simple difference gives a way of identifying whether a soldier was mounted or unmounted in old photographs.

Personal Equipment (webbing): Several types of webbing were in use during the First World War, with Kitchener's New Armies typically issued with the 1914 Pattern leather equipment, and regular and territorial soldiers the canvas 1908 Pattern Web Infantry Equipment (1908PWIE). Designed in 1906 by Major Burrowes of the Royal Irish Fusiliers in collaboration with the Mills Web Equipment Company, the 1908PWIE consisted of a waist belt, cartridge carriers (pair), valise, haversack, brace straps (pair), entrenching tool and cover, helve (entrenching tool handle) and carrier, water bottle and carrier.[21]

Exchanging the leather equipment whenever possible for the more durable canvas webbing,[22] the 1908PWIE was hugely successful and continued in service for 30 years until being replaced prior to the Second World War with the 1937 Pattern Web Infantry Equipment system.

Officers' Uniform

Officers uniforms were redesigned in 1902 and continued to be modified until the 1912 pattern was adopted. Made of a khaki serge wool but of a finer higher quality such as 'Garberdine', 'Whipcord' or 'Barathea', the lighter Garberdine was made from cotton yarn, whereas corded cotton was the basis for Whipcord making it similar in appearance to a fine needle cord fabric. Barathea was the most expensive of the three as here wool was blended with cotton or silk, making it warm and hardwearing and as such the preferred choice.

Tunic: An officer's tunic had two breast pockets with a central pleat and shaped pocket flaps secured with brass buttons. Two large expanding pockets were positioned on the outside of the lower section of the jacket. Two more pocket flaps covered the tops of these and were secured with brass buttons. These buttons and the four buttons that secured the front of the jacket were regimental or GS pattern and were the same size as those worn by rank and file. The collar was of an open neck lapel style and the tunic was worn with a shirt and tie. On each lapel of the collar sat regimental badges (miniature variants of the regimental cap badge often referred to as 'collar dogs'). Sleeves had what was known as 'false cuffs' made up of braid. At the sleeve hem on the front inside edge, braid was used to create a space where cloth crowns and stars known as 'pips' were sewn. Another braid ran around the

Officer in full SD with Sam Browne belt (Author' Collection).

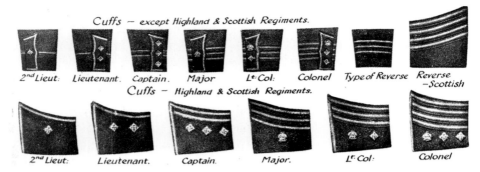

*Illustrations of officer's rank cuff decoration (***The Cutter's Practical Guide to British Military Service Uniforms.** *Anon: 1914 - Author's Collection).*

sleeve, parallel to the hem. This combination of pips, crowns and braid stripe denoted the rank of the officer.

Most tunics were fully or partially lined and could range from cotton drill at the lower price spectrum to silk at the highest. 'Rayon' was also used for lining,[23] though that fabric name appeared just after the war and was called 'viscose - viscose rayon'[24] during the conflict. Commonly known as 'artificial silk', by the outbreak of war viscose was already an established cloth and was a popular choice of lining for both officers' uniforms as well as the civilian clothing trade, though silk remained the preferred fabric for those who could afford it.

These elements were distinctive enough to identify officers as a preferred target for enemy snipers, so to counter this, many officers requested their tailors to move away from the traditional tunic design and instead produce SD jackets in the same pattern as the 'rank and file'.[25] Accepting this variation, the Royal Army Clothing Factory made available to officers' tailors early 1915[26] pattern draft instructions and measurements that allowed the creation of a 'National Guard' sewing pattern that could be used to form the basis for an officers' SD jacket design.

Breeches: Officers' breeches were a combination of the traditional Jodhpur worn in India and the British civilian breeches (knickerbocker) and pantaloons, cut wide over the thigh for free movement when in the saddle. By August 1914, the style of breeches and pantaloons varied according to manufacturer.

Breeches were usually made from Bedford cord with thick leather patches sewn on the inside thigh to add protection if the officer was mounted. They stopped just below the knee where buttons and lacings were used to fasten around the leg. The back waist was cut high which helped to protect the kidneys from the cold or heat. Finally, a button fly front secured the trousers at the waist and two pockets sat just below the waistline.[27]

Cap: Known also as a 'Forage Cap', the standard officers' SD Cap was introduced in 1900 and had a peaked front and stiff crown (Officer SD Cap Model 1902).[28] Made from Whipcord or Garberdine, the colour of the cloth used for the cap changed colour from dark blue to khaki in 1902. Waterproofing the yarn before the fabric was woven, unlike its rank and file equivalent, the officers' SD cap could be lined with a quilted layer or a single layer of silk or viscose. Above the peak sat a leather chin strap and regimental cap badge. Just as with rank and file, as the war progressed a cap was needed that was easier and cheaper to manufacture, and so a softer variation without the wire stiffening and stiff peak was quickly developed.[29]

Shirt: The officers' shirt was single-breasted and long-sleeved with two breast pockets and attached collar made of khaki brown/green cotton. Worn with a necktie of similar colour and fabric, photographs of officers often show them wearing a collar pin that passes underneath the knot of a necktie to hold the two ends of the shirt collar together.

Boots and Puttees: For officers, as for rank and file, short boots were often worn with puttees or with leather 'leggings' (gaiters) if the officer was mounted. There seems, however, to be a variety of boot and puttee combinations depicted in wartime photos, so these items cannot be relied upon as evidence of an officer's regiment or corps (i.e. whether mounted or infantry). The Field boot was very popular, it was made of leather and worn knee length rather like a riding boot. Specification on style did not exist, they just needed to be practical, tough, hardwearing, and made from brown leather.

Puttees were made from a better-quality khaki serge to those of the rank and file, with 'Foxes' puttees being a popular choice. Leather gaiters came in a variety of shapes and styles and could be fastened with straps and buckles, buttons, and laces.

Officer's boots (By kind permission of Gieves & Hawkes Archives, No.1 Savile Row, London W1 - Copyright Gieves & Hawkes Archives).

'Sam Browne' Belt: This was a brown leather belt with a strap worn across the body, and was first designed in 1852 by Sam Browne, an officer in the Indian Army. One of the only parts of an officer's uniform to survive the redesign of 1902, on active service the modified Sam Browne had a pistol holster attached, whilst an optional second strap could be added turning it into the officer's equivalent to the 1908PWIE as carried by rank and file.

A 'New Army'

Before the 'shell scandal' of Spring 1915 when the lack of shells and ammunition supplied to the front reached crisis levels, there was the 'uniform dilemma' of Autumn 1914. Many new soldiers and reservists had to wait for their uniform which added to a despondency and frustration. A Reserve battalion, 4th Company Devon National Reserves, made their feelings known in an unusual way. Novelty comic postcards were printed depicting the lack of uniform but the 4th Devon Reserves took one of these and put their own twist on it to make a point. The postcard depicts a crying baby with a dummy round its neck and wearing only a pair of socks. Written in ink on the top of the card is 'On active service 10 weeks', with the original tag line altered to read 'Has anybody seen *our* uniform'. To make sure it had the greatest impact they sent it to 'The Right Hon Earl Kitchener KCB, The Secretary of State for War, War Office London'.[30] I discovered this postcard in miscellaneous papers of the Army Ordnance Department (AOD) and Army Service Corps whilst researching this book, and although the outcome of their complaint is not known, it speaks volumes about the frustrations felt regarding the lack of uniforms. Indeed, even more extraordinary is the fact that

'Where's My Uniform' *comic postcard* **(Miscellaneous Papers Army Ordnance Corps and Army Service Corps.** *The Royal Logistic Corps Museum Archive - Author's Collection).*

the postcard was deemed worth saving in the first place and is now archived at the Royal Logistics Museum at Deepcut.

In the first months of the war, demand for khaki out-stripped supply and so temporary 'stop gaps' were needed. For large numbers of men their first uniform would be their own civilian clothing. Such problems led to the War Council passing The New Army Order. Men were paid a daily allowance to live at home, feed themselves and wear their own clothes for training and drilling until such time that uniforms could be provided. Reminiscences by an original member of Bristol's Own noted that 'one of the features of these early days was the guard [group of drilled soldiers]. It turned out in civilian dress with rifles.... . Marching ten in number to take up sentry duty at the [Cumberland] Basin [Bristol]. What a figure we used to cut...'.[31] Several drawbacks resulted from this situation. Civilian suits were not hard wearing and it gave the impression that men were not 'doing their bit' - in some instances the absence of uniform led to soldiers being presented with white feathers. The War Office recognised this problem and so, in collaboration with Recruiting Committees, provided badges for enlisted men to show their commitment to fight. Recruits for Bristol's Own were given an enamelled badge denoting they had enlisted. This large and highly visible badge was the first item of uniform they received and was worn with pride.

Another temporary solution was issuing existing stocks of scarlet tunics[32] that languished in regimental stores and depots around the country. It was better to have soldiers train in scarlet than their own civilian suits, in turn saving money by not having to pay the men an allowance. For the War Office and the government, this was a workable solution as it avoided negative press and questions in Parliament about supply. There were alternative temporary uniforms to the scarlet tunics, most notably the 'Kitchener's Blues', arguably the most disliked of all. Surplus blue cloth used in Post Office uniforms was readily available and was put to immediate use. Made from a thick, dark blue serge cloth that was described as shapeless and baggy, men complained they felt like convicts and, in some instances, were mistaken for them.[33] The Jackets had no breast pockets and only two pockets sewn on the inside of the lower front sections. With brass buttons securing the pocket flaps, the collar was the same as the rank and file SD tunic, with five brass buttons securing

Bristol's Own enlistment badge as worn by Pte. George Brace, Ambulance Section (By kind permission of Keith Nickless - Author's Collection).

Kitchener's Blues (Author's Collection).

the front of the jacket. Replacing the service cap with a 'side' cap, men who had answered the call to arms found this temporary uniform offensive and demoralising. It was common for battalions in the same regiment to be dressed in entirely different uniforms. It soon became apparent that men in locally raised battalions and Territorial battalions (such as Bristol's Own) were often clad in full khaki uniforms before both the Reservists and those in Kitchener's New Army. Local Recruiting Committees went to great lengths to fundraise and equip their men at their own expense - the Bristol Citizens Recruiting Committee being no exception.

Finding ingenious ways to raise money for uniforms and equipment, the Bristol Citizens Recruiting Committee persuaded the composer Ivor Novello, writer of the popular wartime song '*Keep the Home Fires Burning*', to pen music for a song for Bristol's Own. With words written by Fred E Weatherly ('*Roses of Picardy*' and '*Danny Boy fame*'), the song was called '*Bravo Bristol*,' and the sheet music sold to raise funds. Printed on the front cover was a message 'The entire proceeds of the sale of this song will be given by the Author and Composer to the regimental fund of the Bristol battalion'.[34] Because of this, and other fundraising efforts, the people of Bristol and surrounding area gave generously, and so Bristol's Own went from a civilian-suited regiment to a fully uniformed and equipped one by 12 December 1914, when they marched past the Lord Mayor and the Sheriff of Bristol.[35] When George attested, and joined Bristol's Own in April 1915,[36] his uniform was provided by the Recruiting Committee as the War Office had not yet taken over the running of the regiment.

The Issue with the 'Issue'

As far back as the Elizabethan period (1558-1603), the supply of uniforms to the rank and file of the British Army had always been dealt with on a local basis. Regiments of the army were owned by the Colonel in charge and it was his responsibility to clothe, equip, train, and feed his men, the cost of which was then deducted from soldiers' pay. This system was open to abuse and fraud by the officers in charge, with fake soldier names added to muster rolls which increased monies received from the army; and soldiers were often deducted more pay than items cost, leading to large profits for the Colonel of the regiment.[37]

In 1745, the 1st Horse Guards bill from the clothier totalled £1,946.00, with deductions from the soldiers' pay being £2,823.00, leaving a profit of £877, a vast sum for the period. This system was abolished in 1855[38] during the Crimean War (1853-1856) when supply inadequacies were reported in the so-called Crimean Scandals of the same year, stating clothing was 'extremely spongy in texture, badly put together and quite unfit to stand the tear and wear of the rough work of the trenches...', before continuing in regard to boots 'like all articles obtained by contract from the lowest bidder, the workmanship was bad and totally unfit for endurances in the tenacious soil of the trenches, or for travelling along muddy roads in which the men were often half leg deep...'.[39]

The Crimean War had been a turning point and, in 1855, a Director of Clothing (DOC) was appointed,[40] laying new foundations for uniform supply. A Contracts Department was now responsible for all supplies to the British Army, with public tendering used to place contracts with firms.[41] Just a few years later, in 1857, the Royal Army Clothing Factory (RACF) was set up at Woolwich to manufacture uniforms initially for the artillery and engineers.[42] In 1863, the factory moved to Pimlico and a new DOC was appointed in 1870, becoming head of the factory, inspection, and depot. The Royal Army Clothing Department (RACD) was formed in 1895, bringing the factory, depot, and clothing sections of the Contracts Department together. In 1899, the role of Director of Clothing was abolished and transferred to the Director General of Ordnance (DGO).[43] Now responsible to the Quartermaster General (QMG), a system was introduced where the supply departments of the army informed the Contracts Department of its requirements, who then in turn placed the contracts with firms to do the work. Still not perfect, this new supply system was nevertheless a step in the right direction.

The Boer War highlighted the need for further reorganisation and the creation of a more 'centralised' way of purchasing supplies. During 1904, this system was dropped in favour of supply departments, under the control of a Director of Equipment and Ordnance Services,[44] who placed orders direct with manufacturers. The results of this change were not successful as direct competition between supply departments led to higher prices being paid. The re-establishment of the army Contracts Department in 1907 brought the supply system back to a centralised concept, changing little up to the outbreak of war in 1914. As a civilian branch of the War Office, the Contracts Department answered to the government's Financial Secretary.[45] The Contracts Department received orders from supply departments, sent enquires to and invited firms to place tenders, negotiate prices then place contracts.[46] Ranging from three months to three years, these contracts could be placed with firms around the world, resulting in thousands of firms catering solely for army orders, earning them the right to be called 'Government Contractor'.[47] Regarded a privilege, this system had the effect of keeping prices down, bringing with it some semblance of order and stability to the supply system.

Monitored by the Contracts Department, any firm found to keep its prices artificially high would lose its contract and be removed from the Government List as punishment, an exile that was almost impossible to reverse.[48] The Director of Army Contracts (DAC) published at the end of the fiscal period to 31 March 1914 a list of contractors, date of orders, quantities and prices paid. During this period 30,000 SD tunics were ordered and supplied, with Table A[49] showing the number of SD jackets supplied in one month.

Qty.	Price Paid Per Item	Name of Contractor	Date
3,600	10s 0d	Compton, J and Sons Ltd	11/12/13
5,000	10s 0d	Hammond, J and Co Ltd	11/12/13
2,000	9s 3d	Harmer, F W and CO	11/12/13
5,000	10s 0d	Smith, J and CO (Derby) Ltd	11/12/13
15,600 Total			

Table A - Compiled from WO 33/1076: Director of Army Contracts: Report.

In the same year contracts were placed for 107,000 and 120,000 pairs of cotton and woollen drawers respectively, 735,000 pairs of worsted seamless socks and a total of 400,000 yards (365,760m) of khaki cloth.[50] Although private contractors were used extensively, some military departments had their own factories where armaments, munitions and uniforms were manufactured to compare the quality of the product from contracted firms. Found throughout the country, these factories had come into existence in the 1880s and were efficiently run.

The RACF establishment at Pimlico, London, was still the main site for uniform manufacture of all types, and the factory's output between 1913 to 1914 saw the production of 102,676 SD jackets and 203,127 pairs of SD trousers[51] made by 1,300 personnel, of which 1,150 were women.[52] This pre-war system worked. It resulted in superior quality items at the best price, with mistakes and errors few if not non-existent. Although an effective way of equipping the army during peace time, manufacture was nevertheless a slow process and one that was put to the ultimate test on the outbreak of war.

Drastic economic changes occurred across supply trade and industries after war was declared in August 1914. It was now prohibited to trade with the enemy, and orders placed prior to war by foreign, now 'enemy' countries were forfeited.

Firms lost money as orders were cancelled and invoices not paid. Overnight, the 'Tweed' industries on the Scottish Borders lost a sizeable percentage of their market, as their tweeds had been popular in Germany. The economic situation combined with Kitchener's appeal for men to enlist put too much pressure on the contracts system, highlighting its inadequacies. As the Contracts Department, various Territorial County Associations and Local Recruiting Committee's all started placing orders for cloth and uniforms, the effect on the textile industry was astonishing. The system soon reached breaking point and speculation on the cost of raw materials such as leather, wool tops and yarn kept prices high. To counteract this, the Contracts Department tried to buy direct from manufacturers to get the best price. This was not always possible, and so the Contracts Department was often forced to buy from middlemen merchants who could place orders with manufacturers within hours, albeit at an inflated price.

The Contracts Department had to consider every one of the hundreds of tenders it received before passing them through separate departments for approval. The Chief Inspectorate, The Chief Ordnance Officer at the Royal Army Clothing Factory, and the Quartermaster representative of the Supply Department and Contracts Department were all part of the decision-making process. If samples of patterns were required or supply departments needed to inspect items, then the entire process could take several months - not an ideal situation with the BEF already in France. With manufacturers quite often withdrawing their initial quotes for products at an agreed 'immediate acceptance' rate due to increased raw material costs, the supply issue was compounded yet further by the fact that in addition to the needs of the British Army, Allied governments were also purchasing uniform supplies from British firms. In August 1914, The *Commission Internationale de Ravitaillement* (International Supply Commission) was established between the British and French Governments, allowing the latter to access firms and manufacturers in Britain. The Commission had around 2,000 representatives from the British and Allied Governments, with military, civilian and business backgrounds[53] who reported expenditure to the Treasury and dealt with the tonnage and organisation of supplying Allied Governments from Britain. Specific requirements and purchasing was dealt with by Inter Allied Committees, who informed the British Government of their own requirements. The British Government then supervised purchases by the Allies to keep control of British supplies, which also extended to controlling purchases from the USA. Depending on whether a country was financially reliant on Britain, such as Russia, priority was given to soldiers from Allied armies and the supply of Kitchener's new recruits.[54]

By October 1914, this over-complex and bureaucratic supply system was nearly crippled, and change was needed. Mr Wintour, a representative of the Board of Trade, was appointed by Kitchener as Director of Army Contracts and in November 1914 proposed vital changes. Suggesting the combining of the Supply Departments and Contracts Department to limit the time spent inspecting goods and issuing contracts, Wintour ordered the re-examination of design specifications, modifying patterns to allow for faster production methods. Maximising the use of cloth, the implementation of small design changes to the SD uniform, when magnified by the need to manufacture hundreds of thousands of garments, led to a faster and more efficient production of the uniform.

Commonly known as the austerity or emergency pattern, the Simplified Pattern uniform emerged because of these changes, and was produced between October 1914 and July 1915 to relieve pressure on supply. Removing the shoulder patches, the chest pockets no longer featured pleats, with plain brass buttons added, although existing stocks of GS or regimental buttons were still used. Trousers no longer had pockets in the side seam and the high back on the waist was lowered. As the manufacturing pressure eased,[55] the original 1907 pattern SD was reintroduced but it was common to see men in the same platoons

wearing both the Simplified as well as 1907 pattern SD jackets. Clearly, the Simplified Pattern uniform does not automatically date a photograph, as men could be seen wearing them in 1918,[56] however it does give a 'terminus post quem'[57] in that the photograph can be no earlier than October 1914.

Rigid army regulations for buying uniforms gave way to more efficient methods used in business. The pressures of war led to the Contracts Department encouraging tenders from firms which would not have been considered before 1914. Employment Exchanges around the country aided this expansion, inspecting woollen and textile mills in Yorkshire for the possible manufacture of khaki and so encouraging these firms to place tenders. The result of this helped increase production as well as securing employment for workers and firms hit economically from lost international trade. From November 1914, the old competitive tendering

Ernest Rowe wearing Emergency Pattern uniform (Author's Collection).

system was simplified. One of the extraordinary things the War Office did was to appeal direct to federations, trade unions and associations, such as the Wholesale Clothiers Associations, for their full co-operation. Writing to manufacturers, clothmakers as well as tailors, the War Office outlined the severity of the pressures on the supply situation, with Lord Kitchener, in an appeal to their sense of patriotism, stating in *The Tailor and Cutter Journal*:

> I earnestly appeal to every employer and employee for the utmost effort they can put forth with a view to augmenting the output of Army Clothing and expediting its delivery. In carrying out the Government work of providing the Army with its equipment, employers and employees alike are doing their duty for their King and country equally with those who have joined the Army for service in the field. I feel confident in making this appeal that I may rely on the same loyal and patriotic support from them as from the Army they are helping to equip....[58]

The response from manufacturers was that the War Office itself needed to become efficient, organise production, and drop the competitive tendering system. Agreements were subsequently made between the federations, trade unions and associations and War Office. For the Wholesale Clothiers Association, there would be a flat rate paid for each article of uniform produced across the whole industry. No matter the size of the manufacturer the War Office would pay the same rate, ensuring that prices stayed constant and the Contracts Department could buy direct from the manufacturer, cutting out the middle man.[59] Not only was the Contracts Department trying to increase production of new uniforms for the new armies, they were also trying to find and place contracts to replace uniform and equipment lost or worn out by the British Expeditionary Force. With the winter of 1914 fast approaching and both sides now 'digging in', the BEF was in urgent need of fresh uniforms, especially greatcoats - during the hasty retreat from Mons in late August 1914 many soldiers abandoned their equipment and stores, with greatcoats and backpacks discarded in favour of fast rapid marches. These marches could be 150 miles (241km) or more, with very few rests, leaving soldiers boots often completely worn out and their feet bleeding.[60]

As 1914 became 1915, the clothing issue was now being addressed and the results of these changes starting to be seen. Uniform production was now increasing. Commentating in February 1915, *The Tailor and Cutter Journal* reported that Kitchener's Blues 'have now been discarded, and new uniforms are being supplied in their place as rapidly as possible...'.[61] The Army Ordnance Department was, to begin with, responsible for the supply of both clothing as well as munitions and was sub-divided into Quartermaster General sections specific to a branch of supply. Clothing came under QMG 7,[62] beneath which

MILEAGE OF CLOTH AS PER STATEMENT.

	ORDERED.					ISSUED.				
	Miles					Miles.				
Cloth	121,159	=	5½ times round the world			95,051	=	3 ⅓ times round the world.		
Buttons	8,651	=	One-third	"	"	6,812	=	.26	"	"	"	"
Eyepieces	3,636	=	One-sixth	"	"	309	=	.0126	"	"	"	"
Sewings	2,693,813	=	112	"	"	54,712	=	2¼	"	"	"	"
Strappings	700	=	.26	"	"	539	=	.0226	"	"	"	"
Tape, etc.	24,392	=	Once	"	"	12,615	=	½	"	"	"	"
Leather	2,038	=	One-twelfth	"	"	2,038	=	One-twelfth	"	"	"
	2,854,189					163,076				

68.8 sq: miles - Cloth miles.

*Mileage of cloth ordered as recorded on 1 February 1915 (***Miscellaneous Papers Army Ordnance Corps and Army Service Corps.*** The Royal Logistic Corps Museum Archive - Author's Collection).*

was the Royal Army Clothing Department. Various branches of the Contracts Department were attached to numbered QMG sections, and handled everything the soldier needed personally (uniform, medical supplies, and food).

Problems nevertheless remained. In the early months of 1915, newspapers broke a story that shocked the nation. Although this had no direct connection with clothing it made the question of supply a national story. Dubbed the 'Shell Scandal' by the newspapers, it led to questions raised in the House of Commons. Unlike clothing contracts that placed tenders with firms not on the previously approved list, to increase supply, Kitchener would not countenance this for the production of high explosive shells, believing it to be dangerous to both workers and soldiers alike.[63] This debate continued into 1915 until a crisis point was reached. A committee was formed of business experts, representatives of the Admiralty, War Office and Cabinet with the aim of finding a solution. What resulted ultimately evolved, in May 1915, into the Ministry of Munitions.

Formed to deal with, and advise on all such issues, the Ministry of Munitions was initially responsible for what the soldier needed in order to fight - small arms, ammunition, mechanical transport, and aeronautical manufacture. This responsibility was to soon expand, with uniform supply now added to their sphere of activity. Making the Ministry of Munitions now in control of ALL war production, prior to the inclusion of clothing into its remit, the Royal Army Clothing Department was the subject of a detailed investigation.

The Debenham Report

A committee headed by Ernest Debenham reviewed the contracts, factory, and depot of the RACD , with several of its proposals instigated throughout 1916.

The doubling up of jobs was found to slow down the administrative process, with the Royal Army Clothing Factory and depot located at Pimlico, with the rest of the department at various sites in Whitehall. To rationalise, the Contracts Department was moved from Totshill Street to Pimlico and remained there until the end of the war.[64] It was further suggested that a Director of Clothing should be advised by two or three businessmen on 'all points concerning the economical and efficient provision, storage, handling of stocks...'.[65]

September 1916 saw the appointment of Lord Rothermere, a newspaper magnate and businessman, to the post of Director General of Army Clothing (DGAC). Chosen by Lloyd George, then Minister of Munitions, the inclusion of business acumen into the process of contracts and supply was crucial in adopting change, although this was a temporary post, for the duration. The report also proposed (and later approved) the specific role the Royal Army Clothing Department should play in the 'determination of the quantities of materials and clothing to be provided and maintained and general questions of policy...',[66] noting that it was also responsible for the 'calculation of the quantities of materials and garments to be ordered from the trade and from the factory...'.[67] Analysis of the army's past requirements combined with other factors such as seasonal variations, future campaigns, and rate of enlistment, were carried out by the establishment of the Statistical Branch, a new office within the Royal Army Clothing Department.

For the RACD to know exactly when to notify the Contracts Department to place new orders, the Statistical Branch needed to compile estimates from supplied goods returned over a given period. Looking at stock held, items due from contractors, and the approximate rate, socks, SD Jackets and trousers etc. were issued per day, per week, per month etc. In a report published on 29 September 1916, the resulting totals were drawn from a six-month period (27 March – 25 September 1915), and showed that the number of SD Jackets held in stock at the RACD and clothing depots totalled 4,406,482 items. Another 1,306,104 items were 'due in' giving an overall total of 5,712,586 Service Jackets held in stock on 25 September 1915. With a rate of issue to the men over a six-month period an average 90,000 items per week, the total number of SD jackets held in stock or 'due in' would have given approximately 11 months' worth of supplies. From these figures, the Statistical Branch and RACD could predict the army's needs.

On 30 October 1915, the Royal Army Clothing Department held in depots some 6,729,000 yards (c.6,153,000m) of khaki serge, which divided by the 1yd 21" (about 1.45m) of cloth needed to make one SD jacket, would produce around 4,250,000 finished SD jackets.[68] Based on a rate of issue of approximately 90,000 items per week over a six-month period, the serge held in the RACD depots equated to approximately 11 months' worth of jackets in one size. This gave the impression that supply was not an issue, but each article of uniform had to come in varying sizes as there was not a standard 'one size fits all.' To manufacture two sizes of SD jacket, for example, would reduce stock levels to just over five months' worth of supply, whilst to make four sizes would cut the total held in stock further to under three months. Add to this the new recruits that needed uniforms in addition to replacement items needed by the BEF, then the several months' supply held in stock would quickly disappear without constant restocking.

Cloth was not the only item which needed careful calculations - trimmings, buttons, and threads (haberdashery) all needed to be held in stock. One of the problems in early 1915 was the bureaucratic process a garment contractor had to follow when requesting the cloth and trimmings they needed. When the Contracts Department had accepted a manufacturer's tender, a contract was sent to the firm who duly signed then returned it to the Contracts Department. The manufacturer would then send several requests for the cloth and haberdashery it required to the RACD depot to enable the manufacture of the garment. Not only did this take too long, it was also a haphazard method of administration that needed to be simplified. New request forms were subsequently introduced in March 1915 and sent out, along with the contract, to the successful manufacturer. Accompanied by instructions on how to complete the new forms, the signed contract and completed request form were then returned to the Contracts Department. Requests for cloth and haberdashery were then passed to the Clothing Factory or Depot, who despatched the items to the manufacturer. It was a small but effective change that was part of a larger administrative shakeup.

Adopting these new clerical procedures, if manufacturers speeded up production to maximise output, then the components to make the garment also needed to be supplied more rapidly. Depots for the Royal Army Clothing Department were based in London (mainly at Pimlico, Battersea and Olympia). In peace time, various mills and factories producing cloth and haberdashery sent their goods to the London depots, who in return issued them to garment factories as per the contract. After manufacture, the finished articles were sent back to the London depots. This system was unfit for purpose in wartime. Multiple, repeat journeys of supplies added to an already strained rail network, under enormous pressure to deliver soldiers, equipment, food, horses and munitions to various locations and ports around the country.

Many cloth mills and garment factories were situated in the same region, however it was found that, in 1915, cloth woven in Bradford was sent to London only to be sent back to garment factories in Leeds, approximately 10 miles (16km) from Bradford. The finished articles were then returned to London for inspection before being sent to stores around the country ready for issue. By de-centralising the process away from London, manufacture could be quickened, substantially cutting railway usage and journey times. Consequently, a depot was soon set up in Leeds to receive the cloth and trimmings from the local mills, inspect the goods then issue the items to local garment factories. Inspectors, who ensured that cloth and trimmings were of the required military specifications, were provided by the Bradford Conditioning House and Manchester Chamber of Commerce. Other depots soon followed across the country, reducing journey times when sending and receiving cloth and garments.

With London depots heavily congested due to the increase in workload, new depots were opened to relieve the pressure and receive finished garments. The process of determining where the finished article eventually ended up was now simplified and changed. Previously, many factories had to send finished garments to different depots, with jackets and trousers being sent to one depot, while greatcoats sent to another. To streamline things, a garment manufacturer would now be appointed a specific depot where all their finished goods were to be sent, keeping details of what entered and left the factory. Not only was there now a firmer grip on the raw materials, but the Contracts Department and Royal Army Clothing Department had a revised contractors list. Between September 1916 and February 1917, existing contractors were classified into different grades A, B, C and D based on their past performance, current contracts and number of rejections by inspectors.[69]

End Game

This new system was a success, but each year of the war brought new obstacles and problems, 1916 being no exception. Military conscription and the 141 days of the Battle of the Somme tested the new supply system to its limit. Despite these pressures, the severe shortages of 1914 were not repeated. But no sooner had manufacturing output increased, a new problem appeared. Without raw materials, nothing could be made and this was a worldwide problem.

Restrictions and export bans on materials essential to war production were introduced by the British Government in 1914. Prohibiting the export of raw wool to countries now considered hostile to the UK, the imposition of restrictions provided the cloth industry with additional consignments of wool previously unavailable in peace time. Despite this sustainable resource, the summer of 1916 nevertheless saw a shortage of Bedford cord for breeches and leather for jerkins.[70] During September 1916, it became clear that stocks of khaki serge were also running low, due mainly to the repercussions of the Battle of the Somme, as well as increased raw material losses at sea from enemy submarine attacks. To improve the situation, agreements were made on 27 November 1916 to buy the whole of Australia's and New Zealand's wool clip left over from their home needs at 10 per cent below market prices.[71]

Witnessing the reorganisation of the Contracts Department during the same year, the Surveyor General of Supplies (SGS) now took over administratively from the Quartermaster General, Director General of Ordnance and Ministry of Munitions. Dividing the Contracts Department into more specialised compartments - Priority branches, Contracts, and Directorate of Raw Materials (DORM), the DORM took over from the Director of Army Contracts in controlling certain raw materials including wool, leather, cotton, jute and hemp. Its function was to source, secure materials then negotiate prices. Part of DORM, the Directorate of Wool Textiles Production (DOWTP) was responsible for the whole cloth manufacturing process and took over Directorate of Raw Materials' responsibilities after the raw wool had been converted into 'tops' (i.e. when it entered the mill). Becoming the largest textile concern in the world, controlling all production of cloth and hosiery, the DOWTP appropriated 75 per cent of the total wool in the country for military needs.

With a purchase rate for the Directorate of Wool Textiles Production totalling over 250,000,000 yards (c.228,600,000m) of cloth, including hosiery, blankets and flannel, the Directorate of Wool Textiles Production's total expenditure in 1917 was £88,000,000[72] (£5,343,229,624.48 in today's money[73]). In addition, a series of control boards and schemes whose specific duties related to a single commodity such as leather, was introduced. Recruiting expert business men from their relevant fields to join these committees and schemes and work closely to solve the raw material difficulties, business efficiency and organisation was soon introduced into the military supply chain.[74]

From 1917 to beyond the Armistice of 11 November 1918, salvaging, repairing old equipment and clothing, grew in importance. What could not be fixed was sold for scrap, raising much needed funds for the war, which by the end of 1917 was raising millions of pounds Sterling each week.[75] At the tail end of the war manufacture was as efficient as it could be given the impact the war was having on the supply and distribution of the world's raw materials.

Officers' Issue

Although the War Office paid an allowance, officers had to provide their own uniform which still had to conform to strict military specification. To maintain continuity from the provincial tailor to the hallowed ground of Saville Row in London, patterns and instructions were made available from the Royal Army Clothing Factory. These mathematical instructions required the tailor to substitute his client's measurements from the given example to create a pattern unique to the client. Blocks of stiff card were made from the drawing and kept so every time an officer needed a new uniform, the 'block' would be taken out and the fabric cut. A number of these uniform blocks still survive as a unique kind of *matériel culture* in some tailoring firms that have continued to trade since the First World War. Forming a visual 'bodily' memorial to a person and

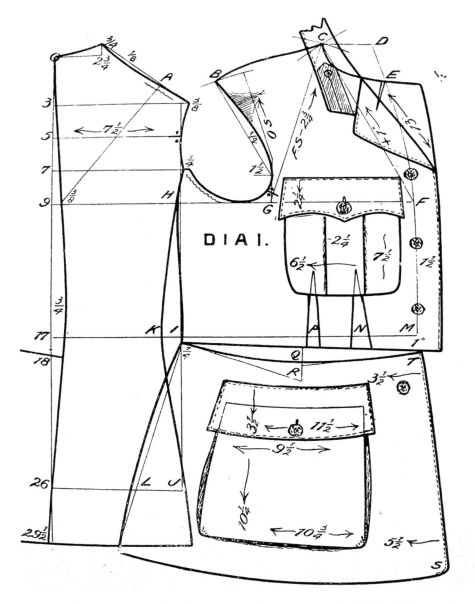

Example drafting instructions for an officer's SD tunic (**The Cutter's Practical Guide to British Military Service Uniforms.** *Anon: 1914 - Author's Collection).*

their past, a century later client confidentiality still prevails and so no examples are presented in this book.

Prior to the outbreak of war, there were tailors who specialised in military tailoring such as 'Gieves and Hawkes' in Saville Row who had, for over

200 years, dressed officers of the Navy (including Nelson) and British Army.[76] For many tailors across the country, their client base catered solely for the civilian trade, often with specialisms in either menswear or ladies wear. With the tailoring profession changing very little over time, the outbreak of war in 1914 was to have an immediate effect on the craft in terms of manpower and consumer trade.

The rush to enlist saw an increase in demand for officers' uniforms, which only benefited those tailors who already specialised in military apparel. For civilian tailors, it was a completely different situation, with clients enlisting and being drafted overseas resulting in orders slackening. This despite the sizeable percentage of the male population still being at home. With clients from the upper and professional classes of society - bankers, teachers, merchants, lawyers[77] - tailoring establishments varied, from the single tailor or father and son business, to the small firm with a few employees. Regardless of whether they were civilian or military, for some companies bankruptcy was inevitable. With a diverse work force in which many of its employees were from continental Europe, the outbreak of war resulted in a skills shortage within the tailoring trade, with many of its employees enlisting themselves, both in the UK as well as abroad in their native country.[78] Frequent press reports regarding the pressures faced by manufacturers left the tailoring trade wondering why they could not get a share of contract work. Responding to a reader's letter in *The Tailor and Cutter Journal* (17 September 1914), the issue of contracts was a concern felt by the trade with the journal continuing to voice one of its biggest contentions:

> Almost every day we have letters of enquiry from tailors who have small workshops, asking where they can obtain a share in the making of uniforms. We can only tell this enquirer to ask for information at the War Office, in the hope that they can give them the name of any contractor in their district where they can obtain employment….[79]

Questioning why it was that large orders were being placed with manufacturers in the USA or Canada, when small tailor workshops in the UK were desperate for work, the fact was the Contracts Department had little choice but to place large orders overseas where mass production could take place. For any small workshop to get a contract, especially when competitive tendering was abolished, it was recognised that they would have to modernise and, in some instances, join forces to gain contracts.[80]

In June 1916, the Master Tailors Association drew to the attention of the Contracts Department that tailors in London and the West End were struggling to obtain enough cloth for Officers' Service Dress. Representatives of the Royal Army Clothing Department looked at how to prioritise cloth to these tailors, with a Director of Textiles controlling the cloth for officers' uniform, fixing an agreed price to be paid between the cloth merchants and tailor. These fixed, flat rate prices which had been established in the garment factories soon filtered down to the tailor, where an officer's uniform could be charged at a fixed price made from army priority cloth. These prices were arranged between the Master Tailor's Association and woollen merchants, with the cloth inspected and passed by the RACD. Now officers were not charged inflated prices for a cloth that was inferior to the peacetime version, or in some cases of a lesser quality than that used for rank and file.[81]

An officer's uniform could also be made in what was termed wholesale tailoring and the Royal Army Clothing Factory had a section specifically for this, making made-to-measure uniforms without the need for a personal skilled fitting that only a tailor could provide. Wholesale uniforms were cheaper to buy than from a tailor and so may have been more popular with new officers of lower rank. Speaking of his promotion from Corporal to 2nd Lieutenant, Basil Sawers wrote 'Then I got my commission, went to the RTO [Railway Transport Officer] and they gave me a chit to go to Poperinghe[82] to 177 [Tunnelling] Company...', adding 'I was still in Corporals uniform. Went to London and within half an hour was on the street in brand new outfit as a Second Lieutenant'.[83]

A State Controlled Country

For the first time in British history, the state had complete control over trade, manufacture and the raw materials needed to supply an army - from an eyelet in a boot, to the spoon he was going to eat with. It extended into buying entire stocks from various countries as well as controlling the labour of many foreign nations.[84] A trade agreement was reached with Iceland,[85] a neutral country, to guarantee a fixed price to buy its entire excess raw wool stocks. Not only was this done to ensure Britain had enough supply, but it also meant that Iceland would not sell to enemy countries.

As the war turned into a conflict of attrition, state control of whole industries, from raw material to finished articles, was a development which increasingly concerned British ministers. From the opening days of war, when the Defence of the Realm Act (DORA) was introduced,[86] the entire economic, trade and wartime production had been transformed from one of near disaster in 1914, to one of complete success by the end of 1917.

Chapter 2

The Real 'Material' Culture

What would man be—what would any man be—without his clothes? As soon as one stops and thinks over that proposition, one realises that without his clothes a man would be nothing at all; that the clothes do not merely make the man, the clothes are the man; that without them he is a cipher, a vacancy, a nobody, a nothing....[1]

The materiality of a cloth garment, together with the unique skills, traditions and lifeways employed to produce it has defined parts of Britain. In turn, these regional textile centres have translated their culture into different types of cloth which have changed little over time. Weaving cloth is an ancient technology. Wall murals in Pompeii depict the process of 'fulling' cloth by people treading woollen cloth in tubs of water.[2] The 'Doomsday Book' recorded the business of wool and cloth from small cottage industries to the large monastic fulling mills.

The first Industrial Revolution in the eighteenth century brought mechanisation and automation which transformed landscapes and turned a largely individual cottage industry to mass manufacture. Evolution of water to steam powered mills and a greater leap forward for the development of machinery occurred throughout the nineteenth century. Looms became larger and faster, and the introduction of machines to replace hand sewing for industrial use saw the whole process become faster and more efficient. As the nineteenth century became the twentieth, machinery and processes changed little, and by the outbreak of the First World War many mills and factories were using machinery that dated back to the nineteenth century. Steam powered mills were in the majority, but waterways and water-wheels were often still in use.

Industrial transformation changed whole areas of countryside and certain districts became known for textile manufacture. Variations of pattern and weaves were as distinct and unique as the districts they were produced in. Worsted fabrics mainly originated from Yorkshire, centred on Bradford, whereas the world-renowned tweed trade of Scotland came from the Island of Harris. Scotland was also the home of shirting and dress goods in Glasgow and hosiery from Harwick. In the south-west of England, mills stretched from the Stroud Valley, Gloucestershire, to Wellington, Somerset, into Devon and across to Wiltshire. These areas were the home of broadcloth, flannels, fancy tweeds, worsted, woollens, serges, and the puttee.[3] In the north and Midlands, Lancashire, well known for cotton production, also wove worsted flannel in Rochdale, blankets in Bury, and hosiery in Leicester. These industries became the heart of industrial landscapes, swallowing up villages which in time became part of towns and cities.

Mills and factories were often the largest employers in an area, where generations of the same families worked. A continual workforce enabled employers to prosper and continue production in some instances for over 150 years. But the family tradition of following the previous generation into the factory changed when the First World War broke out in 1914 - enlistment impacted on the workforce, and some men of course would never return to their jobs. With a closed and divided international market, and a lack of raw materials, many mills and factories were forced to close before the end of the war, forever changing the culture, history and landscape of the textile industry in Britain and the rest of the world.

What is Cloth?

The need to wear clothing has not changed for millennia. It protects against the weather and reflects the individual's place in society. It lies at the heart of social identity, not least in the mass mobilisation of men and women in wartime. Cloth production is, in many ways, a way of creating and communicating status, a process that makes people as much as the things they wear. The same can be said of the manufacture of 'Tommy's' uniform. Generating a collective militarised identity for the wearer, the manufacture of uniform elevated a worker's role to that of vital war work, creating an important workplace identity. Despite this raised status few people know where or indeed how that uniform was made.

Cloth can be made in three different ways: felting, weaving, and knitting. Service dress jackets, trousers, shirts and underwear of 'Tommy's' uniform were made from woven cloth which consisted of two yarns that ran 90 degrees to each other called the 'warp and weft'. Warp runs the length of the fabric and the weft across the width. Made from twisted fibres, whether wool, cotton, linen or synthetic, that was spun into yarn, the fibre types would impact on the quality, finish, appearance and durability of cloth. In woollen cloth, the raw material, the fleece, has fibres that are either long and fine or short and coarse. Coarse fibres produce heavy, thick, rough cloth compared to fine fibres that produce a lighter, softer and finer cloth. Merino fleece, of which Australia and New Zealand were the largest exporters, contained the finest fibres and was used in cloth of the highest quality.[4] In Britain, farmers bred a variety of sheep, such as the long fibred Lincoln and Leicester, whose fleece, although not as fine as Merino, was ideal for hosiery and flannel. Most breeds in Britain were crossbred, producing fleeces that had characteristics of both long and short fibres, and created an average medium weight cloth.[5]

The production of wool fell into two different categories, woollen - heavier thicker, and worsted - a finer thinner cloth. A combination of a worsted warp and woollen weft produced a cloth with the thickness and durability of woollen fibres, yet with the softness and strength of worsted fibres.[6] From December 1915, future contracts for serge cloth stipulated that it was to be made either from an all woollen warp and weft, or from a worsted warp and woollen weft.[7] Cloth made from wool is versatile, and can be woven into a variety of weights, textures and patterns (weaves), such as plain and twill. Providing warmth, cloth from wool is naturally water repellent, flame resistant, durable, and has elasticity and absorbs moisture,[8] making it ideal for army uniforms. Woollen and worsted industries varied in their production, either by sub-division in the case of worsted, or staying in-house in the case of woollen. Although there are some variations in production, the process of turning fleece into a piece of cloth largely remains the same as today.

Cloth Manufacture

It is important to understand the industrial process of making cloth, as this is the first stage in the manufacture of a British Army uniform. Small mills often could only weave the cloth, so the fleece had to be brought from 'top makers' pre-washed and combed. Once woven, these mills sent the cloth to specialist firms for finishing and dyeing, whereas larger mills could process the fleece, weave and finish the cloth all on one site – as at Hainsworth in Yorkshire where the fleece was processed and woven, with the finishing handled by an outside specialist firm. Regardless of the size of mill, the method of weaving stayed the same[9] (see Appendix A for detailed information on the manufacturing process):

Sorting and Grading: Fleece is 'sorted' into wool type based on its qualities and the breed of sheep. It is then 'graded' into different categories dependent on which part of the sheep it came from. Fleece from the neck was the best quality, followed by the back, whereas the hind quarters, legs and belly were of a poorer quality.[10]

Scouring (**Cleaning**): Washing and bleaching fleece to rid it of dirt, impurities and excess lanoline, once treated the fleece would then be passed through a 'willey' machine, turning the detangled fibres into the 'top'.[11]

Scribbling and Carding: Using a 'scribbling' machine to straighten the 'tops' into strands, it would then be passed through a 'carding' machine to produce longer and even-length 'tops', and / or lightly twisted 'roving'.[12]

Spinning: To give strength, the roving would be twisted and wound onto a bobbin to create yarn. Using 'Spinning Mule's' to enable the roving to be spun

Carding and Scribbling Machines at Hainsworth's Temperance and Spring Valley Mills circa 1930s (By kind permission of A W Hainsworth & Sons Ltd - Copyright A W Hainsworth & Sons Ltd).

onto around 1000 bobbins at a time, once spun and wound onto bobbins it was classed as 'yarn'. Eight of these machines were installed in Armley Mills, Leeds, and could spin yarn onto 600 bobbins 24 hours a day, six days a week.[13]

Warping: Winding the yarns onto a 'warping beam', once full, the warps would then be taken to the weaving floors or sheds ready for weaving.

Weaving: Passing the warps through eyelets found in 'heels/heddles' frames, then through the 'reed' which divided the warp threads and 'batted' down the weft threads; the ends of the warps were then taken over the front of the loom and attached to a 'cloth beam'.[14]

   The toughest weave was twill, which has a diagonal pattern across the fabric and was traditionally used for serge cloth and uniforms. To create the weave, a 'flying shuttle' that held the weft thread would travel from side to side across the front of the loom, where heddles would raise to create a 'shed' (gap) between the warp threads. Allowing the shuttle to pass between the warps, once the shuttle had passed, the reed then batted down the weft. Passing the shuttle back, another

Spinning Mules at Hainsworth's Temperance and Spring Valley Mills circa 1930s (By kind permission of A W Hainsworth & Sons Ltd - Copyright A W Hainsworth & Sons Ltd).

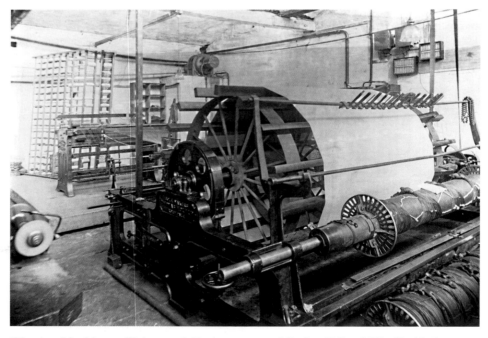

Warping Machine at Hainsworth Temperance and Spring Valley Mills (By kind permission of A W Hainsworth & Sons Ltd - Copyright A W Hainsworth & Sons Ltd).

Weaving looms at Hainsworth's Temperance and Spring Valley Mills circa 1930s (By kind permission of A W Hainsworth & Sons Ltd - Copyright A W Hainsworth & Sons Ltd).

heddle and set of warp threads were then raised to complete the process. By changing the number of heddles, and the order in which they were raised, would create different weaves in the cloth.[15]

Fulling: To wash and shrink worsted, woollen and flannel cloth, the material would undergo 'fulling' to tighten the weave. Thickening the warp and weft to create a thick felted appearance,[16] this was achieved by adding an alkali substance (fullers earth) then continually pounding it whilst in water.

Often found in the bowels of mill buildings, 'fulling stocks' (giant wooden hammers) were sited in large troughs containing water and alkali. Connected by a gearing system that enabled the hammers to be raised and dropped in sequence, this continuous pounding would cause the cloth to shrink.

Still in use during the First World War, most mills by 1914 had moved to 'milling' machines which forced the width of the cloth through a small channel and, combined with heat, alkali, and compression, caused the fabric to shrink.[17] Once 'fulled', the cloth was washed again and stretched out to dry over a frame with hooks on either side.

Fulling stocks preserved at the Stroud
Textile Trust (By kind permission of
Stroud Textile Trust, Dunkirk Mill -
Author's Collection).

Finishing, raising the nap. Armley Mills
Industrial Museum (By kind permission
of the Armley Mills Industrial Museum
Leeds Museums and Galleries - Author's
Collection).

Finishing: To finish, the fabric needed its 'nap' raised. Traditionally using 'teasels,' a tall spiny flowering plant grown in marshes[18] secured into large wooden drums,[19] the hooks would rough and fluff the fabric to create the nap. The cloth would then be machine 'cropped' (cut) to give the nap an even and smooth appearance. The action of the cropping machine inspired the invention that no gardener could now do without, the lawn mower.[20]

Mending and Burling: Before the cloth left the mill or specialist finisher it had to be inspected for flaws, mistakes, or knots. Correcting any imperfections by hand, it was pressed and folded ready to be delivered.[21]

Dyeing: Cloth can be dyed at various stages in its production which created a variety of colour and appearance to the finished fabric. Warp and weft could be dyed before weaving began in either the same colour or in contrast, or when after weaving when the cloth was finished. Roving was dyed before spinning and this was called 'dyed in the wool' and was used in the production of khaki serge.[22]

The dye industry did not escape the problems of the First World War as Germany was the industry leader in the research and manufacture of synthetic dyestuffs. Closed markets cut supplies to Britain, which led to huge shortages that put enormous strain on British dye manufacturers.[23] Some chemicals used to create dyes were also used in the production of munitions, such as Petric Acid. This element was required by the War Office and some dye manufacturers found themselves requisitioned, becoming part of the national munitions factories. In March 1915, to combat war shortages, 'British Dye Limited' was formed as a single company with Government assistance to develop dye making in the UK…'.[24]

The War Office described khaki as 'drab mixture' and it varied in shade. It could be a 'greeny brown', or a 'browny green' or even in some instances, grey in appearance. There seemed to be no set instructions for producing khaki although 'standard khaki is a mixture of five different shades-dark olive, light olive, dark blue, light blue and white. The exact proportions are, of course, a secret…'.[25] The 'secret' for most manufacturers was to mix together whatever quantities they had available from the five colours.[26] Such was the reliance on aniline dyes from Germany that in May 1916 *The Tailor and Cutter Journal* reported on the effects of the war on the industry. It stated the importance of 'state and big manufacturing firms combining to encourage and support research work by the chemists of all our technical schools…'.[27] Khaki was a colour that identified the man as a soldier, it was an important part of the uniform and afforded the wearer a modicum of camouflage and was as important as producing the ammunition for him to fight with. Uniform specifications could be modified to allow for quicker manufacture, the khaki colour couldn't.

'Tommy's' jacket and trousers were made from serge drab mixture, his shirt from flannel and his overcoat from greatcoat serge. The output required was astonishing, with *The Tailor and Cutter Journal* reporting in May 1915 that 'for every million men in the field require 13,000,000 yards of khaki cloth [11,887,000m] …1,200 miles [1931km] of khaki each month, working 24 hours a day, seven days a week…'.[28] In the first nine months of war, the cost per yard of khaki serge had risen from 3s. 11d to 5s (£11.89 to £15.90).[29] Hainsworth alone produced approximately 66,000,000 yards (60,350,000m) of serge drab mixture, 32,000,000 yards (29,260,000m) of greatcoat serge and 231,000,000 yards (211,226,000m) of narrow flannel during the war, a total yardage that would go around the world five and a quarter times at the equator.[30] These figures do not include the Admiralty, Royal Flying Corps, civilian trade, or Allied orders.[31] On 27 July 1916, material made from 100 per cent wool, or which contained a partial percentage of wool, was declared as 'munitions work',[32] thus giving it official war status under the umbrella of the Ministry of Munitions.

Hainsworth Mill

Hainsworth opened its first mill in 1811, and by 1841 provided cloth for the British Army. Expanding its order book in the 1880s to include both the War

Office as well as railway companies and the Post Office, Hainsworth produced their first order for khaki serge in 1899. With a crossbred worsted warp and woollen weft,[33] the company had two manufacturing sites: Spring Valley Mill (for woollen production), and Temperance Mill (for worsted production).[34] Increasing its overall cloth production into the twentieth century, in 1910 a quarter of monthly orders totalling £6,000 were for the War Office.[35]

Between 1910 and August 1914, Spring Valley Mill evolved into a three-storey spinning mill, weaving shed, cloth mill, and mechanics workshops, with boilers and engines added in 1912. Now run by the next generation of the Hainsworth family, Charles and Gaunt Hainsworth, the company joined the Serge Contractors Association for the Royal Navy, where Admiralty orders with standard prices were divided evenly between the Association's twelve members. Like most mills, the outbreak of war led to rapid change and adaptation.

Overseas trade lost to wartime restrictions on imports and exports, insurance for ocean freight, and the cost of imported goods all rose to cover losses at sea. Many orders and invoices were subsequently unpaid as international trade became affected by war, with these debts having to be absorbed by the firm involved. The long association with government contracts could not guarantee work as orders peaked and troughed, leading Gaunt to complain in April 1916 'not many large army orders lately...'.[36]

Uniform Production

Two firms, Waltham and Gardner, and Messer's J Barran and Son Limited,[37] were amongst many garment manufacturers under contract to make uniforms alongside the RACF in Pimlico. Making uniforms for all three services in a readymade standard size for rank and file, or wholesale bespoke for officers, patterns, samples and articles were drawn up from specifications received from army supply departments and the Admiralty. With finished samples and deliveries from contracted firms inspected as part of quality control, paper patterns were subsequently made available to the wholesale clothing factories alongside drafting instructions for tailors. Cataloguing all aspects of uniform production and change in their 'pattern changes ledgers,' factories recorded everything from modifications to existing uniform patterns, orders placed as well as whether the work had been contracted out.[38]

Individual contracts covered everything a soldier would wear or need, from less obvious eyelets for boots, thimbles for Regimental tailors, to trousers and jackets. Despite the beginnings of a 'readymade' industry during the late eighteenth-early nineteenth centuries (when the Napoleonic Wars played a key role in transforming uniform production),[39] it was only from the middle of the nineteenth century onwards that developments and patents for machines took manufacturing from a hand sewn to machine made garment. This further distinguished the tailor from the factory, both of which required two completely different skill sets.

In factories, each element of garment construction was broken down into specialist skills that were repeated, so one person would make pockets, whilst another the sleeves and so on, resulting in one service dress being made by several individuals. This way of working led to 'piecework', a term long associated with factory work where the worker would be required to achieve the construction of a certain number of elements per day. Being slow not only gave the individual less pay, but could hold up production down the line when all the elements would come together as a whole. If one element was missing, delays in finishing meant delays in delivering. Each person in a factory was therefore a 'cog', and all the cogs needed to work together. Machines aided the process but also raised the quantities that potentially could be produced. Just like cloth mills, clothing factories varied in size, numbers employed, type of garment, and whether it was for military or civilian trade.

The Royal Army Clothing Factory

By 1914, the Royal Army Clothing Factory was already a large factory, employing 1300 workers who worked from 8.00am to 6.00pm Monday to Friday, and 8.00pm to 12.15pm on Saturdays. Visiting the factory for the 6 August 1914 issue, a journalist from *The Tailor and Cutter Journal* having been issued a special visitor permit, described in detail the building and the work carried out within it. Stating that before they entered the building 'it looked more like a gentlemen's residence than a factory…', the reporter continued 'entering the main hall, we found ourselves in a magnificent room…'.[40] The various procedures by which the work was carried out can be seen in this outline description, which gives a unique insight into this long-forgotten process.

Factory Floor: The factory was separated into various sections that contained specialist workers and machines. In the centre was a large main hall that measured 200 feet long (61m) and 50 feet high that ended in a large glass roof, and housed the machinists of which between 400 and 500 were women. Additional offices and workrooms were situated around this central space, one of which housed the cutting rooms.[41]

Cloth Arrives: Railways and mechanical transport delivered the bales of cloth from the mills to the depot for inspection. Replacing the cloth taken from existing stocks and sent to contractors as well as the adjoining factory, the subsequent reorganisation of the clothing department later in the war eased the strain in the depot, with mills sending cloth direct to local depots.

Cutting the Cloth: Layers ('lays') of fabric were first placed upon tables and secured together, before the pattern was placed on the top, and the outline chalked out.[42] It should be pointed out that a pattern referred to in a factory setting refers to the shape of the piece required to construct the garment, and thus not to be confused with pattern in the military sense meaning design.

The pile of fabric was then cut by an electric 'cutter' which guided the cloth around a vertical 'band knife'.[43] Cutting with clean edges and smooth curves, the use of a band knife allowed for multiple garments to be cut, with it not being uncommon to cut through twenty layers of fabric in one go. In addition, several cutters would also use metal based handheld band knives that sat flush to a cutting table. Approximately twenty-five yards (22m) long and wide enough to take two widths of fabric on which lays could be placed, the use of a cutting table allowed the fabric to stay in one position whilst the cutter moved the knife around the cloth. The reporter observed artillery tunics being cut out, stating the pattern had 'been arranged so closely and economically that scarcely an inch of material was wasted…'. Detailing the process meticulously, from this the number of tunics cut out can be calculated. Observing 10 cutting machines each with 20 layers of fabric, a single layer

Band knife used to cut multiple lays of cloth. Armley Mills Industrial Museum (By kind permission of the Armley Mills Industrial Museum Leeds Museums and Galleries - Author's Collection).

Hand held electric knives to cut cloth. Armley Mills Industrial Museum (By kind permission of the Armley Mills Industrial Museum Leeds Museums and Galleries - Author's Collection).

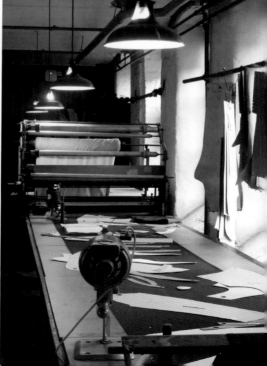

equated to one tunic, therefore 10 men cut 200 tunics. In a top floor room, more cutters were employed on flannel shirts, cutting 50 at a time as this cloth was thinner.[44]

Despite the advantages that cutting machines brought to the factory, some items could only be cut by hand and so two cutters (predominantly women) were employed. Using traditional shears, items such as tartan trousers (tartan needed to be cut in a single layer to ensure the checks matched across trousers), as well as uniforms in the officer's bespoke wholesale tailoring section were cut by hand, the latter to an individual's measurement. Once cut the fabric lays were then passed to the 'rollers' (also mainly women) whose job was to take each lay and roll it up to be sent to the right department.

Trimming: Trimming was also done by women, and involved the attachment of braid, lace, trims and buttons to parts of the uniform. Completed whilst the garment was in pieces (as it was more efficient to attach items when the garment was flat, ensuring the ends were hidden in seams), pockets could also be attached at this point or at the next stage.

Sewing: This was a profession revolutionised by the sewing machine. By 1914 the Singer Manufacturing Company Limited was one of the world largest manufacturers of sewing machines, with its site at Clydebank in Scotland the largest of his factories.[45] Made of cast metal with intricate small cogs and gears attached to shafts, all of which had to turn and work faultlessly with each other, the sewing machine had to be 'timed' correctly.[46] The machinery and engineering skills of many armaments firms were well suited to sewing machine manufacture, and thus ended up making their own machines. Between 1872 and 1877 the Breech Action Manufacturing Company made a machine called the 'Fearnought', a mighty warlike name for a domestic item[47]; whereas Vickers, the machine gun and tank manufacturers produced a domestic machine from 1917 until 1939 that was almost identical to the German made 'Frister and Rossman' sewing machine.[48]

Despite the speed at which garments could be made by machine, they were not wholly engaged in making readymade clothes. Many firms had machines that were more than a decade old when war broke out, so to increase production the government made allowances available to firms on government contracts to buy new specialised machines and expand production. This included the purchase of new industrial sewing machines that could sew up to 3,200 stitches per minute, with a triple stitch machine able to reinforce and add strength to seams by sewing three stitches close together at once (normally the seam was sewn three times on a regular machine). Cylinder arm machines were specifically designed to sew sleeves in, one for left sleeves and one for right sleeves. Sewing buttons on had previously been done by hand until

King George V and Queen Mary visit the sewing room at the Royal Army Clothing Factory, Pimlico (Copyright Public Domain).

Singer's button sewing machine was introduced allowing between 10 and 14 buttons per minute to be sewn on, each with 18 stitches and three fastening stiches for each button. Singer claimed these buttons were sewn on stronger than if by hand. Serging (overlocking) machines neatened raw edges and prevented them from fraying, whereas the Trouser Bottom Felling Machine hemmed curved and straight trousers with ease 'very little practice is required for an operator to become proficient...' .[49] Every stage of garment production was now mechanised. The *Tailor and Cutter Journal* encouraged the use of these new machines and published an in-depth article on the variety offered by the Singer Company.[50]

Quilting, collar stitching, bagging lining, buttonholing, bar tacking, pocket making and binding each by now had their own special machine and were all used to produce uniforms.[51] These machines would all be redundant, however, without the thread essential for sewing the garment together. Traditionally the uniform was sewn together with linen thread which was tough, strong, and didn't break easily. Derived from the flax plant, the principal supplier of flax to Britain was Russia, through Archangel, and into Scotland.[52]

Singer button sewing machine. Armley Mills Industrial Museum (By kind permission of the Armley Mills Industrial Museum Leeds Museums and Galleries - Author's Collection).

The Russian Revolution in March 1917 saw Britain lose its main supply of flax. Other smaller countries had also been exporting flax to Britain prior to 1917, and in December 1916 linen yarn from Ireland, Netherlands, France and Courtrai in Belgium (now Kortrijk) were requisitioned (indeed the War Office went as far as to purchase flax seeds in 1916 to ensure supplies).[53] There was also a new call on the supply of linen thread in the need for sewing the canvas covering of Royal Flying Corps aeroplanes. Such were the unexpected pressures for linen from this new kind of warfare that eventually the government had no alternative but to restrict the use of linen to aeroplane production, which meant that uniforms had now to be sewn together with cotton thread.[54]

Buttons[55]: Several areas of Britain had brass manufacturing industries. Birmingham was one such centre where Firmin and Sons was one of several button manufacturers on a government war contract. Although no records have been found which tell of the total number of buttons produced during the First

World War, a rough estimate can be made. Each rank and file tunic required eleven buttons, so for every million tunics 11 million buttons were needed. Aware that over 31 million[56] SD Jackets were produced for the British Army alone between 1914 and 1919, then it can be calculated that at least 341 million brass buttons were required, not including replacement items.

Pressing and Finishing: Each uniform had to be pressed during and after its production. Large pressing rooms were occupied by a variety of pressing machines 'Rows and rows of women and girls were working foot pressing machines, either gas or electrically heated…'.[57] In the finishing room, each uniform was then inspected for mistakes (e.g. missing buttons), with any excess threads trimmed, size tickets added to each main item of clothing, before being bundled into bales ready to be taken to a depot.

All elements of cloth and haberdashery had to be in the right place, at the right time from whichever type of manufacturer it came from. Failure to meet the contracted deadline had serious knock on effects and caused extra delays. If a mill was late with a contracted delivery, then the garment manufacturer would deliver their finished article late from their agreed contracted date. Through no fault of the garment manufacturer, disputes often occurred and it was not uncommon for them to be settled in court, with compensation paid for loss of contracts or money. The Royal Army Clothing Department could also remove a manufacturer from the contract list for poor quality goods or repeated failure to make deadlines.

Tailoring Trade

Many tailoring companies were family run, and passed down through generations, trading on reputation. Some, such as Gieves Limited and Hawkes & Co, would merge[58] into a large company patronised by some of the important figures of the time. Thomas Hawkes had been an apprentice hatter before starting his business in 1771, specialising in military headgear and uniforms to the British Army. A few of his notable customers were the Duke of Wellington and George V who appointed the company to make and maintain uniforms for the Royal Bodyguard, and Sir Herbert Plumer who took charge of the 2nd British Army in the Ypres[59] Salient in May 1915.[60]

For decades, the method of hand crafting a bespoke garment in tailoring establishments had not changed, with the main workrooms often situated in poorly lit basements and artificial lighting provided, in many instances, by gas.[61] The upgrading to electric light, steam irons[62] and machines such as buttonholers and bar tackers during the war helped the tailor stay productive with a smaller and, potentially, less skilled workforce. In the workroom, everything was done by hand with only a few basic seams sewn by machine. It took approximately forty-five minutes to reinforce pockets by hand with bar tacking, whereas a machine could do it in one minute. These minor changes allowed the tailor to compete for small contracts.[63] Whilst there were subtle differences in the bespoke tailoring trade, especially between male and female attire, the generic process of making a garment was nevertheless the same and would have been identical when constructing officers' uniforms and coats.

The Cutter: Regarded as the highest skilled individual in an establishment,[64] the deftness and skill of the cutter underpinned the quality and reputation of a firm.[65] Whilst they did not physically sew, the cutter fully understood sewing and had extensive knowledge of the different varieties of cloth and their uses.[66] In small workshops, there may have been only one cutter and trimmer, an assistant in training to become a cutter,[67] whereas in larger workrooms there were often a headcutter, 1st cutter, coat cutter and trouser cutter.[68]

Understanding the human figure and how to allow for certain traits,[69] patterns were constructed using mathematical instructions which required the cutter to substitute his client's measurements to create a uniquely personal pattern. Blocks from stiff card were made from the drawings and kept so every time an officer needed a new uniform, the block would be taken out and the fabric cut.[70] Cloth was cut from a single layer and the pattern chalked out first, attention was paid to matching stripes and checks. An officer in any of the services could telegram their requirements from anywhere and the uniform item could be produced and sent to the serving man.[71] The knowledge of the individual by the cutter and tailor[72] would ensure that it would fit the recipient.

Tailor: The tailor was[73] an artist who manipulated, draped and shaped flat cloth into a three-dimensional form - a textile engineer with patience, knowledge, skill and nimble fingers. In the construction of an officer's uniform, the tailor would begin with a 'fit up' which required facings, flaps, welts and collars etc. to be cut.[74] Next the garment was prepped for a fitting with the officer which meant the garment was constructed to a certain point. This was often to a tight schedule as the officer may be home on leave or about to be mobilised to the front. Pieces were basted together with facings and hems pressed under, known as a 'full baste' garment.[75] Any adjustments from the fitting were noted and the full baste could be ripped apart and adjusted, sometimes heading back to the cutter if edges needed re-cutting.

Pockets and flaps were then basted to the garment and correctly aligned, ready to be sewn whether by hand or machine. On the officers' SD jackets, both canvas underlining and fronts were shaped by shrinking and joined together. Any linings or collars would be added and then fronts and backs would be sewn together before the sleeves sewn in by hand.[76]

Tailors sewing in the 'tailor-style' position (Copyright Public Domain).

Pressing: There were two main stages of pressing. The first involved the tailor and the second, the 'pressing off', was undertaken by a skilled operator. Using a 'goose' hand iron, heated by a gas flame[77] to flatten seams open, a damp cloth was placed over the fabric and the iron ran lightly and smoothly over the surface creating steam. If too much water was present in the cloth, then too much steam was produced and the cloth boiled. Once this had occurred the fabric could not be saved as the fibres in the cloth and appearance were damaged.

When the garment was ready, the client had a final fit unless he was abroad, in which case the skill of both cutter and tailor came into their own, as knowing their regular customers enabled them to produce a garment to a very good fit. A regimental tailor would be able to make any adjustments that may be required by an officer. The horrors of war touched every aspect of society and the order books started to show the cost. Gieves Limited, who had already kept prices the same despite increased costs, took an extraordinary decision. For every officer that died and still had a balance to pay, the firm wiped his slate clean, swallowing the cost and choosing not to send a bill to the deceased's family.[78] That was the power of the relationship of the tailor and his client.

*Pressing with a gas iron (*The Tailor and Cutter Journal, 8 June 1916. *Anon:1916.*
By kind permission of Manchester City Galleries: Gallery of Costume, Platt Hall -
Author's Collection).

Labour – A Fine Balancing Act

One of the biggest wartime obstacles to overcome was manpower, as factories
and mills were left with a dwindling workforce as men became soldiers and went
off to fight. A firm in the East End of London advertised for '500 machiners
and machinists for tunics...', the same number for greatcoats, leather jerkins,
200 for breeches and 500 for finishing and felling.[79] Men had voluntarily left
workplaces to enlist, but in January 1916, the Military Service Act gave them
no choice. Single men between the ages of 18 – 41 were now conscripted and
this was extended to married men in May 1916, with 1918 seeing the upper age
limit extended to 51.[80] A man's occupation could exempt him from call up if
it was deemed essential to war work and their job could not be easily done by

anyone else. Tribunals heard these cases along with those seeking exemption on the grounds of occupation, religion, or that they were conscientious objectors. Even with uniform production classed as war work some specialist workers still found themselves conscripted into the army.

The balancing act of labour versus output was a problem manufacturers wrestled with throughout the war. Another issue was the month on month increase in the cost of living. In September 1918, it was recorded at 110 per cent, with the retail cost of food for the working classes up 116 per cent over July 1914.[81] War bonuses to workers failed to keep up with the cost of living, and strikes in all trades and industries took place in pursuit of higher wages. Federations and associations worked with the government to find a balance and agreements. The government now had an enormous vested interest in all of the nation's industrial trades. With increased pressure and workloads, factories and mills began working longer hours. Between January and May 1915, overtime in the woollen and worsted industries was permitted up to nine hours per week which coincided with the severe shortage in uniforms. When the pressure relaxed it was reduced to six hours. But just a few months later in July, overtime was extended from six to eight hours, a fluid reaction to wartime requirements that would continue until 1918.[82] The pressure on factory workers began to take its toll, with the British Association Committee voicing concern over 'war fatigue', the tiring of workers to such an extent it begins to affect manufacturing output.[83]

As the war dragged on more restrictions were placed on the textile industry, so much so that a general ration system was introduced in May 1917. This limited the output, purposes of manufacture, and hours of labour in both the woollen and worsted trade.[84] Restrictions in production continued throughout the year when, in October, wool machines could only be used to prepare Merino or crossbred wool, with further restrictions introduced on the use of Merino other than for military purposes. Only 25 per cent of machinery could be used for the civilian market which proved inadequate as civilian orders started to pile up.[85] At the same time, military clothing factories were placed under the War Office to ensure maximum productivity. This constant ebb and flow of restrictions, hours, cancelled public holidays (such as Easter), would continue through to 1918 and beyond. Britain was running out of raw material and manpower, with the Board of Trade estimating that about half of all industry was on war work.[86]

Prices for goods were fixed and there were restrictions on the number of different types of cloth that could be manufactured for the civilian market. Throughout the war, mills and clothing factories not on government contract required permits and licences to produce, and without them restrictions on imports and exports would limit production. By 1918, from an economic perspective, the war had become one of attrition on the home front as well as on the front line.[87]

The clothing and textile industries used the skills of both sexes, and, indeed, had been employing vast numbers of women even before the war. Spinning mule turners, normally men, maintained and operated the machines whereas women were employed as 'piercers'. This involved mending any breaks in the roving as it was spun. A woman's hand was ideal for this job as they were smaller to get between the strands of roving to mend. Piercers were paid by 'piecework'.[88] At Hainsworth, the wage bill reflects this change rising from £11,000 at the start of the war to more than double this in 1917 at £23,000, when 318 people worked for the firm of which 181 were women aged 16 and over. The number of men aged over 21 was 95 and the remaining 42 youths included men under 21.[89]

With the increased employment of women in factories, especially munitions, to fill staffing shortages, a Women's War Service Register was started at employment exchanges from March 1915 at which 124,000 women were registered.[90] The numbers of women grew with continual encouragement to replace men and many firms that employed them paid the same rates as for men's work. Railway companies also agreed to pay women men's wages,[91] with the Hosiery Knitting Trade going further by adding that this would last 'as long as necessary after the war…'.[92] Noting the exponential increase in women replacing men in industry and commerce, the *Tailor and Cutter Journal* wrote in October 1915 'When this story of this awful war comes to be written it will be found that women factory workers – as well as – men have done their bit. If they have not actually gone to the front and fought in the trenches, they have bravely and unselfishly helped to supply the sinews of war in the shape of uniform for the soldiers, without which no army could fight…'.[93] Proving their worth with war work in factories and elsewhere, by July 1916, the number of women now employed had reached 766,000, a factor that helped women over 30 win the right to vote on 6 February 1918.[94]

Gas Masks - Home Front 'Mass' Manufacture

During the Second Battle of Ypres in April 1915, warfare changed forever when a new weapon was used against which the British Army had no protection. War brings evolution and invention to uniform, the Boer war showed the need for khaki, and the Great War the need for a life-saving mask to counter the deadly new invention of poison gas.

On 22 April 1915 in the Ypres Salient, German troops released chlorine gas with huge and devastating effect.[95] Unprepared and unsure when the next attack would happen, the British Army raced to find protection for hundreds of thousands of men at the front. Initially smoke hoods that were used on board Royal Navy ships were issued to the men, ideal for protection against smoke but completely inadequate against gas.[96] Handkerchiefs soaked with an alkaline solution or with men's own urine were used as a basic gas mask, but the urgent production and issue of an effective gas mask became an unexpected priority. Army divisions at the front commissioned local French and Belgian women to make cotton pad gas masks from locally sourced fabric, with lint bandages made by nuns from the local convent at Poperinghe, near Ypres, some of the first to be used by front line units.[97] On 24 April, just two days after the attack, locally produced gas masks were sent with supplies up the line. The War Office realised that it needed more than what could be manufactured locally, so to fulfil this urgent demand it issued an appeal to the nation:

Liverpool Daily Post – Wednesday 28 April 1915 - 'RESPIRATORS FOR TROOPS – PROTECTION AGAINST POSIONOUS GAS – WAR OFFICE ANNOUNCEMENT.

The War Office issues the following communication: -

As a protection against the asphyxiating gases being used as a weapon of warfare by the Germans supplies of one or both of the following types of respirator are required by the troops at the front. Either can be made easily in any household: - A face piece (to cover mouth and nostrils) formed of an oblong pad of bleached absorbent cotton wool about 5 1/4 inches by 3 inches by ¾ inch, covered with three layers of bleached cotton gauze and fitted with a band to fit around the head to keep the pad in position, consisting of a piece of half inch cotton elastic 16 inches long attached to the narrow end of the pad. A piece of double stockinette 9 ½ inches long, 3 ½ inches wide in the centre, gradually diminishing in width to 2 ½ inches at each end so as to form a loop to pass over the ear. These respirators should be sent in packages of not less than 100 to "Chief Ordnance Officer, Royal Army Clothing Department, Pimlico".[98]

Georgina Lee commented in her diary 'an appeal is launched to all the women of England to make respirators, thousands and millions of them'.[99] Horrified by reports in newspapers of the gas attack, the nation's response was astonishing, with the *Western Daily Press* writing on Friday 30 April 1915 'the press Bureau yesterday afternoon issued the following: - Thanks to the magnificent response already made to the appeal in the Press for respirators for the troops, the War Office is now in position to announce that no more respirators need be made.'[100] It was reported that one million respirators had been made in a day and that during May 1915, British and French troops were supplied with numerous versions of the cotton pad 'respirators' to protect the nose and throat and motoring goggles to protect the eyes.[101]

Development of the gas mask continued with the Hypo (H) helmet by Captain Cluny Macpherson of the Royal Newfoundland Regiment being one of the most notable. Known officially as the 'smoke or H helmet', the Hypo helmet was made from a single layer of flannelette dipped in a neutralising sodium hypo-sulphate solution, with talc eyepieces and a rubber breathing tube. Designed to be worn over the head and tucked into the jacket collar, the Hypo helmet was issued in the beginning of June 1915,[102] with the following announcement appearing in the newspapers:

> The Secretary of the War Office announces that an improved type of respirator has been adopted as the official pattern on the recommendation of a special expert committee. Ample supplies of this respirator are now available at the front and it is undesirable as well as unnecessary, for the public to supply their soldier friends with other patterns.[103]

The Register of Changes Book at the Royal Army Clothing Factory recorded the evolution of the gas mask. Pattern number 8403/1915 was described as Helmets Flannel with film eyepieces and marked as First Pattern. Authorised and sealed by ACD /Pattern 2870 on 28 May 1915, the helmets were unpopular with troops as the impregnated flannel was greasy and breathing through the tube difficult, the eyepieces could break and the single layer of flannel did not give full protection. Modifications were made and pattern number 8417/1915 Helmets flannel with film eye pieces authorised and sealed by ACD/Pattern 2817 on 28 June 1915 and marked 'Improved Pattern.'.[104] Over two and a half million of the Hypo Helmets were issued to soldiers in a waterproof bag that protected it from rips and tears, thus preventing the chemical from evaporating.[105] Priority of manufacture in Britain meant that as soon as a sufficiency was available, each soldier at the front was issued with two Hypo helmets and a third kept in the reserve dump of a division.

Further improvements led to the appearance of the P (Phenate) Helmet.[106] Recorded as a first pattern on 29 July 1915 and described as Helmets Flannelette Double without eye pieces[107] (which would be added later), the helmet was sprayed with compounds of various chemicals for protection. Over nine million of these were issued and reached the front line in November 1915, but within a month further improvement was needed when phosgene gas was used in a German attack on 19 December.[108] Although the P Helmet provided some protection, it was not total and so hexamine, a neutralising compound, was added to protect against phosgene. This became known as the PH (Phenate-Hexamine) Helmet which first appeared January 1916. Over 14 million were issued before it was modified, and in Spring 1916 the Large Box Respirator was issued to soldiers in specific regiments like the Royal Field Artillery. It proved cumbersome and the Small Box Respirator (SBR) soon replaced it,[109] with a mask secured tightly

*General evolution of gas mask (*The Literary Digest History of the World War Volume V. *Halsey: 1919 - Author's Collection).*

around the face by elastic straps and goggles to protect the eyes.[110] A nose clip was provided to ensure the soldier breathed through the mouthpiece, with a tube leading to an absorbent box that contained charcoal, made from coconut husks, combined with soda lime manganite which neutralised the gas.

After August 1916, the SBR was standard issue but was modified in 1917 when celluloid eyepieces were replaced by shatterproof glass, and a small cotton pad was put in the box to protect against toxic smoke.[111] It took a year for the gas mask to evolve from the cotton face mask to a specifically designed integral piece of kit. A year may seem a long time to provide equipment to protect men, but it had taken many more years to develop the khaki tunic from conception in 1901 to the final pattern in 1907. The early cotton pad gas mask is a prime example where mothers, wives, sweethearts, aunts, or grandmothers had a physical direct impact by giving protection to their menfolk at the front.

Soldiers' 'Comforts'

Prompted by such patriotic desires to support the soldiers away on active service, women on the home front became the unofficial suppliers of non-regulation items. Creating popular knitted and sewn 'comforts' such as cardigans, jumpers, scarfs, balaclavas,[112] and body belts (to keep the kidneys warm), this 'cottage industry' could be undertaken anywhere, by anyone of any age - children, women, Belgian refugees,[113] even wounded soldiers played their part. They became an unofficial home front 'army' of individuals, associations and groups that made everything from bandages to clothing.[114] Sapper Albert (Jack) Martin, a signaller in the Royal Engineers, wrote in his diary for 23 March 1917 'When I unfolded it a piece of paper dropped out – I picked it up and read this: Miss Dulcie Bennet,

111 Mansfield Road, Nottingham, wishes the boy who receives this belt (body belt) the best of luck and a safe return to Blighty. xxxxx for luck'.[115]

Additional socks were no doubt the undisputed king of the knitted home-comfort article, symbolising the worst of conditions at the front, with thousands knitted by loved ones. Men went through their issue socks faster than any other article of uniform, lasting on average only seven days on the front line, due to their feet being often ankle deep in water during winter. The topic of socks was raised in Parliament on 17 November 1914 when Mr Hogge posed the question 'Why the knitting of socks, etc., by private enterprise was stopped and an appeal subsequently made for hundreds of thousands?'. To which Mr Tennant replied:

The War Office maintains a sufficient supply of socks for the troops at the front and the knitting of them was not therefore the most useful form the activities of the public could take. It was found however, that there was such a strong wish on the part of the private persons desirous of helping the troops to make and send socks that it became necessary to co-ordinate the efforts, to ensure uniformity of supply and proper distribution.[116]

The War Office used this large informal textile workforce to supplement official production, and throughout the war some 88 million items were produced this way. The 'cottage industry' nature of this supply was also a vital physical and emotional connection between families and soldiers.[117] The private manufacture of socks could, however, be considered as ambiguous as often its production was half-way between official uniform and 'comfort'.

Chapter 3

Factory to Front

George had an interesting route to France. On 23 June 1915, Bristol's Own marched complete with band to Temple Meads train station where it left Bristol for further training at Sutton Coldfield in the West Midlands. They were to be part of Kitchener's Fourth Army under Northern Command. Prior to leaving Bristol, an order had been sent to the Commanding Officer of Bristol's Own from the Assistant Adjutant General, Northern Command. Writing on 12 June 1916, the order stated:

> Captain Bennett Goldney M.P. has under War Office instruction reported himself here, having been directed by the War Office to visit various battalions and brigades of the Fourth New Army with the object of selecting five men as "expert Tunneller" for overseas from each battalion. According to his instructions, these men have to be despatched at once to Chatham, and the necessary procedure will be explained by Captain Bennet Goldney on the spot to the various Commanding Officers from whose battalions these men may be selected.[1]

Out of around 1,000 men in the battalion, George was one of just five selected to be a tunneller[2] as he had previously been a mine examiner.[3] Major Norton Griffiths was the brains behind tunnelling and had permission from the War Office to find men with mining or sewer experience.[4] Accompanied by a mining colleague Alfred Jones, George transferred to Chatham the same day that Bristol's Own left for Sutton Coldfield, though he did not sign his transfer documents as it was noted that he was 'already in France' by the time they were sent. George arrived at Chatham, home of the Royal Engineers on 24 June 1915 and embarked for France just four days later.

Prior to embarkation, George received a complete new issue of kit, with the army form 'Clothing and Necessaries' issued by the New Clothing Store, RE Depot, Chatham, detailing a full list of articles. The Regimental Quartermaster Sergeant placed a tick in red ink next to articles issued. George was given two pairs of boots, one SD cap, two pairs of drawers, one SD jacket, one pair of SD trousers, one pair of puttees, one waistcoat and one greatcoat. Other items included spare bootlaces, hair, tooth and clothes brushes, knife and spoon, boot and brass polish, as well as three pairs of socks and two shirts known as 'necessaries'.[5] The new issue of kit reflected that he was now a sapper in the regular army and his uniform was now provided by the War Office. Supplying millions of items of clothing, uniform and 'comforts' to soldiers like George on the Western Front, it was vital to have an efficient supply chain for supplies and stores, starting on the home front and the factory.

Uniform Supply Chain - Home Front

Logistics are crucial for any army, as the 'function of the fighting troops is to carry out the actual military operations, and all their energies should be concentrated on those duties… [the] function of the administrative services and departments is to provide the fighting troops with the personnel, animals, and material required…'.[6] How much more so for the vast numbers of men involved in the world's first global industrialized conflict.

As soon as the deadline for Britain's ultimatum to Germany passed in August 1914, the machinery of war was set in motion.[7] Initiating the 'War Book,' a document that held everything every government and military department would need to action in the event of war, the book listed the ports that specific stores and supplies, including clothing, would pass through.[8] So began the long journey for uniforms to reach the men at the front.

Factory → Royal Army Clothing Department → Stores: Responsible for clothing, Quartermaster General [branch] 7 (QMG 7) was supervised by Major General Stevens, the Director of Equipment, and Stores. The Royal Army Clothing Department was part of QMG 7, and provided, stored, and supplied clothing for the Chief Ordnance Officer (COO). Receiving the clothing from the factory, uniform was sent from the main central depot at Pimlico, London, to regiments and units across the country. These clothing requirements, known as 'demands,' were sent from Regimental Quartermasters to Pimlico. New 'issue' would be sent from clothing depots, such as Pimlico to the stores of regiments and units for the Quartermaster to issue.

For the battalions of regiments and units in overseas garrisons, a similar system of sending stores abroad was already in place, it just evolved and expanded as the war in Europe continued. In the field, a chain of 'demands' (a list of the army's requirements) was requested from the Commanding Officer of a unit to his superior and so on up the line of command until it reached the Director of Supplies. Describing the total poundage (weight), number of cases, garments or bushels needed, because of the fluid nature of the army's movements, clothing 'demands' were usually made monthly, though they could also be sent three months in advance. These 'demands' were sent to Britain and the Surveyor General of Supplies' office.[9]

Before the uniform started its journey, ALL uniform was inspected after manufacture at the depot[10] for quality control before continuing to London

Bundles of uniforms waiting to be despatched. Royal Army Clothing Depot housed in the Exhibition Hall, Olympia, London (Author's Collection).

storehouses in places such as Olympia and White City. As the war progressed, the inspection section evolved and sent 'viewers' to the factories to check the articles as they were being made. Intended to speed the process up, this enabled the finished items to be bundled and transported direct to the storehouses ready for shipment. During 1915, inspection branches opened at commercial manufacturing centres such as Bradford, Birmingham and Leeds. Inspected by QMG [branch] 9,[11] before long these depots were running out of space. A new storehouse depot was needed on a railway line and so Didcot was opened in June 1915.

Stores → Home Ports: Holding the bulkier stores, Didcot would become the main centre for delivery and distribution, dealing with around 2000 railway trucks[12] a month. With more than 30 miles (48km) of track and sidings, and 1,500,000 square feet (1.39km²) of covered storage space needed, finding enough labour to run the Didcot depot was a problem as many AOC companies initially formed to run them were now posted overseas. Initially run by local volunteers, it was not unusual to see working groups of ladies and pupils from nearby Kingsham Industrial School, with at one point, boys and masters from Eton arriving to volunteer, including His Royal Highness (HRH) Prince Henry. Eventually two Labour companies each consisting of about 500 soldiers, along with 1,560 civilian men and 760 women aided the Army Ordnance Corps staff.

Home Ports → Sea Transport: As part of the logistics chain, certain ports around the country had been charged to despatch specific supplies. Avonmouth, Bristol, despatched motor transport and horses, with one of the largest remount centres in Britain sited at Shirehampton near the port. It was common to see London buses travelling through the streets of Bristol en-route to Avonmouth.[13] At the beginning of the war, stores (including uniform and clothing) and supplies were embarked from Newhaven[14] in Sussex, but in 1915 this changed as the number of embarkation ports grew. After August 1916, the supply of clothing required at the front switched from the Newhaven to Le Havre route to Newhaven to Rouen for armies in France, adding another route from Littlehampton[15] to Calais for armies located in Belgium and the Ypres Salient. The ports of Richborough and Dover were also heavily used, but the most important cargo usually passed through Southampton - the never-ending supply of men. Six divisions of the British Expeditionary Force needed to be transported to France as quickly as possible. Sir Henry Wilson was, in 1910, the Director of Military Operations for the War Office and had at that time planned the mobilisation and movement of men. He revised the railway timetable to get men to Southampton as efficiently as possible. The plan worked, with 65,814 men passing through Southampton to Le Havre by 26 August 1914. Along with their kit, horses, wagons, and weapons, at its height Southampton handled a troop train every twelve minutes, with an empty troop train heading back out within forty minutes.[16]

With the number of shipments increasing,[17] Richborough would by the end of the First World War become one of the largest ports for the import and export of ordnance stores, with vast amounts of salvaged shell cases for recycling returned to Britain through its gates. Pressing into action old French sea barges to transport material from Dover to France, Richborough port was a perfect site due to its flat terrain being ideal for shallow draft barges. The first purpose built barges sailed from Richborough in late 1916.[18] The port was also ideal for purposely designed 'train ferries', constructed to speed up the supply of heavy goods such as artillery guns by having railway lines built into the deck, allowing wagons of mixed stores to be railed straight onto and off the ferry. The manpower needed to move 1000 tons (1016 metric tonnes) of materials from factory to France, using conventional methods, was around 1,500 men. The same tonnage could be handled by only 106 men on the train ferry service. It took around 30 minutes to turn a train ferry around from embarkation to departure. Probably due to the speed and efficiency of this system, it could operate with only two train ferries from Richborough to France, whilst a third from Southampton, was only used as a backup.[19]

Train ferry (Copyright Public Domain).

Sea Transport → France: With the Admiralty responsible for the control of all sea transportation, most clothing stores were shipped by the traditional method from either Newhaven to Rouen or Littlehampton to Calais, depending on where along the front the soldier was serving. There were two main types of ship being operated - Transport that carried units with or without animals, supplies and stores or as hospital ships, and Freight that carried personnel, animals and their attendants or stores.[20] It was essential to know the size of packed goods from clothing to food as each section on the supply line needed to maximise space as efficiently as possible. Clothing was bundled or cased to specific dimensions, the quantities in each determined by the size of the article, and was laid down in the Field Service Pocket Note Book[21] (Table B). Space and tonnage had to be calculated for everything that crossed the English Channel, including men and horses. For long ocean journeys four tons (4.6 metric tonnes) per man and twelve tons (12.19 metric tonnes) per horse were allocated to cover stores, provisions, and equipment required. For short ocean journeys, this was reduced to two tons (2.03 metric tonnes) per man and eight tons (8.12 metric tonnes) per horse.[22]

As navigating the Channel became more dangerous due to U-boat activity, as well as increased cross-Channel traffic, any disruptions to shipping would delay and, in some cases, prevent much needed men and stores, especially ammunition and food, from reaching the front. The British Army on the Western Front depended on its supplies of food and armaments which is why Britain's shipping was targeted by German submarines in an unconstrained campaign in February 1917.[23]

Attrition was fast becoming a weapon of war by 1917. German submarines too often hit their mark and losing a ship full of supplies put ever more strain on the manufacturing front.

Article	How Packed	Size in Inches
Blankets	Bales of 25	18 x 21 x 32
Boots	Cases of 45	38 x 21.5 x 15
Greatcoats (dismounted)	Bales 25	29 x 20 x 29
Dressings, field	Cases of 500	30.5 x 19.5 x 16
Helmets	Cases of 20	36 x 23.5 x 17
Puttees	Bales of 200 pairs	29 x 20 x 21
Service Dress – Jackets	Bales of 50	30 x 20 x 22
Service Dress – Trousers	Bales of 50	25 x 15 x 28
Sheets – ground	Cases of 60	26 x 22 x 19
Shirts, flannel	Bales of 100	26 x 20 x 21
Socks – worsted	Bales of 300 pairs	29 x 16 x 20
Towels	Bales of 200	25 x 21 x 20

Table B - Clothing bundle specifics and quantities (by size of article) Field Service Pocket Note Book - War Establishments. Field Service Pocket Book 1914 (Reprinted Amendments in 1916 and 1917).

Despite the submarine threat, British and Allied ships kept criss-crossing the English Channel. The first two ships to arrive at Calais from Littlehampton were the S.S *Irwell* and S.S *Viscount* on 17 November 1915. The *Irwell* held a mixed cargo of 1023 tons (1039 metric tonnes), of which 268 tons (272 metric tonnes) were clothing, whereas the *Viscount* carried a mixed cargo of 361 tons (366 metric tonnes), of which 235.5 tons (239 metric tonnes) were clothing. On average, a ship carrying some sort of clothing arrived every two days[24] from a British port.

Route to the Front – Western Front[25]

To enable stores to reach the front line, the supply route to the battle zone first had to be set up. Known as 'Lines of Communications', these supply routes would begin at the port of entry and continued into fighting zones. The BEF was a single army and so needed a single Line of Communication. After the retreat from Mons and the First Battle of Aisne in September 1914, France, Britain, Belgium and Germany were drawn into the 'race for the sea' which led directly to the beginnings of trench warfare. When the Second Army arrived in France, and with the First Army now in Belgium, a single 'Northern Line of Communication' could no longer supply both armies at the same time. In Spring 1915, a second 'Southern Line of Communication' was set up. Whilst units and territorial forces were mobilised in Britain, officers and men from administrative services and departments were sent to France.

These early supply arrangements included offices for the Headquarters of the Commander-in-Chief of the Forces in the Field and Inspector General of

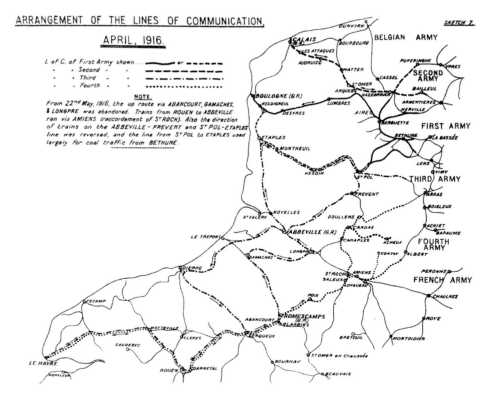

Arrangement of the Line of Communications **(Official History of the Great War. Transportation on the Western Front 1914–1918**. *Henniker: 1937 - Author's Collection).*

Communications (IGC). The latter arranged transportation via railway, road and inland waterways. Storage at Bases, Supply and Ordnance Depots, access to railways and quarters for troops all needed to be found. Working in conjunction with permission of French and Belgian authorities, 'Lines of Communication' were established ahead of the arrival of the fighting men, horses, artillery and equipment. Divided into two categories - fighting troops, and administrative services and departments,[26] the latter of which provided the stores (including clothing) for the armies at the front. This was sub-divided into three main branches:

General Staff: The General Staff were responsible to the Commander-in-Chief, and their main purpose was to decide where the armies, divisions, and brigades were to fight, and to organise the distribution and movement of troops. Arranging draft orders for operations in whichever theatre of operation they were in, General Staff informed the Quartermaster General and the Assistant General (AG) of estimated requirements so troops could be supplied in time.

Adjutant General: The Adjutant General's staff oversaw the administration of military law and its regulations, including issues of pay, promotions, and the spiritual welfare of the British Army. They also dealt with casualties and invalids, the provision of medical equipment, and the burial of the dead as well as administering garrisons, camp duties and Prisoners of War.

Quartermaster General: The Quartermaster General oversaw the many aspects of supply. Arranging administration between field commanders with the IGC dealing with ammunition, equipment, uniform and clothing, and supplies (except medical equipment which came under the AG Branch). Transportation via land, sea and inland waterways[27] as well as railway administration, remounts, veterinary and postal services were also the responsibility of the Quartermaster General[28] (see Appendix B).

These three main branches worked in close co-operation. Allocation of duties governing parts of the Line of Communication to directors and their staff ultimately made it easier to keep the entire system working. Units of the Army Ordnance Department arranged Supply Depots and Railheads, provided vehicles for distribution and issued all stores (including uniform) whereas the Army Service Corps provided the men to deliver it.

The system of supply had a complex network although its basic principle was sound. It is the differing meanings of words, and their context that compounds the complexity. The Field Service Pocket Book 1914 (reprinted in 1916 and 1917) states 'Train – Transport allotted to fighting units for their conveyance of the baggage stored and supplies necessary for their subsistence...';[29] a reference to the carriage of stores and supplies mainly by horse,[30] whereas to most people a train refers to a railway locomotive.[31] In the instance of delivering stores, supplies and clothing to George who by now was at the front and Railway Wood, the 177th Tunnelling Company was supplied with their provisions largely by motor transport.[32]

Ypres and its approaches were well within range of German artillery and by 1915 the town had suffered large scale destruction. A shortage of motor vehicles meant that wear and tear on motor vehicles was huge.[33] In May 1915, lorries assigned to the Royal Engineers around Ypres were taken from vehicles held in reserve at ammunition parks.[34] The retreat from Mons in late summer 1914 led to sections of the original 'Line of Communication's' Base and Supply Depots being evacuated, with stores, clothing and equipment hurriedly transferred south to more secure areas.[35][36] After the front line was redrawn, earlier Bases, Supply Depots and Routes were re-occupied with the re-opening of the 'Northern Line of Communication' in June 1915.[37]

While the fighting war had become static, it had become a war of movement for logistics and the supply of stores (particularly of replacement clothing).[38] A general overview and the ideal locations for each stage of supply were given in Field Service Manuals and Pocket Notebooks, but they were just that, an ideal. George spent most of his war in the Ypres Salient, in the Railway Wood area, and so my focus here will be on the logistical chain that supplied northern France and Belgian, the 'Northern Line of Communication', starting at Calais.

Base Port Depots (France) → ***Advanced Supply Depots:*** In the event of a mainland European conflict, France had pre-assigned three Base Ports for the British Army's use; Calais, Dunkirk and Le Havre. After the retreat from Mons in August-September 1914, Dunkirk and Calais were swiftly closed as the extent of the German advance at that point was not known. Once the war had become entrenched in late 1914-early 1915, Calais re-opened in April 1915, though Dunkirk was still regarded as too close to the front and so remained closed.

Concentrating on Calais, the chain of command at the British Army's storage space and transit sheds was the Base Commandant, the Military Landing Officer (MLO) who communicated with the Inspector General of Communications and the Director of Sea Transport (DOST) When a ship, such as the S.S. *Irwell*, left home port, details of its cargo were sent to both the Inspector General of Communications and Calais. When the ship arrived, the DOST informed the MLO who boarded the ship and checked the cargo. Nothing could be unloaded, including men, until the MLO had arranged its collection from the various departments concerned with a ship's cargo. Once arranged he would issue orders for the unloading. Regarding men, on boarding the ship, the MLO would hand orders to incoming commanders of where they and their men should go.[39] The huge amount of material sent over at this point was then split into two categories:

Supplies: Items such as food, forage and ammunition were needed daily and were called the feeding strength of the armies. Daily estimates of these were requested from the Base Port depots based on war establishment figures, the number of men and animals a unit had. War establishment figures of fighting units were usually taken from their War Diaries,[40] with George's unit, 177th Tunnelling Company, showing a company strength on 31 March 1916 of 21 officers and 323 Other Ranks.[41] Supplies were usually dispatched within 24 hours of receiving the 'demand'.[42]

Stores: Stores were bulky and sizable items, such as clothing and uniforms, that were needed frequently, but not on a daily basis. The term covered all the items not covered by supplies, and included tents, vehicles, medical equipment and clothing. Known as bulk issue, these goods were 'indented' for (ordered) by wire once a week by the Ordnance Officer of the requesting army Formation. Depending on what the item was, bulk issue was dispatched on specific days (Table C) and ready for issue a week later (Table D). It was more efficient and easier to supply a whole division than to send lots of small parcels to individual fighting units.[43] Stores and supplies would be packed on wagons and sent to Regulating Stations using the railway network in France and Belgium. At the end of April 1916, Calais issued a staggering 627,873 items of clothing[44] in just one month (Table E).

By 1917 there were eight Base Depots; Boulogne, Rouen and Le Havre had been set up in August 1914, Dieppe and Marseilles in late 1914, St Valery sur Somme in March 1916, and Cherbourg in November 1917. On 22 July 1915, the Chief Ordnance Officer at Calais received notice that it would issue stores and supplies to the entire Second Army stationed in Belgium which comprised three corps made up of several divisions[45] (see Appendix C). With a division numbering about 20,000 men, Calais needed to provide stores (including clothing) and supplies for a total of around 140,000 men,[46] in addition to goods and equipment for the Belgian and French Armies.[47]

Clothing item	Wire demand	Due at Railhead
Boots	Saturday	Following Wednesday
SD Clothing, Greatcoats, Woollen Drawers, vest, and Puttees.	Tuesday	Following Saturday
Ground sheets, Flannelette, Smoke helmets	Wednesday	Following Saturday
Cotton drawers, Shirts, Socks, Caps, Necessaries, Chevrons	Thursday	Following Monday

Table C - Specified days for bulk Issue of clothing - Compiled from WO 95/4020/5: Lines of Communication. Calais Base: Chief Ordnance Officer: 1916 Apr–1916 Jun.

Stores	Indent to be Sent in on	Available for Issue
Boots, SD Clothing, Greatcoats, Woollen Drawers, Vests and Puttees	Thursday	Thursday Week
Accoutrements, Oil & Grease	Sunday	Monday Week
Picketing Gear, Camp Kettles, Blankets, Ground Sheets, Entrenching Implements, Buckets, Water Canvas, Sponge Cloths, Cotton Waste, Flannelette and Horse Rugs	Monday	Monday Week
Horse Shoes, Clothing, Shirts, Socks and Balance	Saturday	Saturday Week
Winter Clothing	Wednesday	Wednesday Week

Table D - Specified days for Ordnance Stores Indents and availability for issue - Compiled from WO 95/1879 Adjutant and Quarter-Master General.

Service Dress Jackets	88,870
Service Dress Trousers	71,810
Drawers, woollen	32,697 pairs
Shirts, flannel	102,669
Socks, worsted	229,593 pairs
Boots, ankle	102,234 pairs

Table E - Breakdown of garments issued by Calais April 1916 - Compiled from WO 95/4020/5: Lines of Communication. Calais Base: Chief Ordnance Officer: 1916 Apr–1916 Jun.

To make it easier and simpler for stores and supplies to reach the men, the supply of a division was broken down into 'baggage' and 'supply'[48](Table F).

Railways would become a crucial factor in logistics although their use for supply was not new. During the Boer War, supplies and stores were transported by train from the coast inland to the soldiers.[49] Long before the First World War, countries had recognised the importance of railways in any future conflict with a secret Railway European Committee formed in 1912 by Britain outlining contingency plans in the event of a European war. Belgium, with a large railway network of over 4,700 miles (7564km) of track[50] that crossed borders into Germany, France and Luxembourg, drew up its own contingency plans in the years prior to the outbreak of war.

The German 'Schlieffen' plan was to invade France and outflank the French Army by passing through Belgium. Keen to utilise the rail network in this plan,

Germany demanded to use the Belgian railway tracks to transport their troops. On 2 August 1914, as monarch of a neutral country, King Albert I of Belgium refused the German request and on 3 August 1914, he instructed the railway contingency plan be instigated. This involved destroying tunnels, bridges and tracks that led into Germany, France and Luxembourg to prevent a German invasion.[51] The partial success of Belgium's destruction of its railway network did slow down the German advance, allowing the Belgian Army to form a defensive line long enough for reinforcements to arrive from France and Britain. Once the two sides had started to 'dig in,' parts of the railway that had been destroyed needed to be rebuilt.

The French rail system was struggling to cope with the needs of the French, Belgian and British, as everything travelled on these lines - civilians fleeing the

Four Brigades, each of which consisted of…	Divisional Troops	Divisional Ammunition Column	Divisional Train (Motor and Horse Transport)
Infantry Brigade HQ	Divisional HQ	Dealt with by	Dealt with by a Divisional Troop Officer
4 x Battalions	Divisional Artillery HQ	a Divisional	
1 x Field Company R.E.			Divided into two sections – Baggage and Supply.
1 x Field Ambulance	Divisional Engineer HQ	Troop Supply	
1 x Brigade Field Artillery			
1 x Company Divisional Train (First Line Transport which took over transporting from the Divisional Train) Divided into two sections – Baggage and Supply.	Divisional Train HQ	Officer	Baggage – Transported HQ's, camp equipment, soldiers, and Officers' kit when a Division moved to new area or new billets. When stationary could be used in supply section.
	Divisional Mounted Troops	All	
	Army Veterinary Corps	ammunition	
Baggage – Transported HQ's, camp equipment, soldiers, and officers' kit when a Brigade moved to new area or new billets. When stationary could be used in supply section.	Supply Section	was delivered	
	Howitzer Brigade	separately to	Supply – Transported supplies (daily goods such as foods) and stores (such as clothing)
Supply – Transported supplies (daily goods such as foods) and stores (such as clothing)	Heavy Artillery Batteries	other stores	
	Signal Company	and supplies.	

Table F - Divisional Supply - Compiled from An Officer's Manual of the Western Front 1914-1918. War Establishments. Field Service Pocket Book 1914 (Reprinted Amendments in 1916 and 1917).

fighting, troop movements, equipment, daily requirements, supplies, as well as the wounded and sick to hospitals. The Line of Communication Routine Order No 179 explained 'The working of the French Railways remains entirely in the hands of the French Authorities…'.[52] The French commercial railway network was taken over by the French Authorities at the outbreak of war. The British Army's railway requirements were communicated to French military authorities by the Inspector General of Communications. France initially maintained expansion and repair of existing lines, as Britain's offer of help had, at first, been refused. The British Army, during the battle of Marne in September 1914, advanced so quickly that it ended up some 30 miles (48km) in front of the nearest railhead, a distance that took too long for motor transport to cover. Repairs to the railway were not able to keep pace with the advance of the army. On 19 September 1914, the French Director of Railways (*Directeur des Chemins de Fer*) accepted an offer from the Inspector General of Communications for British Railway troops to assist with repairs and extending the rail network, as well as now being responsible for the maintenance of the Northern Line of Communication in Belgium.[53]

Winter Migration: Twice a year, in winter and spring, extra pressure was put on the 'Line of Communication.' In October, winter clothing was issued, with greatcoats, extra jumpers, cardigans, balaclavas, gloves, blankets, socks, woollen underwear and vests, all of which had been in storage for the summer. In spring, winter clothing was returned to Base Ports, from where they were sent to laundries, disinfected, and sent on to Ordnance depots to be stored. Items that needed repairs were sent to clothing workshops.[54] Any items beyond repair would be cut into rags and sold as scrap either in France or shipped back from the Base Ports to Britain as recycled 'salvage.' When the S.S. *Rye* left Calais in 6 April 1916, its cargo included 443 sacks of old rags, totalling over 21 tons (21.3 metric tonnes) and when it docked at Newhaven, these were transported to Messer J Eastwood and Co, in Dewsbury.[55]

Advanced Supply Depots/Field Supply Depots → Regulating Stations: Storage space at Base Port depots was very limited so additional locations were quickly established between the port and Regulating Stations to stockpile stores and supplies. Known as 'Advanced Supply / Field Supply Depots,' these stores were often sited on or near a railway line, though barges would also be used if the depot had a river or canal alongside.[56]

Each Army was allotted a 'Base Port' and several 'Advanced Supply Depots' for their divisions to draw from, with each depot usually holding a specific type of stores or supplies, such as grocery, engineering, wood and clothing - St Omer stored clothing and uniform for the 'Northern Line of Communication'.[57] At Wardrecques, 5 miles (8km) south-east of St Omer and 32 miles (51km) from Calais, a Field Supply Depot was opened in January 1915. Housed in a paper mill and able to hold 17,222ft^2 (c.1,600m^2) under cover and 53,820ft^2 (c.5,000m^2) outside, the Field Supply Depot held a reserve of one day's ration for around 300,00 British troops, 300,000 Indian troops, oats for 100,000 horses, as well as handling surplus supplies left at railheads. With administration offices in small out-buildings and tents providing accommodation until Autumn 1915 (after which local houses were used), Wardrecques was an ideal location for a Field Supply Depot as it had both railway sidings, a canal, and an adjacent road.[58] Not all stores and supplies were sent to 'Advanced or Field Depots' when Wardrecques Field Supply Depot closed in November 1916. Demands from divisions from December 1916 onwards were sent direct from the Base Ports, or from several specific 'Advanced or Field Supply Depots'.

Regulating Stations → ***Railhead (Railways)***: In a phrase taken from the French regulations for the maintenance by rail of an army in the field, 'Regulating Stations' are described as 'places where railway trains are marshalled',[59] and were where railway trains from Base Port and 'Advanced or Field Supply Depots' converged. Unloaded by the Army Service Corps, the stores for a Formation would then be collated from several trains to form a single railway train. A system of easy identification of stores within the wagons was needed to assist the Railway Transport Officer (RTO) in verifying and checking the goods. Initially each Formation was given a colour code, either a single colour or combination. Letters, either single or grouped, were printed over the colour and this identified the contents of the wagon and to which Formation it was destined. Later in the war as the number of Formations and units grew this system changed to numbers that had been allotted to divisions or brigades.[60] Once loaded, the railway train was despatched to the Railhead allotted for a formation, division or brigade to draw from.

An exception to this practice was the Tunnelling Companies, which bypassed the standard chain of command that divisions and brigades adhered to. Classed as Army Troops, Tunnelling Companies answered directly to the Corps or Army Headquarters.[61] Rapid growth in the number of Tunnelling Companies in 1915 and 1916 brought administrative challenges. On 1 January 1916, the post of Inspector of Mines (IOM) was created and under his command were Controllers of Mines (COM). Tasked with liaising between the Tunnelling Companies and the Army to which they belonged, the Controller of Mines ensured the supply and issue of equipment and materials could be more efficiently administered.[62] Tunnelling Companies answered to the Inspector of Mines who had the power to visit any mine on the Western Front without any notice given to division or brigade Headquarters. The only other person with this power was the Commander-in-Chief of the Armies in the Field.[63] This meant that although the Tunnelling Companies worked closely with division and brigades, they were not commanded by them.

As the 177th Tunnelling Company War Diary shows, each month they were assigned to a different corps, division, and brigade, and so all their stores (engineering, equipment, and clothing etc)[64] needed to come together to form a single baggage and supply train and this happened at Regulating Stations.[65] With their daily supplies and stores coming up the line through the divisional route, currently it is impossible to determine if their bulk stores were supplied through army, corps or divisional level. For administrative purposes, the Tunnelling Companies were attached to divisions and brigades, which would suggest they received daily and bulk issue in the same way as the infantry soldier. If supplied on a corps troop basis, then Corps Supply Columns collected stores from the railhead and proceeded to Corps 'Dumps', where it was divided up and delivered direct to units.[66] For the 177th Tunnelling Company, their 'dump' was Hellfire Corner.[67] This command structure caused some confusion, as Tunnelling Company officers had to work with the officers of infantry battalions, both operationally as well as sorting out their men's requirements.

Railhead → Rendezvous → Refilling Point (Supply Columns of Motor Transport): 'Railheads' on the Belgian front were often at stations in large towns such as Poperinghe or in smaller villages such as Proven which was at the end of a spur line. Constructed off the main broad-gauge line at various locations such Ouderdom, Dickebusch, Vlamertinghe were specific stores such as those for stone or wood. Other sites, like Remy Sidings, had stores such as that for clothing sited next to the Divisional Rest Camps and Casualty Clearing Stations. Each division would be assigned a railhead from which they collected their stores and supplies, resulting in several divisions all drawing from one railhead. When the divisional railway train arrived at the railhead, each wagon had identifying marks indicating which division they were for. On arrival, the Railway Transport Officer handed the documentation to the Railway Supply Officer, (RSO) who checked it then wrote out a 'chit' [receipt] on behalf of the intended recipients. Each receipt listed the commodity to be issued to the different sections of a division.[68] Lorries then met the railway trains at the railhead.[69]

Supervised by an NCO from each section, each lorry was loaded and checked. Accompanying them, the Brigade Senior Supply Officer (BSSO) of the division would confirm the issue of stores and supplies on the Railway Supply Officer paperwork once loaded. The lorries then took their freight to one of two locations depending on whether the division was on the march or in camp. In special circumstances lorries were authorised to carry stores greater distances. Such was the case 29 November 1916 when 'An urgent demand received from the 51st Division for 3,000 pairs of trousers and 3,000 pairs of drawers' woollen, approved by QMG and stores despatched by special motor transport by road'.[70]

A 'Rendezvous' was mainly used when a division was on the move. It could take days to move the 20,000 men, horses, vehicles and equipment of a division

Truck loading from train at Railhead (Author's Collection).

to a new area. Supplies were required daily so the motor transport would collect its supplies from the nearest railhead, then proceed to a rendezvous point to meet their division. The Brigade Senior Supply Officer sent the baggage section and ammunition column to the billets and the lorries for the brigades and divisional troops to their respective 'Refilling Point'.

Officers Shops: During the British retreat from Mons in August-September 1914, the stocking of officers' uniforms had become a significant issue. In response, the War Office at once set about acquiring jackets, shirts, and caps in the officer's pattern ready for immediate dispatch. Charging the officers for any articles they needed, this method of supply worked well and was popular. During the Summer of 1916, an 'Officer's Shop' was set up in each Army area and run by the Army Ordnance Department. Stocking item of uniform an officer would need from collar studs to field boots. Officers now had the choice of either ordering a new uniform direct from their tailors back in Britain, or for the first time, purchase everything over the counter from the new shop. These proved popular, with one Officers Shop in Poperinghe selling thousands of pounds Sterling of stock in a single month.[71]

Every day, food, water and ammunition (supplies) followed this route to the front. General clothing and uniform such as SD trousers, SD jackets, shirts, and underwear (not socks) would stop short of proceeding any further to the trenches, normally reaching as far forward as the railhead or Refilling Point. When men came out the line they collected items of clothing which had been issued to them from Company headquarters, as well as any 'comforts' posted from home. In the case of George and the 177th Tunnelling Company, this would have been at a site north-west of Poperinghe, just off the Proven road.

Refilling Point → Wagon Lines (Quartermaster Stores – Train, Section Supply Horses, Mules and Wagons) → Trench Dumps: Refilling Points were simple and basic constructions, just a place where stores and supplies were handed over divided into four 'dumps', one for each brigade of a division.[72] When a division was in one area for any length of time, the motor transport would proceed to a 'park' and stay overnight before its onward journey to the Refilling Point. Each Division was assigned a Refilling Point from which the four brigades of a division would draw, and which the divisional horse transport would take to each brigade.

Wagon Lines (Quartermaster Stores): Receiving the supplies and stores from the Brigade Supply Officer, the Brigade Quartermaster issued them to the four Company Quartermaster Sergeants of each battalion, who in turn issued the stores and supplies to each platoon. The first line transport of a battalion (consisting of horse and wagons) would then transport to trench 'dumps';[73] [74] though congestion, condition of roads and German artillery impacted on the movement of goods,[75] meaning other modes of transport were frequently needed. *Decauville Light Railways*: The Decauville Light Railways were an ingenious development of the Frenchman Paul Decauville in 1870. A portable system with prefabricated tracks that could be laid easily and quickly, the light railways consisted of three gauges - 40cm, 50cm and 60cm – and were designed for industrial use both outside as well as inside buildings. Their usefulness was soon developed for military purposes, when artillery Captain Prosper Pechot in 1888 recognised it's potential and designed locomotives to be used on the railway. Utilising the 60cm gauge for military purposes, the Decauville Light Railways transported bulky and heavier items of stores and equipment to soldiers in areas standard gauge railways could not reach.

Extensively used by the French in their own areas, the prefabricated sections of track could be laid fast and quickly over almost any terrain. Employing a host of railway trucks, water tanks and locomotives in many sizes, they were used to get food and ammunition up to the forward trench systems and to evacuate wounded soldiers out. Steam locomotives were used initially, but were soon replaced by petrol-driven versions to avoid the smoke being used by the

*Light Railway, somewhere on the Western Front (*The War Illustrated Album de Luxe – Volume III The Autumn Campaign of 1916. *Hammerton (Ed): 1917 - Author's Collection).*

Germans to target the trains. The petrol version came in various guises, such as a Model T Ford car engine, steering wheel and front seats mounted on a railway carriage. The advantage of the Decauville light railway was that multiple items of food and ammunition could get to the trench far more quickly, and avoid the loss of mules.

The Decauville light railway was initially rejected in many areas by the British Army which preferred to use horse trains and motor vehicles. As the war became more entrenched and the landscape shelled into impassable morass, the effectiveness of the Decauville became clear. Depositing the stores on or near the roadside ready for onward transportation, this method of transferring supplies to the front helped prevent traffic congestion on the roads. The Brigade Senior Supply Officer supervised the unloading and issued stores and supplies to the Quartermasters of each brigade. Stores were loaded onto horse transport before proceeding to the Brigade Wagon Lines, (Quartermaster stores). If a railhead was close to the front, as at Ypres, then the Refilling Point could be sited within the railhead where it could be loaded straight onto horse transport and onto the wagon lines.

If the railways were the arteries of the transport system, then horse and mule transportation were the veins. These animals were a valuable commodity and the backbone of the British Army.[76] Large and heavy draught horses were ideally suited for pulling wagons and carts. The General Service (GS) Wagon was a common sight, with each unit allotted their own supply train sometimes referred to as a 'Section Train'[77] (Table G). Horse transport requirements for Cavalry, Field Artillery, Field Ambulances, Army Service Corps, Army Ordnance Corps, and Royal Engineers were attached to brigades and had their own war establishment of

A two horsed GS Wagon, location unknown (Author's Collection).

horses and wagons. Mules were not the only animals given the title 'pack animals'. Others included pack horses, camels, cattle and donkeys according to the theatre of operations. Interestingly, men were also included in this category and were estimated to be able to carry up to 50lbs(23kg) in weight.[78] A General Service Wagon could carry extensive loads such as 400 blankets, four hospital marquees and 600 ground sheets cased or 900 uncased. A wagon with four horses could pull up to 3,000lbs (1361kg) of weight and a two-horse cart 1,500 lbs (680kg).[79]

	Personnel		Horses				Carts		Wagons		
Units	Officers	Other ranks	Riding	Draught	Heavy Draught	Pack	1- horse	2-horse	2-horse	4-horse	6-horse
1 x Divisional Ammunition Column	15	553	56	625	28	-	1	2	1	6	94
1 x Divisional Train	26	153	153	10	2	2	1	16	125	-	-
3 x Infantry Brigades	372	11,793	195	336	102	108	12	99	84	6	-
4 x Battalions	120	3,908	52	104	32	36	4	32	28	-	-

Table G - Section Trains – Compiled from War Establishments. Field Service Pocket Book 1914 (Reprinted Amendments in 1916 and 1917). London: His Majesty's Stationery Office.

Trench Dumps → Front Line: Each platoon had its own trench 'dump' as near to the trenches as possible, and each dump was sub-divided into four, one for each section of a platoon. 'Ration parties' from each section carried everything by hand through the communication trenches, past the reserve and support lines, and into the front-line trenches. The type of store or supplies would dictate how far forward into the trenches it would be taken. Special arrangements were sometimes made for items of clothing such as dry socks, to

*Basic Sketch of route to front from base port (*General Scheme of Supply of a Division from the Bases to the Trenches.*** *The Royal Logistic Corps Museum Archive - Author's Collection).*

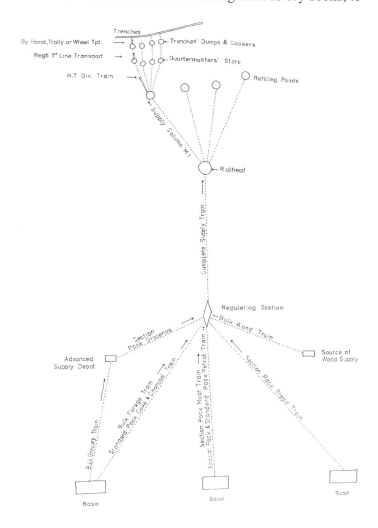

GENERAL SCHEME OF SUPPLY
FROM THE BASES TO
THE TRENCHES

be sent forward up the line in waterproof bags and into the front-line trenches when conditions were particularly wet.[80]

Trench Stores: General items used for maintaining the trench system such as wood, pick axes, shovels and barbed wire were held in trench stores. Restocked as needed, several items of vital uniform and equipment did however get supplied to the infantry in the front firing trenches, one such item being gas masks, especially those incorporating new modifications. Corps Routine Order 571 issued 6 February 1916 stated, 'It has been decided to issue as soon as possible the new pattern P.H. Tube Smoke Helmet on the scale of one per officer and man, in replacement of one of the P Tube helmets now carried.'[81]

Another vitally important piece of equipment was the steel helmet whose replacement of the earlier soft caps was arguably the single most important development in soldiers' uniforms of the entire war. The first British ones were issued in January 1916 to soldiers in the Ypres Salient. One million were expected to be delivered to the Second Army area by the end of April 1916. Top priority was given to the fighting units in the frontline trenches, and trench stores would hold enough helmets for every soldier.

The initial rarity of this precious life-saving item was such that the helmet, along with thigh-length gumboots, leather jerkins, and goatskin jerkins, had to be handed over to the incoming troops when a section of a battalion was relieved at the front.[82] Furthermore, soldiers were routinely reminded to remove these items from any casualties before they proceeded back up the line. Routine Order 606 reaffirmed this by stating:

> Steel helmets. It has been brought to notice that casualties have been evacuated from the corps area with steel helmets in their possession. Divisions will take steps to collect steel helmets from casualties at the earliest opportunity and re-issue them to the fighting troops as soon as possible. Arrangements should also be made to collect helmets left by casualties at Dressing Stations, Field Ambulances, and Casualty Clearing Stations....[83]

This order remained in force until each man was issued their own steel helmet.

Finding Space

As ever more nations from the British Empire arrived in France, they all required their own supply chain. Some Canadian divisions drew their stores from Calais, and the Indian Army through Marseilles with its Advanced Base at Rouen.[84]

On the Italian Front, stores were transported through the Base Port of Rouen before travelling south through France and into Italy. Packages and parcels from families and organisations also needed transportation to the front, as did the return of a soldier's possessions. In late August 1914, an officer of the Army Service Corps was given the job of dealing with soldiers' comforts, parcels, and newspapers. The sheer number of items sent to the troops led to the creation of the Military Forwarding Department (MFD) within which different branches dealt with the kit of deceased, sick and wounded men. With their personal effects dealt with by another branch of the MFD, the Military Forwarding Department kept the accounts for the items on behalf of the Expeditionary Force Canteens (EFC), YMCA and other organisations.

In October, the Inspector General of Communications received notification from the War Office regarding plum puddings for Christmas, which would be sent by individuals and organisations in Britain to the troops abroad. The Directorates of Transport and Supply duly arranged for the puddings and Princess Mary's Gift Fund Boxes[85] to reach the soldiers in time. These Military Forwarding Department branches were sited at Base Ports, large establishments and at some Regulating Stations, and utilised the same supply routes as stores and supplies to railheads. For parcels, notifications were sent to the unit recipient who then organised for its delivery. Almost 50,000 separate consignments had passed through the MFD by the end of 1914. From the initial two officers and eight other ranks in 1914, the Military Forwarding Department grew to 18 officers and 500 other ranks by 1918, and were dealing with more than 20,000 packages a day.

Every commodity such as food, ammunition, boots, steel helmets, SD uniform or gas mask were all manufactured and passed through hundreds of pairs of hands to supply one fighting man. All to sustain the soldier and make life at the front as bearable as possible. The eventual and extraordinary complexity of the 'Line of Communication' network in 1918 could never have been envisioned four years earlier. The First World War proved the theory behind the physical, since regardless of the size of conflict the system could grow quickly and easily and was not restricted by the number of Base Ports, Supply Depots and Refilling Points used. It adapted and changed according to country, circumstances, and conditions. To define a 'Line of Communication' as being one thing or another is impossible. It had to physically move and flex.

The administrative process of indenting for stores was well documented in Army Regulations, while, in comparison, the actual physical location of all the Supply Depots, Stores and their route through the Western Front landscape, are still somewhat uncertain, despite the static nature of the war. Akin to archaeology, the location of all the stores can be considered as an 'unknown' within a 'known', i.e. we know how the supply chain worked but not where all the stores were sited in France and Belgium. Evidence of stores' locations can be found in the landscape today, with railway stations at St Omer, Poperinghe and Ypres still in the same location, just with new façades. The old broad gauge main line that connected St Omer, Hazebrouck and Poperinghe can be explored and viewed in the landscape today. While it no longer carries locomotives, cars pass by Remy Sidings where Ambulance Trains once stopped at the Casualty Clearing Station, and its cemetery marks the spot. Near Poperinghe, the road deviates onto a new stretch of carriageway, but the old railway line can still be followed on foot through modern housing estates, across roads and into Poperinghe. There are even old railway sleepers that have been used to make a small bridge across a tiny stream, a recycled relic of the war. Part of the old railway line around Ypres has become a modern main road helping to ease traffic around the city. A modern map has indications of the lost 'Line of Communication' such as the 'Railway dugouts' south of Ypres, near Zillebeke lake, the location of a spur line that ran into several sidings and where goods and men unloaded to make their way up to the trenches.

British Army regiments received equipment and clothing so regularly that they could not appreciate what a truly vast amount of organisation and effort was involved in its supply. 'That they should get what they needed was treated as a matter of course, they troubled not about how or whence…'.[86]

Remains in the landscape of the main railway line into Poperinghe, now a foot and cycle path. The Poperinghe Old Military Cemetery can just be seen on the left (Author's Collection).

Chapter 4
Laundering the War

Whether above ground or below, a solider and his uniform endured a daily life that is hard to imagine today - 'A soldier's khaki uniform, consisting of service jacket, trousers, greatcoat, cap and puttee…, lasted about a year and the greatcoat from four to five years. Since the outbreak of war, the average duration of wear, it appears cannot be stated, owing to the conditions of service…'.[1]

The Western Front ran in a continuous zigzag line that sliced its way through countries and landscapes, from the Belgian coast to the French border with Switzerland. Of the 475 mile (764km) 'front', five British Armies would eventually occupy about 120 miles (193km).[2] Sub-dividing the line into sectors, it could be weeks before men would get any rest and in Spring 1915 a rotation system was introduced in which battalions were moved through the lines so men could rest.[3] The front was in fact a series of parallel crenelated trench systems aligned north-south. The fire trench looked out over no man's land, behind which were the support lines, and then the reserve lines. Communication trenches zigzagged their way between the fire, support, and reserve trenches to connect them together. The rotation system enabled men, equipment, munitions, stores, and rations to move up to the front as well as facilitating the evacuation of the wounded. It also allowed men four to six days at a Regimental Rest Camp behind the lines. Moving battalions up to the first set of communication trenches from where they entered the Reserve lines, after four days or so, they passed through the next set of communication trenches to the support lines. They spent another four days there before heading up to the front-line fire trench, where they spent about eight days before being rotated back through the lines until they reached the rest camps.

Each sector was re-supplied mainly at night[4] when stores and supplies were brought up from the support trenches. Depending on location and intensity of fighting, the number of days men spent at each point in the rotation would vary. In the trenches, daily life quickly became monotonous, as trench routine stayed constant. Men in the fire trenches would 'stand to' before dawn ready to face an enemy attack. 'Stood down' a few hours later; there was breakfast, inspections, maintenance of the trench and weaponry, and the cleaning and repairing of uniform and equipment. There was a second 'stand to' at dusk, after which men continued to repair trenches, uniform, undertook personal administrative duties, as well as patrolled into no man's land to repair gaps in the barbed wire.[5]

A mud-caked, cold, and wet soldier eating at the 'café de l'Europe' (The War Illustrated Album de Luxe – Volume III The Spring Campaign - 1915. Hammerton (Ed): 1915 - Author's Collection).

At the Front

The misery of being wet, cold and filthy was a daily endurance in winter months. In a letter to his fiancée, Private Jack Sweeney wrote:

> I will tell you just one thing that happened to me on the Somme in the early hours of 14 September. I was wet to the skin, no overcoat, no water sheet, I had about three inches of clay clinging to my clothes and it was cold. I was in an open dug out and do you know what I did, I sat down in the mud and cried. I do not think I have cried like that since I was a child....[6]

Mud, blood, sweat and tears were absorbed into soldiers' uniforms. Men could wash their own socks and shirts in the reserve lines, especially in fine weather, but at the front it was different. A letter home written by Lance-Corporal Roland Mountfort describes life at the front, beginning 'I don't like writing other than a cheerful letter, but if I could compose one now I should be one of the most deserving VC [Victoria Cross] heroes of the war', and he continues:

> It has been raining here every day this week which makes things very uncomfortable, heaps of mud and lice including rats of course, but getting quite use to same now, my skin is quite raw owing to keeping on rubbing myself, haven't had chance of getting water to wash a shirt out but hope to do something towards comfort tomorrow.[7]

Wear and tear on the uniform was extreme and it is a testament to the durability of serge cloth and knitted wool items that they lasted as long as they did in such conditions.

Sapper Jack Martin's diary captured the sights, smells and conditions of the war. He recalled that on 12 August 1917, while trying to sleep in a dugout with a thick gas curtain at the entrance and a ventilation shaft covered in case of gas attack:

> The air in the tunnels becomes most fetid. Seventy or eighty men crowd in one of these galleries, mainly with wet clothes, and all in a filthy dirty condition, breathing the same air over and over again, their bodies strewn in the close, damp atmosphere and exuding all manner of noxious odours – this alone is sufficient to make us all ill...foul air is better than poison gas, and dugouts are preferred to shell holes.[8]

Socks, so important to the men at the front who wore them and the womenfolk back home who made them, were small articles of clothing which endured the greatest wear and tear, and were no friend to prolonged water exposure. Sapper Martin had a view on this too:

> I removed my socks for the first time in three weeks. All the time we were in the line we were not supposed to take off even our boots and puttees but we generally got these off each night. My socks have been soaked through time after time with rain and mud and perspiration so that it was impossible to take them off in the ordinary way. I had to cut them and tear them and removed them from my feet in pieces; the soles were as hard as boards....[9]

During winter, an extra pair of socks was given each day to each man. Between 4 August 1914 to 31 March 1919 at total number of 136,396,000 pairs of socks were issued.[10]

Other kinds of clothing damage were more dramatic. A feature of trench warfare was the night-time raiding party, where men crept out into No Man's Land to reconnoitre enemy positions, attack their trenches and bring back prisoners, and also to repair barbed wire. Endless rows of barbed wire were positioned in front of enemy and allied trenches, and the landscape was ripped by shell holes and jagged shrapnel. Under the cover of darkness men crawled, crept and snaked their way into the battlefield, each time snagging and ripping their clothing,[11] damage which they then had to repair with their canvas-covered sew kit called the 'hussif' (known as 'housewife'). Small rips and holes could be patched up in the trench until the opportunity arose for it to be properly repaired or replaced. If a replacement article of clothing was required it was reported to the Officer-in-Command of a company who, once satisfied the old item was no longer serviceable, passed the request onto the Commanding Officer of the battalion. They in turn authorised the request and passed it to the Quartermaster of the regiment who issued the item. Small stocks of clothing were held with the Quartermaster and once issued, he requested to General Headquarters a demand to replenish from the nearest ordnance depot.[12]

It was possibly during one of these raids in late 1916, early 1917 that George earned his Military Medal. The only family story attached to it was that it was for' leading his men out of no man's land.' There is, sadly, no proof or record of a citation, a factor which was common for other ranks. It was, however mentioned in the *Western Daily Press*, Bristol and *London Gazette* April 1917.

Life as a Tunneller

Tunnellers were sent to France knowing only that they were now sappers in the Royal Engineers. Tunnelling was secret and it was crucial that it stayed that way.[13] George arrived in France on 28 June 1915 and was at once re-mustered as a 'Tunneller's Mate' in the 177th Tunnelling Company. Promoted to 'Tunneller'[14] three days later,[15] George was sent to the front line at Railway Wood.

Life underground was harsh, with Tunnellers working day and night in two 12-hour shifts, four days on and four off.[16] Four sections of men worked three to four separate mine galleries in different directions and depths. Tunnellers, also known as 'clay kickers',[17] worked at the mine face and earned six shillings (£18.92) per day. Behind the Tunnellers, the Tunnellers' Mates built gallery supports and disposed of the spoil from the gallery face, earning two shillings and two pence (£6.57) per day. These men were paid higher than the infantry who earned approximately one shilling and three pence (£3.79) per day.[18]

Men were required to dig by hand for twelve hours per shift and in silence – sometimes muffling their studded boots by tying sandbags around them. With candles for light, the tunnels and galleries were small, with dimensions varying from 4ft by 2ft (1.22m x 1.38m) to 5ft by 4ft (1.53m x 1.22m).[19] Equipped with pickaxes for chalky geology or special spades in clay areas, the men often

worked stripped to the waist or in a shirt with sleeves rolled up. Sturdy protective leather knee pads could also be worn. In some locations, water continually seeped into the tunnels, galleries, and shafts. In the Ypres Salient, the water table was so high that parts of the ground were described as 'slurry', a liquid of mud and

Royal Engineers Tunnellers at Messines Ridge, near Ypres (Author's Collection).

water.[20] Describing the 177th Tunnelling Company's first winter at the front and Railway Wood Winter 1915-1916, Lieutenant Sawers wrote:

> I don't suppose any troops anywhere else had the discomfort we had in the Ypres Salient. In the infantry, no individual would stay more than two days. We had no reliefs. We were there all the time in the wet and mud.... We lived in gumboots. Had a little Tamboule that winter in which the two officers had to live; 2 feet of water on the floor, blankets were sopping wet. One fellow claimed he had 35 days at a stretch up there. We only got back to camp once in a while for a bath and clean underwear. The rest of the time we were plastered in mud. Gumboots were the only special clothing we had for the job – we wore an ordinary uniform.[21]

Sinking mine shafts was not easy and a method was developed to freeze the ground, sink corrugated curved sheets 'piling' then dig out the middle.[22] Once the required area for a mine blow had been reached by shafts and tunnels, it was packed with explosives[23] and detonated.[24] Listening posts were situated in the tunnel galleries to catch any enemy sound, if a noise was detected the officer in charge was alerted. One typical encounter was 'Huns reported working two yards from our gallery, which meant yours truly lying on his tummy in sodden clay for half an hour and hearing nothing....' [25] If the enemy was located nearby the aim would be to destroy their workings, and in the absence of an officer an NCO calculated and fired the explosives.[26] George, who had been a Coal Face Examiner,[27] was in charge of a section of Tunnellers underground and, as part of his civilian job, had some knowledge of explosives as well as the safety of his men underground. Once promoted to Sergeant, an NCO rank, there may have been times when he would have had to 'fire' the explosives in lieu of an officer.

Daily life as a Tunneller, enduring frequent bombardment, difficult working conditions, and the constant threat of being buried alive took its toll[28] physically and mentally. Men from infantry battalions moving in and out of the lines were attached to Tunnelling Companies, and were mainly employed to remove the spoil from underground diggings, collect stores, and transport materials through the trenches.[29]

Reaching the Line

Ypres was an ideal location for brigade and battalion headquarters, despite being well within shelling distance of German artillery. Cellars already existed in sections of the town's ramparts and had stored artillery ammunition in the nineteenth century.[30] The British Army transformed these cellars into battalion headquarters and billets for infantry brigades. It was the 177th Tunnelling Company in August 1915, however, which constructed the first tunnelled dugouts in the Salient for billets and offices.[31] Writing of a visit to the dugouts adjacent to Menin Gate on 12 September 1915, Major S Hunter Cowan, Officer Commanding 175th Tunnelling Company wrote 'Bliss[32] took me to see some dugouts his Coy. [Company] are making in the old ramparts of Ypres. They are very good indeed with I suppose 15 or 20 feet of earth cover….'[33]

The billets in the ramparts were 3 miles (5km) from Railway Wood, an area that became synonymous with tunnelling and the 177th Tunnelling Company, and with no accommodation for the Tunnellers at the front, George and his fellow sappers walked back to their billets in Ypres along the Menin Road in full knowledge they were within range of German guns. Shelled daily, all troops changed shift at dusk, making the journey even more perilous. Due to the dangerous conditions of getting to the front, their Commanding Officer did not care how they got to their positions, as long it was in time to start their shift.[34] George's service records show he was absent without leave for 45 minutes at the start of one shift for which he was reprimanded without punishment or pay deduction.

Getting to the front was creating ever more casualties. In Alfred Jones' record is an interesting report on injuries received whilst returning to Ypres. A report on 'Accidental or Self-Inflicted Injuries' was directed to Alfred's injury, stating its nature, location, how it was received and whether or not it was self-inflicted. On 24 June 1917, the report concluded that Alfred suffered a 'Contusion to the Chest severe', that was witnessed by Sapper Homes. Writing in his statement, Homes states 'Sapper Jones was proceeding with his relief from Railway Wood to the ramparts, Ypres via the Menin Road when he tripped over and fell into a shell hole. The enemy were bombarding the Menin road and the vicinity with gas shell and the men were obliged to resort to the gas masks thus hampering their vision.' At this point in the war, box-respirators were used as gas masks and were worn strapped to the front of the chest. When Alfred tripped, he fell onto his chest resulting in the contusion and it was concluded that it was in the performance of military duty.[35]

No sooner had the 177th finished constructing their dugouts in the Ypres ramparts, then work on accommodation just 100m from the front line was started by them at Cambridge Road dugouts on the edge of Railway Wood. From late January 1916, George and his fellow Tunnellers would spend four days 'on' at the front, living in their new dugouts, and four days 'off', living in the ramparts at Ypres.[36]

Adapt and Overcome

The static nature of trench warfare required adaption and evolution of the uniform. Some adaptations were unofficial and rudimentary by individuals or from official channels. Cold was always an issue, Jerkins and jackets made from leather and goat skins were sent to the front in various styles to help combat freezing temperatures. Writing in December 1916, Sapper Jack Martin wrote 'We have been issued out with leather jerkins. Some of the men have furry ones and look like bears, but I have a plain brown one; when dressed up with a tin helmet, jerkin and gumboots my closest friends at home would hardly recognise me – I only need a spear and shield to transform me into a medieval warrior….'[37]

Unofficial knitted 'comforts' sent from home also helped conquer the cold and included body belts, balaclavas and waistcoats. To combat water and mud, waterproof clothing and footwear was required. Wool has inherent waterproof properties and the greatcoat would protect the wearer to a certain extent. Soldiers were first issued with a rectangular groundsheet that could be worn around the shoulders to provide some protection, but it was not perfect. A rubberised cape replaced it in 1917 and had a collar that could be pulled up to protect the neck. Wrapped around the body, the cape buttoned up at the front to secure it. Completely waterproof and a square shape allowed it to work as a ground sheet, and multiple capes could be joined together to create a shelter.[38]

As the war dragged on trenches turned into quagmires, and men could spend days standing ankle deep in water. Thigh high gumboots known as 'trench waders' were attached to the waist, and were issued with standard gumboots (like Wellington Boots). The relief of being provided with this footwear had a great impact. In Ypres, soldiers collected waders and gumboots from trench stores in the cellars of the ruined infantry barracks en-route to the

Army Service Corps sergeant wearing a Goat skin jerkin (Author's Collection).

front, returning them on their way back. Writing in the war diary on 1 October 1915, the Commanding Officer, 7th Battalion East Yorkshire Regiment wrote:

> There was a welcomed sight, fifty pairs of thigh boots arrived tonight by our transport and are upon as a God send....' The following day he expanded by stating 'Remaining 200 more thigh boots arrived tonight and were given out. A difference was immediately noticed amongst the men who were eager to get on with their nightly fatigues...without complaint of the conditions now that they could wade with impunity....[39]

Although trench waders and gumboots solved one problem, the length of the greatcoat created another. Men could sink up to their knees in trenches and the calf-length greatcoat dragged in the mud. Belgian mud would cling and not let go, and once saturated with water, weighed down an already heavy coat even further, seriously hampering movement. A solution came about in the field, with soldiers cutting their coats to knee length. Whilst not commonplace throughout the British Army, in mud and clay sectors such as the Ypres Salient it was almost essential.

Summer didn't always bring much relief. The disappearance of mud was welcomed although in some sectors it never quite dried up. Dust clung to uniforms, and khaki serge was warm to wear, especially on a hot summers day. With only a tin helmet for shade, men did what they could to stay cool, jackets were removed and shirt sleeves rolled up to 'short sleeve order', but only with the permission of the Commanding Officer. Some men even unpicked the side seam of their trousers to their knee and, by securing the lower corners to the upper part of the trouser leg with buttons, created a rudimentary long pair of shorts. Such adaptations did not conform to any army specifications.

Rats and 'Chats'

Vermin added to the soldier's discomfort at the front. Rats were a constant companion in the trenches, disturbing sleep, and eating food and equipment; whilst the summer brought swarms of flies converging on the dead, especially after an offensive. The real enemy of the soldier however was lice. Known as 'chats' Captain Milne, 1/4th Leicester noted on his return to billets in Ouderdom:

> The 'chat' as the species of louse in question is called, was no respecter of persons. He paid his respects to the Colonel; visited the Adjutant; called on the Company Commanders, became attached to the Platoon Sergeants for rations, but no discipline; and fraternised only too freely with the rank and file. In some dug-outs men itched as soon as they sat down as bathing facilities were entirely absent in the trenches they had to be content to scratch....[40]

Lice spread by close contact between men, so cramped trenches and dugouts were the ideal conditions to jump from one soldier to another. They infested men's underclothes and the seams of jackets, trousers and shirts, and it was estimated that 97% of men in the trenches suffered with them.[41] They fed on skin and their bites caused rashes which made men itch, and it wasn't uncommon for men to be sent to hospital to recover from the effects. By the summer of 1917, trench fever was eventually traced to infected lice bites,[42] with the main symptom including headache, inflamed eyes and leg pain. Five to six days in a Divisional Rest Station normally allowed the soldier to recover.[43] Subaltern Second Lieutenant James Dale, 2nd Battalion Liverpool Scottish, wrote 'I have become a Base Depot for sundry lesser fauna who crawl and bite...'.[44]

An unofficial daily routine of trench life was the attempt to remove lice from clothing. Private Peter McGregor recalled 'I had a lice hunt this forenoon and oh my I caught thousands quite big fat ones - and wee fellows - they get into the folds of your kilt, down the seams of your shirt the devils, how they get there I don't know, nothing kills them, powders etc....have no effect'.[45] These powders could be purchased from chemists back home and sent to the front, bought in local towns or supplied by the Quartermaster. Perhaps the most effective (and somewhat satisfying) method of removal was heat via a candle or match flame run under the seams of the uniform[46] until the pop and crackle indicated their fiery destruction. This solution gave men a temporary psychological boost until they could get to a bath house and have their uniform properly deloused. In places where this was impossible mobile disinfectors were mounted on the back of Foden steam lorries and sent to camps.

Bathing

After about two weeks at the front, the detritus of war, mud, and lice clung to man and cloth. Washing in the front firing line was difficult but men had to shave as a requirement of the British Army regulations. Hot water was needed and old tins or mess tins were used to heat water. Often the first chance to wash underclothes and bathe was when back in the reserve lines, and men were billeted wherever a place could be found. Buckets[47] and old petrol tins made useful washbasins, giving men the chance to divest themselves of jacket, shirt and vest and try to get clean. Water for the ablutions often came from streams and rivers and in the worst-case scenarios, shell holes.[48] Soldiers lived in dugouts set into embankments, ruined villages, house, cellars, or in woods, barns or stables.

In the Ypres Salient, some of the reserve lines snaked through the ruins of the city, mostly in cellars of shattered buildings occupied by soldiers. Dotted throughout Ypres were bath houses, with one situated in the old brick casements of the ramparts and called the 'moat bath house'.[49] Out of the line bathing conditions improved. Army Orders stated that once battalions returned from the front one of the first things they should do was bathe, and each battalion was given a time, date and location for this. Divisional Baths were often temporary wooden structures or located in existing buildings, with breweries commonly used as at Poperinghe. Describing the bathing process, Rifleman W. Worrell wrote:

There were three huge vats in the brewery and between them there were planks. The first vat was full of hot, dirty, soapy water, the next one had hot water, not quite so dirty. The last one had cold water, fairly clean. You started at one end and you stripped off. You tied your khaki uniform up in a bundle and tied your boots to it and your cap. Your underclothes were taken away to go in the fumigator, but it didn't usually do so. You went up and there were ropes across the vat, so you pulled yourself across the rope to the other side, climbed out on the next plank into the next vat, jumped in there, washed the worst of the dirt off, and then into the last vat. When you got out the other end, you picked up a towel, wiped down and then looked around. Where's my hat. It was the only way you could find your own bundle, with your hat and identity disc attached to it. Then you were issued with underclothes. If you were lucky you got some that nearly fitted you, but of course, I was the wrong size for that and it would always happen to me that I got huge underwear. They were all long johns in those days and by the time I'd done them up they were right around my chest, and I'd also have to take about three folds in the bottom of the legs. That would be topped by a vest hanging down below my knees. On the other hand, a fellow who was a

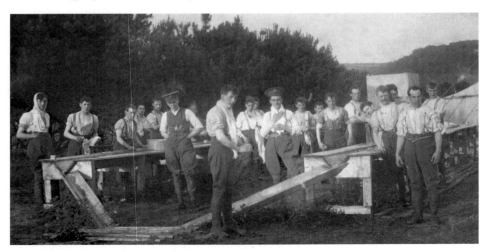

A chance of some decent ablutions 'out of the lines' (Author's Collection).

The Brewery at Poperinghe which doubled as a bathhouse. Now redeveloped into flats (Author's Collection).

six-footer would be issued with a set so small that he could hardly get into it at all, so we had to swap around as best we could. Sometimes the language got pretty fruity. We had some laughs. The odd thing that you forgot the bad times. It's happy memories, the silly things that stick with you – like prancing about in that ridiculous underwear.[50]

In more basic bathhouse facilities men were issued with fresh underclothes and their trousers and jackets ironed in a not wholly successful attempt to exterminate lice. At Harbonniers, France, the Assistant Director of Medical Services arranged to pay rent of 10 francs per day to the owner of the brewery for use as a bath house and laundry which employed 40 French women working three hours per day.[51]

The organisation of soldiers' bathing and delousing facilities evolved as the war progressed and the Army Service Corps developed large timber-built central delousing and bathing stations. They were designed almost as a production line, the largest accommodating 3,000 men, the smallest, 1,500 men during a 10-hour working day. The footprint of the largest structure was about c.120ft x 84ft (36.57m x 25.60m), with smaller buildings connected by walkways that housed clothing disinfectors. A strict timetable was adhered to enabling 200 men to be washed and their clothing deloused every 40 minutes.

As one soldier entered he was given two disks, one to be attached to his clothing and one he kept to reclaim it. In the undressing room, he was allotted 10 minutes to undress and hand his uniform, except boots, through a hatch in an internal wall. He then handed over his personnel belongings into the valuables room, and used the latrines if necessary, and then entered a medical inspection room. Boots were placed upon racks and men were allotted 30 minutes to shower with 10 men per shower in a total of 24 showers. Afterwards, he collected his boots and a clean towel from the towel store, then entered the heated drying room. On his way to the dressing room, he surrendered his disc and received back his now deloused uniform. Collecting new underclothing from the adjacent store, he then had 10 minutes to dry and put them on, with a further 10 minutes to dress in his uniform. As he left the bath house, he walked around the outside of the building to a small window through which he collected his valuables.

The whole business took an hour, although bathing and delousing took just 40 minutes. As the first group of 200 men dressed and left, so the next group arrived. A second production line of delousing uniforms was extremely efficient. In the centre of the bath house was a large room with six Decauville rail tracks running along its width and a longer track down the centre. Trollies were pushed along these rails and where they intersected a miniature turntable rotated them onto the main rail track. The soldiers' uniforms were put into the trollies and pushed outside to one of the six delousing chambers into which disinfectors pumped chemicals. This process took 40 minutes, and once completed the clothing was taken back inside the building, rotating at the turntables to the emptying side of the room.[52]

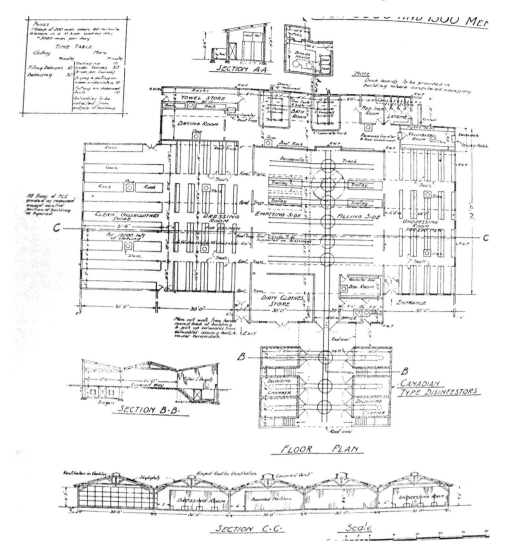

*Plans for a Central Delousing and Bathhouse for 3,000 men (***Miscellaneous
Papers Plans for Central Delousing and Bathing Stations.** The Royal Logistic
Corps Museum Archive - Author's Collection).*

Laundries

Near the road from Poperinghe to Proven, west of Ypres, ran a railway line
operated by the British Second Army which served the Corps headquarters at
Châteaux La Lovie, Divisional headquarters at Châteaux Couthove, and had a

siding for the nearby hospital and Divisional Rest Station.[53] To reach the hospital Sister Alison Macfie remembered:

> The lane leading to the hospital is easily called to mind as on one corner was the Military Laundry and on the other the De-Lousing Station. I shall never forget a visit we paid to the laundry and the sight of large heaps of socks in every stage of decay being turned over by two old women, who picked out any which were capable of further use....[54]

Sanitation, health and disinfecting of soldiers and their uniforms fell under the remit of the Royal Army Medical Corps (RAMC). Each Division had three Field Ambulances, two served in the line and one was in reserve. In the line, they formed part of the chain of the evacuation of casualties, out of the line they were allocated special tasks such as operating Divisional Rest Stations, bath houses, laundries, delousing and scabies stations.[55] At the start of the war the idea of a purpose-built laundry capable of serving five armies was never envisioned.

As winter arrived in late 1914 following the First Battle of Ypres,[56] Divisions and Corps of the BEF soon realised that arrangements had to be made for the mass cleaning of specific items of soldiers' uniform, predominantly under-clothing (shirts were classed as under-clothing as they were worn under the service jacket). To facilitate this, the early war organisation of laundering saw local women in small villages and towns, as well as civilian laundries employed under contract to clean the uniforms. Women in Poperinghe for example were photographed hanging out hundreds of shirts to dry. Residents displayed signs to show that they were, as Sapper Jack Martin recorded in his diary, 'authorised to wash for soldiers... I hand in my dirty clothes and get back the lot I left for washing on the previous occasion. The woman does a lot of washing but has some system of marking so that she always brings out the right set...'.[57]

Often described as '*blanchisseries*' – French for Laundry - one of the first large scale laundries set up during the winter of 1914-1915 was the Divisional baths, laundry and disinfesting plant at Pont de Nieppe, France. Allowing some 1,200 men to bathe, be disinfested, and have their clothes washed in one day, Pont de Nieppe employed one officer, two sergeants and 65 other ranks from the No. 1 New Zealand Field Ambulance, and 185 local women to wash, iron and mend uniforms. The women were instructed in how to search for and destroy lice by disinfesting the uniforms by ironing with hot irons and brushing with special steel brushes. All under-clothing was boiled in disinfectants, washed, dried and repaired, with the wool of old socks unravelled then used in the mending of those that could be made serviceable. During the last two weeks of May 1916, Pont de Nieppe saw 446 officers and 21,675 men bathed; and 13,779 shirts, 13,746 pairs of socks and 99,066 items of under-clothing washed.[58]

Civilian laundries continued to deal with the increasing number of uniform items, and were paid 3½ d. (35 French centimes)[59] per man per week to wash one shirt, handkerchief, towel, vest, pair of pants and one pair of socks. However, if a Division or Corps moved to another part of the line, their washing often got left behind. New issues of uniform items would therefore have to be 'demanded' once the Division or Corps had completed their move, leading to huge amounts of waste.[60] Another disadvantage was the cost which varied from laundry to laundry and between Divisions.[61] In Doullens, France, the 61st Division had a contract with a laundry to wash 2,000 items a day consisting of shirts, drawers and vest to be charged at 25 centimes per item; whereas the charges levied at the 51st Division laundry at Abbeville were for 4,500 items to be washed per day at 35 centimes each for one shirt, pair of pants and vest, and 15 centimes each for a pair of socks and a towel. A total of 1 Franc 35 centimes per soldier.[62]

Transporting washing by horse and motorised transport caused further problems. Sometimes lorries travelled over 40 miles (64km) to and from laundries and camps. With demand soon outstripping supply as the number of armies and men steadily increased along the Western Front, the rising expenditure and over issue of replacement uniform had to be addressed. During October,

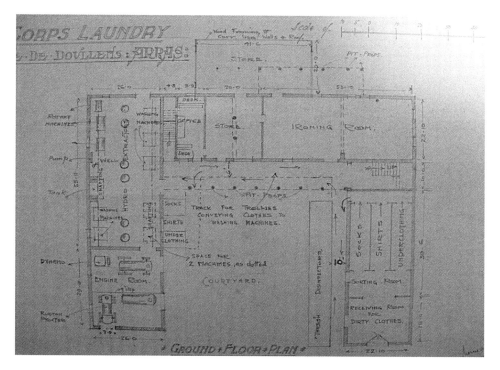

VII Corps Laundry at Arras **(Miscellaneous Papers-Proposed Army Laundry.**
The Royal Logistic Corps Museum Archive - Author's Collection).

November and December 1916, the expenditure by Divisions on laundering was not only high but highly variable. For example, the 63rd Division of II Corp spent 3,804.10 Francs while 31st Division, XIII Corp spent 16,612.60 Francs. Across 11 Divisions from various Corps, there was a total cost of 837,648 Francs per annum, which equated to £29,916 (£1,816,455.20 today) for around 22,600 items of clothing per day.[63] To replace this convoluted early war organisation of Divisional and Corps laundries, a more efficient and economical laundering system sufficient for current army needs was proposed December 1916.[64]

Siting these new large Army area laundries on the Line of Communication and near rest camp areas, Divisional Rest Stations, and hospitals,[65] the first laundry was authorised and built in Abbeville by 2nd Lieutenant Ritchie RE,[66] who, in civilian life, had designed and built laundries. In charge was Captain Allom, a man well versed in business and organisation[67] and Lance Corporal Heyworth, a laundry manager in civil life, who was made laundry foreman.[68] In July, a statistical report revealed that the laundry was a success – the figures were impressive - 50 washing machines, 10 Hydro Extractors (spin dryers) washed around 170,000 items each day and 14 drying rooms on a continuous flow, were drying 250 articles at a time.[69] The laundry was manned by 50 men, judged unfit for the front, Prisoners of War, and around 100 local women to carry out most of the work, leaving five men as managers and clerks.[70] In the first month of operation (April to May 1917), a total of 214, 814 items were washed at a cost (including staff pay) of 13,692.23 Francs. The same number of items sent to the local civilian laundry would have cost 36, 681.36 Francs, a staggering difference of 22,989.13 Francs.[71] This was not to say that all earlier Divisional, Corps or civilian laundries ceased to exist, but clearly there was immense potential for significant future savings, though one disadvantage was the large number of men required to operate these laundries.

Out of the Line

Even at rest, a soldier was not idle. Parades, fatigues, uniform repair and billet inspections were the norm throughout the four to six days officially out of the front line. It was nevertheless a break from the front and men waxed lyrical about it. Detailing his battalion's withdrawal to rest billets, Captain Cockburn, 10th King's Royal Rifle Corps wrote:

There is no more delightful sensation these days, than marching on a good hard road under a bright moon to rest billet far behind the line. You were so glad to be away from the shells: you could look forward to sleeping in a bed, perhaps between sheets… You might wear your soft cap again, instead of the steel helmet which was such a fearful weight. Your peace of mind was only interrupted by thoughts of what the Battalion was, when it last came out for a rest.[72]

Many rest camps were established in and around Poperinghe, some 12km to the west of Ypres. Taken over by the British Army from the French in 1915, Poperinghe was the nearest town to Ypres where soldiers could buy food, clothing such as shirts, personal items, souvenirs and postcards to send home. With the front 20km away it also became home to Belgian refugees from villages and farms caught in the path of the fighting. For the duration of the war it was a home for both soldier and civilian alike, and a town that never slept. Private Allen Tobson wrote:

If Ypres was the key to the Salient, Poperinghe was the key to Ypres, for the one main road that passed through its centre was the one and only way in which troops and transports could pass along to their destination until a 'switch' road was built to relieve traffic congestion. From a soldier's point of view, it was a city of refuge.[73]

There was nothing that Poperinghe did not offer the soldier - restaurants such as *L'Espérance, Cyrilles* and *La Poupée* (known as "Ginger's) were some of Tommy's favourites, where egg and chips was a popular cheap meal. Shops provided a strange mix of everyday essentials and souvenirs. Soldiers that walked up *Casselstraat* towards the brewery for a bath would have passed a small shop that sold English newspapers. The Priem family owned a shop opposite Talbot House that sold postcards, boot polish, shaving cream and brushes, razors, soap, everything a soldier could need or want.[74]

Many soldiers spent time and money hunting for souvenirs to send home to their loved ones. These included sweetheart brooches made from buttons and badges, trench art, handkerchiefs printed with patriotic songs, Belgian lace, with the most popular incorporating a traditional kind of textile - the silk embroidered postcard.[75] When Germany advanced into Belgium there was a significant impact on the traditional lacemaking industry. Belgian lace had been regarded as some of the best in the world. Civilians of towns and cities taken over by Allied forces needed a way to earn a living and for the lace makers and embroiderers of Belgium and France, souvenir silk embroidered postcards offered a lucrative option. First appearing early 1915, their designs appealed to the 'Tommy', with regimental badges, patriotic flags, greetings and flowers. All of these were designs that could be repeated up to 25 times along a strip of silk then sent to factories, cut between each design and mounted into card blanks.[76]

A contradiction in war is that such a beautiful and delicate silk card could come from a place that could be described as 'hell on earth', George sent one of these silk postcards home to his daughter Alice who kept and treasured it all

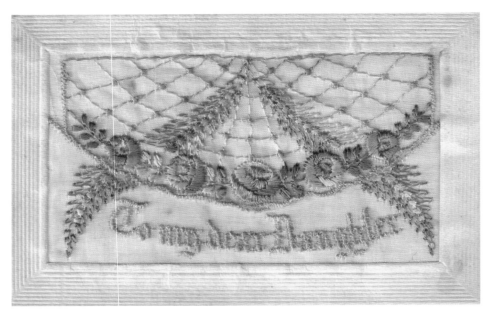

Silk postcard sent to Alice from George (Author's Collection).

her life. Embroidered with delicate pink roses on a tiny envelope flap in which
a printed card read 'All Kind Thoughts', and underneath was embroidered the
words 'To my dear daughter'; on the reverse in beautiful Edwardian handwriting
George wrote 'My dear little girl. For Alice from Dad'.[77]

Photographic postcards captured a moment in time in a more immediate
way. Civilian photographers travelled throughout France and Belgium setting
up portable studios in areas occupied by Allied Forces. The only picture of
George in uniform was as a result of visiting one of these studios. When a
photograph was taken abroad it usually had '*Postcarte*' printed on the reverse,
but the picture we have of George is a copy taken from the original decades
ago. There are clues, however, that tell us it was taken abroad - the men's
demeanour, studio background and their uniform.[78] There are crude tiles on
the floor, a single chair, and some sort of wooden branch as the impromptu
scenery, none of the men are wearing service caps, their pockets are full, there
are creases and signs of wear on the uniform, and their boots and puttees are
spattered with mud.

George stands on the left, with the right arm of his SD jacket bearing the
single stripe of a Lance Corporal. Entering service in the British Army as a
Private, then Sapper upon transfer to the Royal Engineers, George was promoted
to Lance Corporal on 19 January 1916 and then Corporal on 21 August 1916.[79]
This picture therefore must have been taken between these dates. The 177th
Headquarters opposite Châteaux Couthove, was also home to the Tunnelling and

Mine Rescue School.[80] Additional instruction and training would have been provided to promoted NCO's. On 14 January 1916, George was admitted to the 18th Field Ambulance, promoted to Lance Corporal on 19 January to complete establishment, then discharged back to duty from 6th Divisional Rest Station (sited in fields behind Châteaux Couthove)[81] on 22 January 1916. Two weeks later he re-joined his old unit on 5 February 1916.[82] This suggests that during that fortnight, he was, as a newly promoted NCO receiving training at the Mine School. It seems likely that this is when George had his photograph taken and bought the silk postcard for Alice, sending both home in time for her birthday on 17 February 1916. All this information is gleaned from the image of George and by identifying features on his uniform.

Picture of George (left) taken early 1916 at the studio of René Matton, Proven, Belgium (Author's Collection).

In Proven, just 3km from the Tunnelling and Mine Rescue School, many houses were billets for officers and men, and had their capacity of those who could be accommodated painted onto the front of the house.[83] Rest camps, hospitals, Divisional Rest Stations and headquarters were allocated in fields, woods and copses around Proven and down to Poperinghe almost 4 km away. A small area was occupied by vast numbers of men from around the world, including a large number of Chinese Labour Corps in their own camp. In Proven, René Matton, a clockmaker prior to the war, spotted an opportunity when the army moved in. Matton became a photographer and turned his porch and back garden into a rudimentary studio with only two painted scenic backdrops strung up with rope, one a landscape with a tree and the other an interior with a draped curtain and pole. The latter was the background of George's photo. René Matton became a renowned photographer, and some of his photographs have become iconic First World War images, one of which is a Chinese labourer posing with René's own son.[84]

'Toc H' (Talbot House) - A Home from Home

Through an elaborate, iron-grilled doorway I could hear the sound of laughter and music, and pushing the door I found myself at once in a different world. It was amazing, I felt like Alice [in Wonderland] when she stepped through the looking-glass. There were soldiers all around me, of course, and army slang in the air, but, in stepping across the threshold, I seemed to have left behind all the depression and weariness of the street. There were walls with paper on them – clean paper, too! -carpeted stairs, pictures on the walls and vases with flowers in them.[85]

A place to rest and socialise was needed in Poperinghe as an alternative venue to bars and cafes. Senior Padre Neville Talbot found a town house that the owners were prepared to rent to the British Army. He appointed Padre Philip Clayton, known as Tubby, to run the house. Although run by the Church of England it welcomed soldiers from every denomination. It was named Talbot House after its founder and opened on 11 December 1915.[86] Known to all as the Everyman's Club or 'Toc H' (gunners signalling code), it had a small chapel in the attic for church services, silent retreat, prayer, and the baptism of men who were about to go up to the front line, some of whom would not return.[87] This refuge from the war was the only place where 'Rank was left at the door,' as elsewhere in the town, clubs for officers and men were kept strictly apart. Only at Talbot House did they all mix, mingle, laugh and socialise together.

Creating a small theatre in the building next door, travelling entertainers put on shows, films of Charlie Chaplin, lectures, and talks; whereas in the house men could continue their pre-war hobbies of gardening and music in the garden club and the in-house band. There were rooms for games, billiards, library and a canteen where soldiers were welcomed with a cup of tea. Each Christmas soldiers held a party for the children of Poperinghe, something to bring happiness and comfort to children missing their fathers, and soldiers missing their own children. A friendship board was set up by Tubby which was 'reserved for the use of men who wish to get in touch with friends, who may possibly see a message left for them'.[88] A common message was for information regarding a brother, father or friend in a different regiment.

No army rules existed inside Talbot House, but Tubby, through notices, spelt out with wit the house rules: 'Don't leave cycles outside, they will be scrounged by passers-by. Don't leave cycles in the hall, they will be borrowed by the chaplain. You may leave cycles in the garden where it is hoped they will be safe'.[89] Tubby was the constant of Talbot House and was always there for any man who needed him, regardless of faith. A place of rest, but not safety, as Poperinghe was within range of German artillery. A tally undertaken by Toc H staff in 1917 recorded 117 men visited in just one ten-minute period.[90]

There is no official record of George ever visiting Talbot House during his time in the Ypres Salient.[91] That said, with his Company HQ and the Tunnelling

Soldiers relaxing in the gardens at Talbot House (By kind permission of Talbot House Museum, Poperinghe – Copyright vzw Talbot House).

and Mine Rescue School nearby, and the fact he spent a brief time possibly convalescing at the 6th Divisional Rest Station just off the Proven Road, then there is every likelihood that he did indeed have a welcoming cup of tea at 'Toc H'.

Talbot House, YMCAs, cafés and estaminets (small café bars) in towns and villages throughout France and Belgium were hugely important to life at the front. They helped give some sort of temporary relief, whether to wash, a chance to relax or find some sort of peace from the physical and psychological pressures of war. Writing in September 1917 during the Third Battle of Ypres ('Passchendaele'), an unknown soldier of 58th Division noted:

I was sad and lonely when I re-entered "Everyman's Club". During the preceding three weeks I had lived in a land of mud and death. Many of my best friends had passed over, others I had seen mangled, wounded and in agony. The noise of the bombardment still dinned in my ears and I could not rid myself of the sights and smells of battle. I passed through the house, into the garden and sat down awhile to rest. From a neighbouring house the voices of women, busy in the ordinary duties of the day could be heard. The grass was almost unbelievably green. The leaves had scarcely begun to fall, the branches moved gently in a passing wind and a bird was singing in the tree-top.[92]

Chapter 5

Salvage and Recycling – Materials and Men

Salvaging was a necessity, epic in scale, and grew exponentially as the war progressed. The story of salvage can be divided into wartime and post-war parts, evolving by accident and design. It grew to astonishing proportions; millions of pounds Sterling were saved and the system highlighted how efficient the British Army was in recycling its waste. Clothing and equipment had always been repaired in army workshops at home and at overseas garrisons, but organised salvage of everything to save money and raw materials was a new concept in 1914. General wear and tear always occurred but with static warfare came other problems.

The first salvage collection took place after the retreat from Mons to the Marne at the end of September 1914. Equipment and clothing had been abandoned in favour of a fast retreat. Two Sergeants were sent over some retreated ground to collect anything they could find, and in one church in Coulommiers, France, 500 greatcoats were discovered. There was no economic reason for this collecting other than to re-equip the men.[1] Returning stores for re-issue was a valuable resource the army could draw on and included repairable and unserviceable (scrap) uniform and personal equipment (webbing etc), small arms and empty artillery shell cases.[2] As a result, a new systematic collection of salvage was begun by the 4th Division in May 1915.

After the Second Battle of Ypres, a party of men under the Deputy Assistant Director of Supplies collected items dumped in Ypres by men returning from the front. What could be used was kept, and the rest was sent to the railhead,[3] before continuing to the Base Depot, where its original issuing department sorted it again. For some reason, this was not technically referred to as salvage.[4] In 1915, Divisional Salvage Companies were formed within Divisions,[5] but independent from overall army organisation. Mainly composed of personnel deemed as 'temporarily unfit' or 'under-aged men of the infantry battalions',[6] they searched billets and rear areas for anything that could be useful - small arms, munitions, spent shell cases, equipment, and uniforms etc. Competition between units was encouraged and statistics[7] of Divisional Salvage Companies were soon published.[8] Owing to the success of the operation, Divisional Employment Companies were formed in 1917 to give salvage work and its personnel a more definite status, and comprised of one officer and 50 Other Ranks sub-divided into Divisional Salvage Sections.[9]

This work became known as 'Routine Salvage' and would become part of the soldier's daily life. Encouraged to collect any left-over material and bring it with them when they rotated out of the line, such items were deposited at Collecting Stations (known also as Salvage Receiving Stations), and transport that would have been returning empty from delivering ammunition or rations would pick it up. No transport ever returned empty from delivering stores. In addition, Divisional Salvage Sections emptied Collecting Stations and transported the material to the Railhead and Central Dumps.[10] Forty-four other ranks and one officer were additionally formed into Area Employment Companies, sub-divided into Corps Salvage Sections, to work in Corps areas. Attached to a Corps Headquarters, the Corps Salvage Sections role was the maintenance of one or more large Main Dumps on the broad-gauge railway system; while 19 other ranks and an officer were sent to Army Headquarters to carry out similar work in rear areas.

This new and efficient system was primarily used in Belgium and northern France. Further south, the system differed mainly because of the Battle of the Somme in 1916. This battle, and the Germany Army's withdrawal to the *Siegfried-Stellung* (Hindenburg Line) in Spring 1917, highlighted the amount of abandoned and used items left in areas immediately behind the fighting front. Due to the large geographical area involved, and sheer amount of debris,

'Save our Stores' *(Author's Collection).*

the Somme was designated a 'Special Salvage Area' in Summer 1917. The Quartermaster General issued instructions on how to clear the area, and a Special Area Salvage Officer supervised the work undertaken by Divisional and Corps Salvage Sections.[11] While this was happening, soldiers were still responsible for routine salvage from the lines and immediate back areas. Divisional Salvage Sections collected the material and took it to salvage Sub-Dumps, before the Corps Salvage Sections transported it to the main dumps, which they ran. Items were sorted into different categories and sent onwards to workshops or Base Depots.[12]

To keep pace with the evolving organisation of salvage collection, great strides were taken to deal with the salvaged material at the Bases. All material not required for local re-issue was sent by rail from salvage dumps in forward areas to the Depots of the services of supply from which the stores originated. To consolidate this dispersal of salvaged material and so maximise efforts to reclaim, reuse and ultimately save money, early 1918 saw salvage work become organised and controlled right across the British Army. Appointing Staff Captains for Salvage to each Army and Corps Headquarters, a Controller of Salvage was appointed to oversee and deal with all matters of salvage, and was based, along with his staff, at General Headquarters.[13] In addition, Autumn 1918 saw Salvage Sections created within Labour Companies. Comprising one officer and 40 other ranks, one section was attached to each Division and Corps, while a further 18 sections were planned to be held in reserve at General Headquarters, ready to be sent to any Army area or to assist the Area Salvage Officer.[14] Only three of these planned 18 sections had been formed by the time the Armistice was signed.[15]

Collection Day

As far as you can see is a wilderness of torn up soil intersected with ruined trenches: it is like a man's face after small pox or a telescopic view of the moon. The shell holes overlap and run into each other; some are mere scratches, some would hide a haystack; here and there a few distorted posts form all that remain of barbed wire entanglement. But the most startling feature is the debris that is lying scattered on the surface and thick in the trenches. Sets of equipment, rifles, bayonets, shovels, shrapnel, helmets, respirators, shell cases, iron posts, overcoats, groundsheets, bombs (in hundreds) – I don't suppose there is a square yard without some sort of relic and the reminder of the awful waste of war.[16]

As the business of salvage expanded, guidelines on how to collect and transport the material were drawn up. Routine salvage was divided into two distinct areas, the first 'zone of operations', and the second 'zone occupied by troops in camps

The detritus of war (Author's Collection).

and billets'.[17] In the former, Salvage Officers of Divisional Salvage Sections were in constant touch with unit Commanding Officers. Co-operation was required as transport used to get supplies to the front was also needed to bring the salvage back. Salvage Officers assisted by making it as easy as possible for men to deposit salvage when they brought it out of the lines. In the front-line trenches, empty sandbags could be placed within the trench systems at certain points and were well suited to collect small articles. It was assumed that no fit man would leave the trench system without bringing something back with him.

Salvage Receiving Stations (known also as Collecting Stations): These were positioned next to roads, light railways, duckboards or at any point on the communication route to and from the trench systems. This was because it was believed that 'a tired man was far more likely to bring, say an abandoned rifle if he knew that he had not to carry it far before he could leave it to be cleared by the personnel of the salvage organisation'.[18] Salvage Receiving Stations were situated as close to the front as possible and were clearly marked with a notice,[19] and perhaps somewhat grimly, it was not unusual to find them next to First Aid Posts. This was the day-to-day routine of salvage, the reality of living in a trench system part, in a sense, of 'trench culture'. Battle zones were a valuable source of salvage and the way it was collected varied between quiet periods or during military action. During quiet periods, the area was divided up to make it easier to search, everything was collected, there being no distinction between types of salvage.

During military action, the type of salvage collected was stipulated, with items such as rifles and steel helmets considered of highest priority. A Salvage Officer would have known where operations were to take place and where the heaviest fighting had taken place in order to arrange for the retrieval of salvage.[20] Collections from battlefields occurred as soon as the fighting allowed, especially in the wake of a successful advance. The Salvage Officer reconnoitred the area, then mapped and planned the search, dividing the area into sub-areas. Collection in such an area required more men than searching gun positions, but whatever the circumstances most salvage had to be carried out by hand, due to the conditions of the battlefield.[21] Salvage made its way back to the Receiving Stations and beyond to the salvage dumps.[22] This system varied along parts of the line due to local conditions and the availability of light railway systems, but it formed the basis of a system which could be adapted.[23]

Collection in' Special Salvage Areas' such as the Somme required a different way of working. It depended on the military operations in place and could not

be carried out daily like routine salvage. Removal of defensive positions, hutted camps as well as the debris of an advance all made up the salvage in these areas. Labour battalions from different parts of the world were also enlisted to work salvage. The Chinese Labour Corps was one of the largest and provided men to work in all areas along the Line of Communication, and Prisoners of War helped maximise this workforce.[24] The Special Area Salvage Officer mapped the area and divided it into squares.[25] Each square was sub-divided dependent on road, railway and amount of debris and allocated to a labour company.[26] Groups of between eight and 12 men were given two sandbags and searched their allotted squares. If an area was suspected of having heavy items, then a Decauville railway was laid. As the men worked outwards from the nearest roads, they were instructed to check trenches, dugouts and mines, the latter being checked first for booby traps and explosives. Everything had to be collected, but there was an exception where great care and respect was required.

*Temporary battlefield marker (*Trench Art. *Saunders: 2001. By kind permission of Nicholas Saunders – Author's Collection).*

Under no circumstances was anything removed that marked the location of a grave before it was recorded. Soldiers showed respect and marked graves with anything they could find, such as an upturned rifle with the bayonet into the earth sometimes accompanied by a helmet. Empty artillery shell casings had been another popular choice for soldiers to mark the grave or used to make a cross. Graves would be recorded and sent to the Graves Registration Officer, white stones were then used to mark the grave before the article was taken away.[27] This practice was recognised by the War Office and even with salvaging activities in full swing - any item used to mark a burial was not removed, no matter how valuable the material was.[28]

Once collected, salvage was transported via Decauville light railways, mechanical or horse transport to a Sub-Dump to be sorted. Great care was taken when using horses, no further than 12 miles (19km) was to be travelled, ferrying goods back and forth from collection area to Sub-Dump. Extra precautions were taken if items were transported by lorries - wooden cases and lids had to have all the nails removed in case the vibrations loosened them and fell onto the road, thus potentially injuring a horse or mule.

Sub-Dumps to Main Salvage Dumps

Under Routine Salvage, material was collected from a Salvage Receiving Station via returning transport and taken to main dumps which were often at railheads and Advanced Railheads. At the Main Dump, usually within a Corps area, material was sorted into different categories, ordnance stores which included clothing, engineering, and Army Service Corps stores. The Salvage Officer sent items dependent on whether they were repairable either back to main Bases like Calais or on to workshops in Paris.[29]

In 'Special Salvage Areas,' the salvage unit at a 'dump' was required to sort material debris as well as arrange transport to move it. At the Sub-Dump, the NCO in charge completed a returns form for the amount received, which was forwarded to the main dump. Perishable articles such as clothing and tentage were kept under cover at these temporary Sub-Dumps. Salvage cans and boxes formed walls and corrugated iron sheets a roof, which could itself be collected after the Sub-Dump was closed.[30] Trones Wood, on the Somme, was an excellent example. It had been occupied by German forces until the 14 July 1916 when after six days of heavy fighting, British forces captured it.[31] Nearly a year to the day later, the British had advanced forward enough for the area to become part of the 'Special Salvage Area' and Trones Wood became a salvage dump on 12 July 1917.[32] It was an ideal location as a light railway already existed, connecting Pozieres and Aveluy to Trones.[33]

Salvage continued apace until the Spring of 1918, when the German offensive threatened to regain the ground it had previously lost. On 23 March, all salvage work in the area was suspended and the men of Trones Wood were now unloading ammunition that had been sent down the line. Once completed, they loaded up the empty railway truck with ordnance stores only and on the following day Trones Wood was evacuated. The 'Special Salvage Area' fell into the hands of German forces when they retook the ground in May.[34] Salvage parties were now drawing on men from all nationalities and units - British, Australian, Egyptian, Chinese and Canadian, and Labour Companies, Infantry Battalions, and Tunnelling Companies.[35]

Labour Battalion camps were often located next to Sub-Dumps so that the waste from the camp could be put straight into it.[36] The siting of Main Salvage Dumps, however, was crucial in order to maximise use of established transport lines. Such a major dump had to have at least one broad gauge railway siding that connected to a main line, a wide metalled road in good condition, the use of Decauville light railway system and ideally, be located next to a canal. Many sites like this had already been used for Supply Depots, as already described, and turning them into salvage dumps could be done quickly.[37] Dividing the Main Salvage Dump into 11 sections with notice boards denoting where each salvaged commodity was to go, any captured enemy materials were sent direct to General Ordnance Stores. Provided with an elementary layout of what a Main Salvage Dump should comprise (including areas which could be expanded if required and there was space), a road was to run every 200 yards (180m) at a right angle to the light railway sidings, and repeated for broad gauge sidings at 100 yards (90m) intervals. For heavy salvage, dedicated spur lines from the Decauville railway were laid direct to the relevant salvage section.

Most salvage could be sorted and left in the open, clothing, as a perishable classification, was stored under cover in sheds,[38] where it was sorted and if repairable, kept separate from the unserviceable. Anything destined for

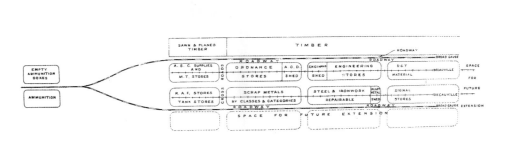

An example of a Salvage Dump plan (WO 107/72: **History of the Organisation and Development of the Quartermaster General's Services.** *The National Archives (OGL) - Author's Collection).*

Britain, such as rags, had to be sorted into woollen and cotton, with men issued a list to help identify the cloth. Then it was carefully packed.[39] Blankets for example were gathered in bundles of 10, pairs of boots tied together and put into sacks the quantity of which was shown on the outside, odd pairs were sorted into left and right and put in separate sacks, and greatcoats bundled together five at a time.[40] Salvage Depots did not exist so any excess[41] or scrap material was sent back to the main issuing Base or Sub-Depots specific to that item.

Over a four-week period leading up to 28 September 1918, the figures give an indication to the effectiveness of salvage. Over 164,000 articles of clothing, boots, accoutrements, camp and hospital stores, rags and waste were collected, which equated to 109 tons (109,000kg). The value of those articles that were sent back to the Base was over £139,000 and those immediately re-issued was over £27,000[42] (Table H).

Article of Clothing	Quantity Salvaged in a Four-Week Period up to 28 September 1918
Service Dress Jacket	27,107
Trousers and Pantaloons	23,172
Greatcoats	19,307
Shirts	33,018
Socks, pairs	55,377
Drawers	16,829

Table H - Break down of individual clothing articles salvaged – Compiled from WO 107/72: Quartermaster General's Department: History of the Organisation and Development of the Quartermaster General's Services (British Armies in France). Salvage - Appendix 2.

Valdelievre: Depot and Workshop

The efficiency of the Salvage Sections in not wasting anything greatly impressed newspaper correspondents when visiting depots on the Western Front. While there were few comments on the efficiency of getting stores to soldiers at the front, it was how salvage was repaired that was regarded as the most astounding feat. On the Western Front, two huge depots were created for this purpose, Graville (Le Havre), from where clothing was moved to Rouen for the southern line, and Valdelievre (Calais) for the northern line.[43]

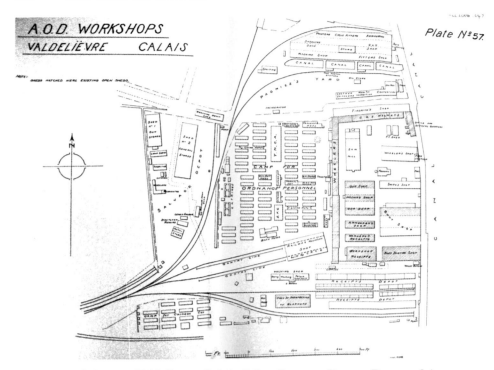

*Plan of workshops at Valdelievre, Calais (*Miscellaneous Papers-Proposed Army Laundry. *The Royal Logistic Corps Museum Archive - Author's Collection).*

In November 1916, at Valdelievre, 1,328 covered railway wagons were received, 904 contained returned stores of which 428 held spent artillery shell cases and ammunition boxes.[44] Clothing was sorted into repairable and unserviceable which included surplus and obsolete patterns, then consigned to the relevant ordnance depot. Repairable items went to workshops within the Base Depot, to Paris, or sent back to Britain, whereas unserviceable materials were 'reduced to produce' and sold as rags in Britain.[45] In some instances, what remained had to be burned but this was only a small percentage.[46] When Valdelievre started operation in Calais it drew from the experience of Graville at Le Havre. It had large workrooms with specialist equipment which allowed for greater productivity with a limited workforce.[47]

Workshops of the Army Ordnance Department made full use of employing British and local women. French and Belgian women were not just employed for the women's work of sewing and washing, but also wherever and whenever they were needed. Cleaning wagons, rifles, unloading barges, carpentry, and office work were all jobs that these women could be asked to undertake. A newspaper correspondent at the time noted this and reported 'but it is not, I think yet known how very useful their aid is proving in France and how many are being employed within the circle of War Office departments…'.[48] Mr Danchenko wrote in *The Times*, 'Here some thousands of French women whose fathers, husbands and brothers have gone to the war earn a handsome living of which they could not dream in peace time'.[49] In addition to local female labour, the question had been raised of using women from Britain to replace men on the Line of Communication, in Bases and Depots, leading the Chief Ordnance Officer of Calais to note in his war diary 'it is estimated that 140 women [from Britain] can be taken in the Ordnance Depot at Calais as clerks in offices and in clerical positions in storehouses'.[50]

'Smoke [Hypo] Helmet' Repair Factory, Valdelievre: In June 1915, following the establishment of a workshop in Abbeville, the Valdelievre repair factory was tasked to repair and re-impregnate the then newly-issued 'smoke [Hypo] helmet' style gas mask. Hypo [H] helmets were made of flannelette and impregnated with sodium hypo-sulphate which would evaporate, after approximately three months, rendering the gas mask ineffective.[51] The Smoke Helmet repair workshop had large boilers to heat water for washing and centrifugal drums that were able to spin the excess water out of the flannelette. Hypo Helmets were placed in drying rooms that were artificially heated, where rips and tears were repaired and eyepieces refitted. Helmets were re-dipped in a sodium hypo-sulphate solution under a Medical Officers supervision, before an expiry date was added to show when the helmet's next treatment was needed. A cross over period existed when the helmet style of gas masks was used at the same time as the small box respirator, but in time the helmet mask was superseded and the repair workshop gradually closed. Despite the temporariness, the importance of this workshop cannot be underestimated, it repaired and re-impregnated over 7½ million 'Smoke Helmet' gas masks.[52]

All the workshop's processes were carried out by 20 French women[53] - one forewoman at 25 francs a week, 10 machinists at 40 centimes per hour, and nine packers at 35 centimes per hour. In overall charge were several Lady Superintendents - Miss Morgan, who arrived from Britain to supervise the workshop on 9 September 1915,[54] Miss Beavor and Mrs Barocchi[55] who arrived soon after. Attached to the Army Ordnance Corps, they were the first British women to be employed by the British Army in France.[56] All three had worked in Branch 8 of the Quartermaster General in Britain and as they had served in a war zone from 1915, were issued the 1914/1915 star, Victory Medal, and War Medal.[57]

Boot Repair Factory, Valdelievre: The boot repair factory was set up in September 1915 with 180 bootmakers that repaired 350 pairs of boots per week. In two years, this workforce had risen to 800 bootmakers and an astounding repair rate of 30,000 per week. French and Belgian women worked alongside the men, sorting and pairing boots together, cleaning as well as re-oiling them.[58]

A bootmaker had a target of 30 pairs a day and if he exceeded that he received a bonus. Using machines to re-sole and renew eyelets, the bootmakers worked in teams of five, with any bonuses shared amongst them, an incentive that showed a return of around 900 pairs per man.[59] To maximise the output for British forces, Prisoners of War were utilised in the repair of boots,[60] with shoemaker's tools along with hob nails, rivets, heels and leather soles sent to the Prisoner of War camps.[61] The Calais (Valdelievre) and Le Havre (Graville) Base workshops returned around four million pairs of boots back to depots for re-issue.[62]

Divisional and Regimental Boot [Work]Shops: These were small workshops sited near ordnance dumps and catered to the needs of a Division of around 630 pairs of boots. Regularly inspected by officers and repaired when needed, the aim was to make boots last as long as possible. Supervised by the Deputy Assistant Director of Supplies, the most common repair was re-soling and re-heeling, but if they arrived in bad condition then a wooden sole would be attached so they could be used as clogs in muddy wagon lines.[63]

Regimental boot workshops catered for a regiment's battalions and each had its own.[64] Bags of shoemaker's tools were issued to some units that were not part of the infantry, such as Tunnelling Companies, which received two shoemaker's tool bags per company.[65] Boots that needed extensive repairs and re-conditioning were sent back to the large workshop at the main supply Base. Boots could be repaired several times before they were classed as unserviceable, and men generally preferred repaired boots, as they were already broken in and more comfortable.[66] Authorities also made use of soldiers in military prisons to repair boots for units who didn't have access to a workshop. Units would contact the prison governor and boots were sent tied together with the soldier's name and number attached. It took two days from when they were received for batches or 25 to 50 pairs to be returned to the unit.[67] Other Divisional workshops included saddlers, carpenters, blacksmith and tailors.

Divisional and Regimental Tailors: Each Divisional tailoring workshop employed three tailors to repair clothing including sewing together the best quality segments of puttees. They could manufacture whatever a Division needed, even a workshop producing nosebags for horses.[68] Each regiment also had its own tailor. Reusing and repairing on such an extensive level could not always be achieved within the Divisional tailoring workshops and so would be carried out in larger establishments. An official photograph released by the Press Bureau in August 1916 shows the far from ideal conditions that tailors worked in. Four tailors are shown sitting cross-legged on the ground, a traditional posture for tailors in workrooms at home. Three of the men are stitching and the fourth pressing, and all are sitting close together outside a tent, oblivious to the comings and goings around them. Behind them is a pile of steel helmets and in the distance a field artillery troop of horses and men are pulling a gun and limber.[69]

After the Boer War of 1899-1902, an outbreak of enteric (intestinal problem) on a training ship had been traced to old blankets that had been sold as surplus

Example of a Divisional / Regimental Tailoring Workshop (Author's Collection).

*Making and repairing uniforms 'behind the lines' (*The Tailor and Cutter Journal, *10 August 1916. Anon:1916. By kind permission of Manchester City Galleries: Gallery of Costume, Platt Hall - Author's Collection).*

stock. Preventing disease and the spread of lice when transporting clothes for repair was crucial, and medical authorities had objected to old clothes being sent back to Britain as they might contain diseases. Another concern was that lousy (lice-infested) and filthy uniforms would be conveyed in wagons that would later transport food. Before large-scale salvage and repairing began, garments had been burnt - a huge waste of money, as even rags had value. As the Line of Communication became more efficient and depots expanded, the Director of Supplies included soldiers' old worn clothing in the salvage effort. Expansion of bath houses, laundries and delousing facilities aided this and locomotive wagons were disinfected before any food or other supplies were transported in them. In the summer of 1916, worn clothing was bundled into sacks and sent to main Bases at Le Havre and Calais, or on to *Quai de Javel* in Paris.[70]

Quai De Javel

Colonel Thomas Heron, Deputy Director Ordnance Services Northern 'Line of Communication' recognised how important salvage could be after he observed several blankets and greatcoats at Le Havre during the winter of 1914-1915. Spattered with the muck of war, he felt that if laundered and repaired they could be reused. A trial contract was placed in March 1915 with the firm *Joly Fils* in Paris to launder and mend at a fixed price. Once this had been done, they needed to be stored, and a large warehouse was found nearby at 79 Quai de Javel.[71] As its name suggests, the warehouse was situated on the River Seine, and had a quayside where barges could load and offload.[72] A railway line also ran along the quayside with its own siding, and so altogether this was a perfect location.

Corps staff under Colonel H Keddie were sent to establish the new warehouse. All greatcoats, blankets and horse rugs were sent direct to Paris from the front, laundered, repaired and stored until re-issue the following autumn. The British company 'Debenham and Freedbody' soon installed a fur-cleaning plant for the special laundering of sheepskin lined coats, fur undercoats and leather jerkins. This saw the items being revolved in large drums with sawdust impregnated with cresyl and formaldehyde, a process later taken over by the Army Ordnance Corps who increased the output by fitting powerful exhausts to allow waste gases to expel quicker. The amount of clothing sent to Paris gathered momentum as the amount of salvage increased, so much so that contracts were placed with other laundries to relieve the pressure on Joly Fils.[73] From April to June 1916 over 55,000 items were sent from the Rouen Base to Paris.[74] The Paris depots were becoming congested with cleaned and repaired clothing as well as with storing winter clothing. After a visit from the Chief Ordnance Officer of Calais, he mentioned the need for ordnance depots on the Line of Communication to start taking winter garments and underclothing at an earlier date.[75]

At the Quai de Javel, vast workrooms had hundreds of women repairing and fixing uniforms. Shoulder titles and rank badges were removed, holes patched and darned by hand or when repairs required something more, by sewing machine, of which a request for 'More sewing machines wanted. Supplies from England very slow – have to buy locally' was sent on 12 August 1917[76] due to the increased workload. Ripped and torn sleeves could be unpicked from one jacket and replaced with good ones that had been unpicked from unserviceable jackets. Other lessons were learned - dry-cleaning the service dress prevented shrinkage and those badly stained were dyed blue to be reused by the Chinese Labour Corps or Prisoners of War. It was cheaper to establish an Ordnance run workroom for all sewing repairs with local women, especially as Paris had a lot of skilled dressmakers that had previously worked in pre-war *ateliers* (workshops). When the Prince of Wales visited, some 2,000 women were employed and had repaired over 10 million blankets, three and a half million pairs of drawers, one and half million greatcoats and over one million service dress jackets. These herculean efforts saved the British over eight million pounds Sterling.[77] Ordnance depots and laundries sprang up all round Paris and new premises were rented for the purpose. Parisian workrooms and laundries also did contract work for the British Army.

French women sorting and cutting off buttons from soldiers clothing, Ordnance Depot, Quai de Javel, Paris, April 1917 (IWM Q29383. Licenced by kind permission of The Imperial War Museum Archives. © Crown Copyright. IWM).

French women operating machines in the SD department, Ordnance Depot, Quai de Javel, Paris, April 1917 (IWM Q29394. Licenced by kind permission of The Imperial War Museum Archives. © Crown Copyright. IWM).

French women operating sewing machines in the SD department, Ordnance Depot, Quai de Javel, Paris, April 1917 (IWM Q29392. Licenced by kind permission of The Imperial War Museum Archives. © Crown Copyright. IWM).

Expansion: Expanding from the Quai de Javel, a gumboot workshop was set up in the north-eastern Parisian district of Pantin. Here, repairs were carried out, gumboots could be easily washed but the main problem was how to dry the insides. It was an Ordnance Engineering Officer who invented a piece of equipment that blew hot air into the boot, and which could dry around 1,500 pairs of boots per day.[78] All the Ordnance workshops and warehouse in Paris were under the control of the Chief Ordnance Officer (Paris) who liaised with the French War Office to purchase any local goods required.[79] This included buying celluloid film which was sent to the Calais (Valdelievre) smoke helmet repair factory to replace the celluloid eyepieces in the helmet gas masks.[80]

Rags to Riches

Unserviceable clothes were still commodities with commercial value. Uniforms were cut into rags and used by some workshops in France and Belgium to make camouflage netting, but the majority were sent back to Britain. Clothing was separated into unserviceable or repairable at source by regimental officers when they authorised a new issue. Guidelines were issued to officers to help them decide what were truly rags and what could be repaired:

Greatcoats: Greatcoats were expensive garments, made of thicker cloth and able to withstand more extensive repairs than Service Dress jackets and trousers. Provided the greatcoat was not threadbare, damage of two or three holes measuring several square inches (cm^2) each or a missing collar or sleeve, was not enough to condemn the item. Blood stained garments and those hopelessly cut by barbed wire would be condemned, but staining caused by equipment straps were repairable.

SD Jackets and Trousers: A far greater proportion of Service Dress jackets and trousers had to be condemned; the material was thinner and more often became threadbare. However, rips could be mended, small holes patched or darned, and buttonholes remade. Bloodstained garments had to be condemned but those with other stains were generally recycled.

Underclothing: Repairs to underclothing included the sewing on of buttons, renewal of binding, patching of holes where the article was otherwise good, and the darning of small holes. When the sleeves of cardigans and vests were beyond repair, they were cut off, and the garment made sleeveless. The waistbands of drawers were replaced if the garments were otherwise in good condition'.[81] Once classified as unserviceable, all buttons and hooks were removed and the articles bagged according to type (e.g. trousers or jackets), then sent to ordnance depots who forwarded them onto the Base Port. From here, they were loaded onto ships and returned to Britain. One ship, the S.S. *Rother* returned to Newhaven on the 17 April 1916 with a cargo full of unserviceable and repairable goods, including gumboots and gas helmets for the Royal Army Clothing Department, and 251 sacks of rags destined for the rag merchant Messer's J Eastwood and Company in Dewsbury.[82]

'Shoddy'

Long before the First World War, rags from wool and cotton had been recombed and spun into yarn, then woven into 'shoddy cloth'. Fabric can be made wholly with shoddy yarn on the warp and weft, or mixed with shoddy on the weft and new wool on the warp. It was classed as inferior in quality, lustre and wear, and the pre-First World War expression itself is still used to describe something that is not well made. In the early years of the war, some manufacturers had tried to pass off shoddy fabric as top quality and sold it at high prices. The subject was raised in parliament November 1914 and the *Tailor and Cutter Journal* voiced its own opinion, writing on 29 October 1914:

> We are not surprised that there has been an outcry against the shoddy garments, especially the overcoats, supplied to the recruits, for Kitchener's new army. Almost every tailor is aware of the "diddling" which has been practised on the authorities in their endeavour to secure garments to meet an emergency. It is to be regretted that many of our manufacturers see in a great national crisis the means of adding to their wealth. We can only describe these people and the firms they belong, as being of the class who are constantly "on the make" .... [83]

However, as raw material shortages developed and worn-out clothing was returned from the front, the need for shoddy became important. A decision was taken in May 1916 for a central depot of salvage to be sited in the town of Dewsbury, Yorkshire - already known for its production of shoddy. This became one of numerous salvage depots to be established throughout the country.[84]

In order to make use of shoddy cloth, changes had to be made to the specifications laid down by the Contracts Department for its use in the production of army cloth.[85] By the end of 1916, it became apparent that the army would need to fix the price and control the shoddy market. Prior to this, clothing manufacturers sold their cuttings to rag merchants who then sold it to mills to make into shoddy.[86] As with raw materials, the price of this resource grew and the Contracts Department stepped in. Now rag merchants in Dewsbury and the Stroud Valley (another area known for its production of shoddy), could purchase cuttings direct from the Contracts Department through the depot at Dewsbury, who purchased the cuttings from the clothing manufacturers.[87] The government now had control of the rag trade, but it was a necessary step as prices were kept low ensuring the continued supply of cloth. Trousers, puttees, jackets, socks, underwear and caps that were worn-out were classed as woollen rags. The amount handled was extraordinary. In less than a year, five million jackets and trousers alone had been handled in the Dewsbury Depot.[88]

The End is Only the Beginning – Clearing the Debris of War

Britain had a joint responsibility for clearing the battlefields of the Western Front once the Armistice[89] was signed. Packing up all its Armies and heading 'home' was not an option. As salvage had grown in importance during the war, after the Armistice the clearing of material from France and Belgium became the Salvage Section's main purpose and was known as 'intensive collection.'[90] Economic necessity and the post-war shortage of raw materials were not the only factors - the old battlefields of the Western Front needed to be cleared. By January 1919 this grim task was in full swing, with scrap, abandoned items, and surplus stores being collected, including ordnance stores, mechanical transport, horses and mules. And many of these, of course, were freely mixed with human remains. The aim was to clear the battlefields and rear areas, working from east to west as the army would slowly withdraw to the main Bases.

Agreements were reached between Britain, France and Belgium on collection of salvage within their own areas. Belgian authorities allowed Britain to continue salvage work, whereas anything the French discovered that was British was handed over to them and Britain reciprocated.[91] At GHQ, a salvage depot was established in January 1919 at Zeneghem Yard[92] near Calais, which for most of the war had been a large ammunition depot. It had numerous broad gauge railway sidings that converged onto a main line and benefited from bordering the Aa River and Calais canal. The collection of salvage intensified and was now considered part of surplus government stock. With the Salvage Control department now absorbed as a section of the Quartermaster General, a disposals board was created in March 1919 to oversee the sale of all excess Government stock both at home and abroad.[93]

In April 1919, the five British Armies that had been fighting up until 11 November 1918 were reconfigured – two became the Army of the Rhine, tasked to follow the retreat of German forces and monitor the terms of the Armistice, with the Line of Communication needed to be kept open to supply them. The three remaining armies were divided across the old battlefields that had been controlled by Britain, becoming Army Troops in France and Flanders.[94] The British Army had two main objectives, clearing battlefields and rear areas, and demobilisation. It was a double-edged sword, intensive collection required manpower but sending men home, especially those who had served from 1914 was the priority. Manpower in industry at home was another consideration, and the combination of time served abroad with the importance of a soldier's pre-war occupation prioritised who was to go home first. Some Tunnelling Companies had already been assigned to salvage as early as 1917,[95] and after the Armistice their particular skills were called on to search mines and dugouts for timber and other materials. Nevertheless, most skilled miners were soon required for the coal mines back home. Local civilians were also employed, as were Prisoners of War and overseas Labour battalions before their repatriation.

The Treaty of Versailles was signed on 7 May 1919, and on 19 May orders arrived stating 'only material to be salvaged considered likely to repay cost of collection.'[96] This included enemy munitions and all kinds of expended bullet and artillery shell casings. All salvage operations were transferred to the Ministry of Munitions in July 1919, and its wartime role now changed to completing the collection of salvage from dumps. This marked the end of salvage on the Western Front.[97]

The British Army's wartime ingenuity in converting, repairing, and utilising everything was unparalleled. It was in effect the largest recycling exercise the world had seen up to that point. The requirements of five British Armies on the Western Front were prodigious, and to this had to be added those of British armies serving abroad. Fat was extracted from cook houses and sent home by the ton and turned into propellant for 18-pounder artillery shells, old canvas tents were cut up and turned into horse nosebags and cooks' clothing. Ration bags and cap covers that needed to be waterproofed were made from old worn out waterproof capes. In modern terms, recycle and reuse does not come close to the achievements of the First World War British Army, the masters of salvage. As Forbes memorably observed:

Without these salvage operations, all the sheep farms of Australia and all the cotton fields of America could not have produced the raw materials we needed; nor, even had shipping been available to carry them to England, could all the looms of Yorkshire and Lancashire have sufficed to weave cotton and woollen goods for our armies and civil population beside Allies that we clad.[98]

Chapter 6
Coming Home

George was one of millions of First World War casualties. His first visit to hospital was 14 November 1915, just five months after arriving in Belgium, where his service record states that, when admitted to the 17th Casualty Clearing Station he was N.Y.D (condition 'Not Yet Diagnosed) which indicates he didn't suffer any obvious external wounds. Nevertheless, he remained in hospital for seven days, transferring at some point to the 12th Casualty Clearing Station at Rue des Prés, Hazebrouck – sited within a requisitioned lace factory.[1] However, after having been discharged on 22 November 1915, he was re-admitted to hospital soon afterwards on 14 January 1916, this time to the 18th Field Ambulance. Taking over Divisional Rest Stations duties from 16th Field Ambulance at Proven, he was again discharged fit to return to duty on 22 January.[2]

George's Route Home

In February 1918, the 177th Tunnelling Company moved from the Ypres Salient to join the Fifth Army in the Le Hamel area of the Somme.[3] Shifting the 177th's role from mining to the construction of dug outs, machine gun pits, and the preparation of roads and bridges for demolition, the Fifth Army area bore the brunt of the opening phase of Germany's 'Spring Offensive', the *Kaiserschlacht* launched on 21 March 1918.[4] This was a period during which George's life changed forever. On 29 May, George reported having 'giddiness and headache along with shortness of breath and paralysis on the left side'.[5] What caused these symptoms is not known, but we do know that George left the front line and his mates never to return.

George's wartime sufferings were the same for millions of men, as were his experiences of battlefield medical treatment. Only basic first aid could be given in the trenches. Stitched inside the right side of each SD jacket tunic was a small pocket which held a khaki cotton cloth field dressing. Inside each cloth dressing was a linen casing covering two dressings each composed of 2.5 yards (2.28m) of bandages, gauze and a safety pin housed within khaki cotton cloth.[6] If a man could walk with or without the aid of others he would return through the trenches - for those who couldn't, stretcher bearers carried them out through the lines to Regimental Aid Post.

Regimental Aid Post: Regimental Aid Posts were situated close to the fighting in deep dugouts than ran underneath trench systems, ruined buildings and cellars; Regimental Stretcher Bearer's deposited wounded men in these comparatively safe places before returning to collect more wounded men. For the seriously wounded, a Regimental Medical Officer and orderlies from the Royal Army Medical Corps examined, stabilised, and provided additional dressings and morphine. Each patient had a 'Field Medical Card' attached to their clothing on which any morphine dosage was written.[7] Men with minor injuries were patched up and, if no further treatment was required sent back to their units.

By the end of the war, light railways were transporting the wounded back across the shelled landscape. In some areas, a trolley system existed based on the same principle as chain ferries, with large slings attached to an overhead cable carrying a single stretcher case allowing it to be guided and propelled by hand. Casualties were sent to the larger Advanced Dressing Stations, sometimes via a series of Bearer Relay Posts (also known as Bearer Collecting Posts), where care for the wounded soldier was taken over by the RAMC. These posts were set up to help avoid congestion allowing stretcher bearers to 'relay' casualties to the next post and then onto the Advanced Dressing Stations. During major offensives casualties could be sent direct to either the Advanced Dressing Stations or the Field Ambulance. The former allowed for further treatment, after which casualties were returned to their units or passed along the chain of evacuation to the Main Dressing Station.[8]

Field Ambulance: Field Ambulances were mobile medical units attached to infantry and cavalry formations rather than the vehicles we associate with the term today, though its role could be considered a modern ambulance: to collect and transport patients for specialised treatment and care, whilst ensuring their condition remained stable in transit.

Providing staff for the Bearer Relay Posts, Advanced-Main Dressing Stations, and Walking Wounded Collecting Posts, three Field Ambulances were attached to each Division and comprised of 39 officers, 495 other ranks RAMC, 180 other ranks attached,[9] 45 draught, and 111 heavy draught horses, 21 two-horsed and 48 four-horsed wagons.[10] Each Field Ambulance had its own transport so casualties could be taken to the nearest Casualty Clearing Station. Motor ambulances were also used in which there could be 40 to 50 motor ambulances within a convoy, or via railway if nearby. Away from the front, a Field Ambulance's role was to keep the soldier fit and healthy, setting up Divisional Rest Stations and bath houses.[11] On 29th May 1918, George was admitted to the 91st Field Ambulance (part of the 32nd Division), with symptoms recorded as 'Giddiness and headache together with shortness of breath and paralysis left side.'[12]

Advanced Dressing Stations: Optimally situated approximately one mile (1.61km) from the Regimental Aid Post, the Advanced Dressing was established as far forward as military conditions permitted.[13] This was the first location where men (approximately 50) could be housed and treated for up to a week before they returned to their units or moved on to the Main Dressing Station. This was where the soldier's details, his injuries and any diagnosis were first documented using information from his medical card. Although they did not possess operating theatres, Advanced Dressing Stations could perform lifesaving surgery if required.[14] The more seriously injured were examined and the sick diagnosed.[15]

Main Dressing Stations: Formed by the headquarters of a Field Ambulance, Main Dressing Stations were a greater distance from the front (2-5 miles (3.2-8km)), and were generally organised into: Receiving, Recording, Resuscitation, Dressing, Gas and Evacuation Sections, Mortuary, Pack Store, Salvage Dump, Exchange Dump, Living Accommodation for officers/ORs, Cookhouse/Ablutions and Latrines, Hard Standing for horses/vehicles, the office of the Commanding Officer and the Quartermaster's Stores. Main Dressing Stations were better equipped than Advanced Dressing Stations, and could undertake urgent operations.

Walking Wounded Collecting Posts: Set up during major offensives, Walking Wounded Collecting Posts were located on routes along which the walking wounded were likely to take, and easily accessible to the Advanced Dressing Station and roads leading to a Casualty Clearing Station. They were organised along similar lines to Main Dressing Stations - Reception, Recording, Dressing and Evacuation Sections, though no operations or complicated dressing were done, and patients requiring this attention were either evacuated to the Main Dressing Stations or Casualty Clearing Stations.[16]

Casualty Clearing Stations: Casualty Clearing Stations were part of Army troops rather than a Divisional or Corps unit, and were a welcome sight for the wounded as they were the first place to resemble anything like a hospital. Each Division had one Casualty Clearing Station though they were usually clustered in groups of two, three or four, and located further back behind the line to avoid long range shelling. They were nevertheless close enough to hear artillery bombardment and to be attacked by enemy aeroplanes. Each Casualty Clearing Station had a minimum of 50 beds and 150 stretchers that could cater for around 200 wounded or sick men, hospitalising them for up to four weeks.

Casualty Clearing Station staff performed major and complicated operations. The stations themselves comprised a mix of wooden huts, marquee tents, operating theatres, dispensary, mortuary, kitchens, medical and surgical facilities as well as staff accommodation. With seven Medical Officers, one Quartermaster and 77 other ranks forming the main staff complement, these locations were the furthest forward positions that female nurses were allowed to serve in.[17]

The days of camp followers had long since passed by 1914, but the unique relationship between nurse and soldier survived and developed during the war. Professional nurses from the Queen Alexandra's Imperial Military Nursing Service (QAIMNS), Voluntary Aid Detachment (VADs) (provided mainly from The Red Cross and St John's Ambulance), and the First Aid Nursing Yeomanry (FANY) were just some of the women who tended the war's casualties. Some women, such as the extraordinary Elsie Knocker,[18] nursed the wounded much nearer the front lines at Regimental Aid Posts but they were the exception not the rule.

Infection was a deadly threat as men had reached this point covered in mud and dirt - an ideal breeding ground for germs. After a battle, it was difficult and dangerous to retrieve the injured as the army was advancing over No Man's Land under fire. A man wounded going over the top would, unless he could crawl back to his own lines, remain where he fell until under cover of darkness stretcher bearers could recover him. Even during more quiet times in the trenches, the threat of injury was real due to shrapnel from exploding shells, snipers, and trench raids. Any penetrating wound could turn from a relatively minor if painful injury to an amputation or loss of life due to infection from a soiled scrap of clothing.

Small fragments of dirty or lice-infested uniform that contained bacteria could be dragged into open wounds, with the infection resulting in gas gangrene. Not to be confused with injuries caused by poison phosgene or mustard gases, or even with trench foot, gas gangrene is caused by anaerobic bacteria, *Clostridia,*[19] and could kill a man in 24 to 48 hours, with terrible symptoms - air under the skin, blisters with foul smelling gas discharge, and pale skin that turned a grey, brownish red.[20] Often the only possible treatment was to surgically remove the dead tissue as the infection did not survive in fresh bleeding tissue. Sir Anthony Bowlby, a consulting surgeon to the BEF stated 'It is absolutely essential for success that wound excision should be done as soon as possible… It is therefore necessary to operate on such cases before the patient is sent by train to the base'.[21] If left untreated, gas gangrene would spread throughout the body, and many soldiers had to have limbs amputated as the infection had spread too far. This problem was so severe that in 1916, experiments in pre-treating uniforms with chemicals to inhibit the growth of the gas-forming bacteria were undertaken.

These experiments discovered that a solution of seven percent Monochlor-cresol when dissolved in alcohol and covered with earth arrested infection in the wound, and that the area surrounding a fragment of cloth lodged in the wound was also free of bacterial growth.[22] Nevertheless, dirt dislodged from the cloth in the wound did form bacterial growth, and so further tests were carried out to measure the effects of repeated washing and of irritation to the wearer. Other experiments included the treatment of lice on all kinds of soldiers' clothing. Pouches of lice were sewn into pre-treated uniforms and worn for six days. Nearly all the lice were killed within 18 hours on garments worn next to the skin, and within just a few hours on outer garments. Unfortunately, in both instances the effectiveness of the treated cloth wore off after six days.

Summarising the results of these experiments, Colonel William H Horrocks, expert in the field of hygiene and then Honorary Surgeon to King George V, concluded that Monochlor-cresol and Copper Monochlor-cresol were effective in preventing gas gangrene bacteria from forming, and that 'Monochlor-cresol has a destructive action on lice' and 'that experiments should be on large scale in the field'.[23] There are no records to show whether these further large-scale experiments took place. A plausible explanation is that in view of the need to re-treat the cloth once the effectiveness wore off, it would be impossible to implement this practice under wartime conditions. What these experiments and results show however is the intimate relationship between soldiers' uniforms, the nature of wounds caused by modern industrialized weapons, and the increasing sophistication of medical knowledge.

Men classed as 'walking wounded' and who required non-urgent medical treatment at a hospital were often put onto an Ambulance Train at a Casualty Clearing Station and transported direct to a port for onward transportation to a General Hospital somewhere in Britain. For many other men sent to Casualty Clearing Stations, their wounds were not of the physical (bleeding) kind, but rather were the equally destructive effects of gas, poison, carbon monoxide, random accidents, and shell shock (often referred to as 'Neurasthenia' during the war, and today as Post Traumatic Stress Disorder (PTSD)).[24] On 30 May 1918,

Location of the 43rd Casualty Clearing Station at Bac du Sud, Near Arras, France, where George was sent. Only the cemetery today remains (Author's Collection).

a day after being admitted to the Field Ambulance, George was sent to the 43rd Casualty Clearing Station at Bac-Du-Sud, near Arras. To his initial diagnosis of 'Giddiness and headache together with shortness of breath and paralysis left side' was added 'mitral heart murmur, enlargement of heart, loss of control. No neurological symptoms'.[25] It was clear that he needed to be moved to a better-equipped base hospital via one of the ambulance trains that departed from the adjacent station.

Stationary and General (Base) Hospitals: There were two Stationary Hospitals for each Army Division, set further back from the front than the Casualty Clearing Stations, and each could accommodate up to 400 men.[26] For some reason, George bypassed these and was recorded as headed for a General (Base) hospital, whose facilities were located nearer the coast and so within easy access to Channel ports. Located near the army's principal bases and resembling a General Hospital in peacetime, these establishments could accommodate up to 1,200[27] patients, and were staffed by 35 officers, 80 QAIMNS and 229 mostly RAMC other ranks.[28]

George ended up at the No. 47 General Hospital at Le Treport, north-east of Dieppe, and was sent back to England on 14 June 1918. He travelled by hospital ship and ambulance train to Maudsley Neurological Clearing Hospital, London on 15 June 1918.[29]

Maudsley Military Hospital, London[30]: George spent almost two months at Maudsley Hospital – a subsidiary of Kings College Hospital (No.4 London General Hospital), dealing with injured and disabled soldiers. It had opened in 1915, and following requisition by the War Office, soon began treating men suffering with 'shell shock'.

On 6 July 1918, approximately three weeks after admission to Maudsley, George's diagnosis was given as Hemiplegia, a paralysis of half of the body due to brain injury, one of the most common causes of which is a stroke possibly caused by a cerebral haemorrhage. Body paralysis is a major symptom of shell shock, though delayed concussion can also cause similar headaches and dizziness. Exactly why George stayed at Maudsley for so long will never be known, but there is little doubt that along with heart disease and stroke, he likely also had shell shock. Prior to George's last transfer, his case was presented to a medical board, as doctors knew he was 'physically unfit for military service' and should be discharged. The Medical Board gave its approval and George was awarded a pension before being discharged on the 28 August 1918 to the Bristol General Hospital[31] in his home city.

Travelling back on an ambulance train along with hundreds of other soldiers, many of whom were still in their uniforms, George arrived at Bristol Temple Meads Station. The Bristol branch of the Red Cross, along with

St John's Ambulance, helped organise and run the reception of ambulance trains at Temple Meads, and VADs helped provide refreshments as soldiers waited to be transported.[32] Every soldier was given cigarettes, a postcard of Bristol to send to a loved one, and a clean handkerchief.[33] George was issued a demob suit that consisted of a suit, waistcoat, drawers, vest, great coat, shoes and hat – a clear visual sign of his change of status. A clue that his condition had deteriorated prior to leaving Maudsley can be observed on his discharge form, as George was unable to sign for these clothes, and in such cases, a doctor or orderly would have signed on his behalf.[34]

Bristol General Hospital was a large Georgian building built close to the quayside in the city docks. Overlooking the quayside ran a balcony where patients were moved for fresh air. Alice recalled how her guardian Mrs Jones took her to the quayside below this balcony to wave and blow a kiss to her father. Whether George was there, we shall never know, but the men that were, waved and blew kisses back. It was a memory that stayed with Alice all her life. She believed that she had waved to her father and he had waved back.[35] This belief likely brought some measure of comfort to her, as George died on 18 September 1918, just 20 days after finally coming home. His death was recorded as Hemiplegia (stroke).[36]

As George died in a Bristol Hospital he was entitled to be buried in 'Soldier's Corner' at Arnos Vale Cemetery, Bristol, where the Red Cross Society had, with donated monies, purchased a plot of land. Alice, aged 11, remembered walking

Bristol General Hospital circa 1900s (Author's Collection).

Soldier's Corner, Arnos Vale Cemetery as it is today. The final resting place of George (Author's Collection).

behind a gun carriage that carried her father to Arnos Vale. All men buried in Soldiers Corner were given the honour of a full military burial. Interestingly, while Canadian, Newfoundland, and Australian soldiers were interred in individual graves, up to five British soldiers could occupy a single plot. George shares his with:

Royal Navy Volunteer Reserve, Ordinary Seaman Herbert Sidney Eyles,
Private A. R Straford, 2nd Battalion, Royal Sussex Regiment,
Company Quartermaster Sergeant H.G. Symington. Somerset Light Infantry, and Private Harold Darby, Royal Dublin Fusiliers.[37]

Beyond the Grave: Finding the Missing

Fabian Ware, a man too old for military service on the outbreak of war, volunteered for the Red Cross Society. On 19 September 1914, he travelled to France taking with him volunteer drivers and a collection of vehicles to create a mobile unit and Field Hospital. During his work, both he and the Red Cross recognised the need to record names and burial locations of the dead. As early as 1914, it was acknowledged that next of kin would want to know where their loved one had fallen.

Wherever possible, fellow soldiers buried their dead comrades in a grave marked in any way they could as we have seen. Small impromptu cemeteries began as soldiers tried to bury the fallen together, but for those who fell in No Man's land there would often be a long wait until the end of the war.

Fabian Ware and his team recorded the location of graves, but also started caring for them. Convincing the Red Cross that he should be able to take control of finding, marking and caring for all British graves, the War Office acknowledged this role in February 1915 and incorporated this work into the British Army. Fabian Ware was given the rank of Major, and his two assistants, Messer and Cazalet as Captains. Ware's mobile unit was given the official title of Graves Registration Commission on 2 March 1915. In just six months, they recorded 31,182 graves while working under the BEF's Adjutant General Macready. Ware was also ordered to approach the French Government to acquire land for British war cemeteries and received an offer not only of

Fabian Ware (By kind permission of the Commonwealth War Graves Commission – Copyright Commonwealth War Graves Commission).

land, but also of care for the graves. The British gratefully accepted the land, but felt it was their moral duty to care for the graves of their own men.

The work of Ware's Graves Registration Commission did not go unnoticed back in Britain. The Joint War Committee of the Red Cross Society and St John Ambulance started to receive requests from next of kin that asked for, and in some cases pleaded for locations, and if possible photographs of individual graves. What started as a few letters became a deluge, an indication of the un-assuaged grief felt at home. Photographing the graves was considered unfeasible as some were close to the fighting, but as requests grew, Fabian Ware decided to act and despatched three professional photographers who by the middle of August 1915 had photographed over 6,000 graves.[38] In reply to an enquiry, the next of kin received a print of the photograph indicating the grave of their loved one, details as to where he was buried, and the name and location of the nearest railway station so they could visit once the war was over.

As the conflict intensified so did the role of Ware's Commission which, in 1916, became the Directorate of Graves Registration and Enquiries, mainly due to the huge number of enquiries that were being received. The Directorate's work was extended to Egypt, Salonika and Mesopotamia. The Directorate was part of the British Army, but it soon became clear that it needed to become independent of the War Office. In response, an organisation was created whose sole responsibility was to care for all graves, of all members of the armed forces, from all faiths, across the British Empire.

The Imperial War Graves Commission (IWGC) was founded in May 1917 by Royal Charter and recognised the religion of the fallen as of prime concern. Forming a sub-committee to advise on all faiths including Muslim, Hindu and Jewish, regardless of rank, all men were to be buried equally, with inscriptions on grave markers comprising name, faith, rank, regiment and date of death (if known).

War doesn't end when the guns fall silent, and in some respects that silence is deafening. In the immediate months and years following the war, Britain faced an enormous task. Hundreds of thousands of men needed to be discharged, but the battlefields of the Western Front needed to be cleaned up. Salvage parties were removing ammunition but the dead still lying in the battlefields needed to be located and reburied. In 1918, the IWGC announced that:

> Over 150,000 such scattered graves are known in France and Belgium. In certain districts, notably those of Ypres and the Somme battlefields, they are thickly strewn over areas measuring several miles in length and breadth. These areas will shortly be restored to cultivation, or possibly afforested, and the bodies cannot remain undisturbed. They must therefore be removed to cemeteries where they can be reverently cared for. The Commission felt that any other course of action would be excessively painful to relatives and discreditable to the country and would place the cultivators of land throughout an enormous extant of territory in a most unfair position.[39]

Exhumation of remains was the responsibility of the British Army and to organise this grim activity Graves Detachment (or Concentration) Units were established. Because of the nature of this work, the Army did not order men to these units, instead they asked for volunteers who were willing to delay their demobilisation. This was to be the last but most important duty for hundreds for men. Those who volunteered scoured the battlefields for the missing. An area was divided into sections and a detachment of men was allotted to each one. Sub-divided into squares and working under one NCO, 12 men[40] walked slowly up and down the squares, placing a flag when a grave or remains were found, the number of which was marked on maps.[41]

When a body was found, it was recorded then removed to one of the cemeteries nearby. If multiple graves were found, they were reburied where they already lay, and a new cemetery established. Men of the Graves Detachment units felt

A Graves Detachment Unit at work (By kind permission of the Commonwealth War Graves Commission – Copyright Commonwealth War Graves Commission).

it was their duty to stay behind and find them. The words of Harry Whiting, an Australian soldier who had volunteered conveys such experiences in a letter home dated 17 April 1919:

We have left Belgium and come back to France. The reasons for evacuating Belgium was because 10 of us volunteered for the Graves Detachment Battn [Battalion] which is composed of 1,100 men, a few from each Battn. Stan Merv and myself volunteered for to assist in the raising of the bodies of our dead comrades and place them in the ground which we have surveyed for this purpose…. We are raising the bodies of Tommie's, Yanks, Canadians, N [New] Zealand and Australians. We started on Monday last and I can assure you it is a very unpleasant undertaking. Nearly all the men we have raised up to date have been killed 12 months and they are far from being decayed properly, so you can guess the constitution one needs. I have felt sick dozens of times, but we carry on knowing that we are identifying Australian boys who have never been identified. They nearly all have some means of identification on them and we make a careful research for some, as it is cruel for their people minds not to set at rest to know their sons have been located. Many Mothers picture their sons blown to pieces and no record, so now we

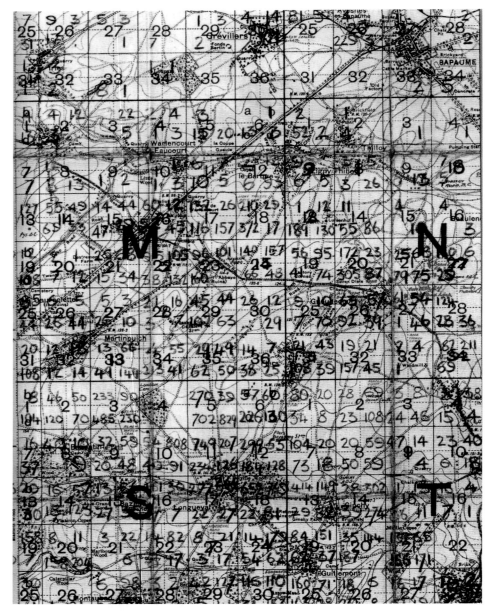

Map depicting in blue the number of graves found by the Graves Detachment Units (Copyright Public Domain).

hope to be able to identify 90% of the missing. Hilda it is heart breaking to see the way the poor fellows are buried, perhaps I should not tell you, then again it's to no harm, but we find dozens of them just in one big lump with all their coats equipment gas helmet and all on and a heap of earth placed over them. Today I dug two up that were buried together one was a Tommie and one an Aussie…. We will be a hard-hearted crowd when we get back, after the sights we see and the many thousands we will have raised by that time. All bodies are placed separately in large bags and buried that way… . I think you will think this is a gruesome letter Hilda but the job we are now on which I believe will last 6 to 8 months is equal to it… We could have been home by August, had we not volunteered for this, but many reasons are already explained, so God strengthen those who are awaiting our return. We will feel that we have completed our duty when this most important job finished.[42]

From the beginning, Fabian Ware had instructed his men to make notes regarding uniform colour, regimental badges, anything that could help identify the remains. This was continued by the men of the Graves Detachment Units.[43] Upon finding a body, detailed records were taken that included measuring the height of the man or noting any distinguishing marks that could be compared to enlistment forms. The body was checked for identity discs, pay book, papers or anything else that could be used in identification, then the body was wrapped in a blanket, sewn up and marked with an identifying tag. When combined with regimental information, identification was sometimes possible without identity discs.[44]

A soldier's paper pay book (Army Form AB64) had been the primary method of identification before 1914. At the start of the First World War a more resilient method was required and so the first identity disc was created using a single aluminium disc stamped with the name, rank, service number, unit details and religion. Prior to burial, these tags and personal papers (including AB64) were removed from the body as per Field Service Regulations.[45] These items were used by Regiment or Corps in notifying the next of kin of their relative's death. However, problems arose when, due to the static nature of warfare and repeated shell fire, temporary battlefield graves markers were frequently destroyed thus leaving the buried man unknown. To rectify this, the War Office issued on 26 July 1916 orders that:

On the recommendation of the Director of Graves Registration and Enquiries approval has been given for the issue of a second identity disc per man, on the same system as obtains in the French Army, so that in the event of death one disc may be removed from the body as evidence of death and the other left on the body for identification of the body when burial takes place. The second disc should be worn round the left wrist attached by a light chain and swivel hook instead of being fastened to the first disc and worn round the neck….[46]

Further evolution occurred in September 1916 when the two-disc system was redesigned to be worn around the neck. Made from compressed fibreboard 'the upper disc will be known as 'Disc identity No:1 green'; the lower one as

'Disc identity No: 2 red'. The former will be issued with 6" of cord attached....'[47] The green disc remained with the body and the red was removed along with the pay book and sent back to the unit. This wasn't always a perfect solution[48] as German soldiers were under orders to remove identity disc(s) from any deceased they found. Forwarded to the Red Cross along with a general location, their actions showed respect for an enemy soldier but ultimately left him nameless.

Uniforms played a key role here, as they could offer additional information when identity discs were missing. Men of the Graves Detachment Units could distinguish between different shades of khaki, badges, shoulder titles and tartan from various units and regiments.[49] They worked from 8.00 am to 1.00 pm on the battlefields, the remainder of the day taken as rest.[50] From November 1918 to September 1921 men of the Graves Detachment Units recovered 204,650 bodies and reburied them in nearby cemeteries. Soon, however the work would take its psychological toll, and they returned home. The story of these men, their achievements and courage are today largely overlooked or forgotten. What they witnessed and did, they would never forget, and without them, the cemeteries that today define the Western Front would not exist. The new cemeteries with their temporary wooden-cross grave markers needed to be tended and the IWGC utilised female labour from the Women's Auxiliary Army Corps (WAAC), renamed Queens Mary's Army Auxiliary Corps (QMAAC) in 1918. They continued to assist visitors and tend to graves into the 1920s.

The design for British Imperial and Commonwealth war cemeteries was given careful consideration, where uniformity was the watchword. Flowers were planted to resemble an English Garden, and Portland stone used for the cross of sacrifice and the final permanent headstones (replacing the wooden crosses). Initially each of these was engraved manually with hammer and chisel before an early form of headstone engraving machine appeared in the 1920s.

Compressed fibreboard identity discs (**Miscellaneous Papers Army Ordnance Corps and Army Service Corps.** *The Royal Logistic Corps Museum Archive - Author's Collection*).

Headstones inscribed with rank, name and regiment indicate the body was found accompanied by some form of unequivocal identification. An inscription that read, for example, 'a Private of the Sussex Regiment' suggests that only enough of his uniform remained to identify him as such, and that shoulder titles or a cap badge denoted the regiment. The role of a soldier's uniform therefore reached beyond death. Minimally, it seems, remnants of cloth, badges, pieces of leather boot, and hob nails were enough to identify the remains as belonging to British and Imperial Forces, and thereby to qualify him for burial in a British cemetery but only as 'Known unto God'. For those who were identified by name, a further inscription could be added by relatives, and carved at the base of the headstone. These extra words were initially charged per letter but this was later changed to giving a donation.

In 1920, an unidentified soldier's body was repatriated back to Britain with solemnity, ceremony and dignity, to be buried as the Unknown Soldier amongst the nation's Kings in Westminster Abbey. An initial suggestion for this in Parliament was considered unsuitable by both Government and the King, with the idea of a symbolic funeral viewed as somewhat belated. The newly completed, and soon to be unveiled, Cenotaph would be sufficient. Newspaper reports on the matter soon generated an unexpected national outpouring of support for the idea,[51] showing how much it resonated with the public mood. Less than five days later, human remains confirmed by remnants of the uniform[52] as British, were chosen 'from a grave which had been marked unknown British Soldier and that the soldier must have fallen in the early years of the war, as the natural process of decomposition had rendered the body unidentifiable'.[53] Placed in a specially designed coffin, the unknown warrior was accompanied by four soldiers who stood at each corner of the coffin for the journey across from France. The coffin was then transferred to the same railway carriage that the year previously carried the body of the executed British nurse Edith Cavell back home to London and then Norfolk. The use of the same railway carriage was emblematic as following her execution in Brussels on 12 October 1915, she was to become a propaganda figure for recruitment.

The Unknown Soldier's train's route to London Victoria Station had been published in the press, and the roof of the carriage painted white so that the thousands who lined the track could identify it. As the grieving nation's symbolic everyman, the Unknown Soldier was given a state funeral on 11 November 1920, with his coffin placed on a gun carriage for the journey to Westminster Abbey. At the eleventh hour on the eleventh day of the eleventh month the procession paused at Edwin Lutyen's imposing Cenotaph where King George V placed a wreath on the coffin, and then unveiled the new memorial.[54] After the Cenotaph ceremony, the funeral service was held in Westminster Abbey and the Unknown Soldier was buried with soil from France and Belgium,[55] soon becoming the focus for a nation's grief still raw in 1920. For many, of course, the Unknown Soldier could have been their own missing husband, son, brother, father, or lover. This was to be the enduring power of the symbolism which has lasted to the present.

Rebuilding the Front

Men and women, military and civilian, knew that the Western Front would become a shrine. To make a pilgrimage, to pay respects, began as early as 1919,[56] usually consisting of relatives seeking the graves of loved ones. In 1917, before the war had even ended, Michelin published a '*Guide to the Western Front*,[57] whilst in 1920, *The Western Front Battlefields, A Guide to the British Front Line* was published. It recommended places to visit, what to avoid, what to wear, and even what souvenirs to acquire.

> Old shells and bombs. Some of these souvenirs are still lying about in unexplored places. They have a nasty way of waking up even after long years of repose… I also know of a lady who, in stooping to pick up what she imagined to be a souvenir sustained a great shock in discovering that it was really an old boot, and that inside the boot were human bones.[58]

Such pilgrimages were easily affordable for the wealthy, but not the average bereaved family. Charity organisations began to aid the poor, particularly widows. Movement around the old battlefields required a permit, and a special pass issued by the Graves Registration Unit was needed to visit graves and cemeteries. The front lines were still visible, and cemeteries were not the white headstone grassed areas familiar today. This new influx of British visitors kickstarted an industry that continues today, and just as soldiers looked for souvenirs and pictures, so did the visitors that came after.[59] For the local civilian population battlefield tourism was a curse and blessing, bringing money to an area with coachloads of tourists[60] and yet having centuries of their history defined by just four years of war.

Many areas along the Western Front had to be rebuilt. In the aftermath of the war, it was decided to rebuild Ypres' most famous landmark – the once magnificent medieval Cloth Hall. Erected during the 13th century, it had been a combined market and warehouse for Flemish cloth merchants and weavers.[61] It was a monumental testament to cloth whose image of its burning destruction became an iconic symbol of the war, and an ironic emblem of this book. In 1928 the Cloth Hall began to rise again like a Phoenix from the ashes of a terrible conflagration. Yet its completion was overshadowed by the dark clouds of another war and it was only finally rebuilt as a replica after 39 years, when the final stone was laid in 1967.[62] It seems tragic yet somehow fitting that a war

Amidst the devastated landscape, an early Imperial War Graves Cemetery at Morval, France (By kind permission of the Commonwealth War Graves Commission – Copyright Commonwealth War Graves Commission).

which produced such extraordinary advances in creating, supplying, mending, and recycling millions of items of clothing should, by historical coincidence, have its own unofficial memorial – a rebuilt 'cathedral to cloth' - which today contains the In-Flanders Fields Museum which chronicles the events of the very same war.

The war left scars, and many were never totally healed. Some were open wounds that lasted down the generations. Yet lives had to begin anew, relationships to be rebuilt, and families adapted to changed circumstances. More men survived the conflict than died, but many had been changed physically, psychologically and emotionally by the war years. Whether physical or emotional, able bodied or disabled, life would be a reminder of those years for many. The ability to work would no longer be an option for many wounded men, but Britain had to rebuild.

Chapter 7

Finding George - The Afterlife of Military Clothing

Would that every brick and stone there [Ypres] could be swallowed up in the earth tomorrow, if that would help us to forget what they have seen! Those narrow streets of ruins, the crumpled water tower, the daredevil prison standing up there until it should be knocked down; the dingy cellar where we played the gramophone; the mangled bodies of those two officers who were killed in the street outside the door that afternoon; the abandoned switch canal all covered with long weeds, and leaning miserably over all, the gaunt maimed Cathedral tower and Cloth hall, left to be as great a mockery of civilisation as the world will ever see. I suppose that men will flock to see the ghastly remains of that city. Let them walk with reverent and humble step.[1]

Visit the Somme and the surrounding landscape is dominated by the Commonwealth War Grave Commission's (CWGC) Thiepval Memorial. Look

out from its central arch over the lush green former battlefields and it is hard not to be moved. The silence is deafening, no matter your age the effect is profound. Thiepval is dedicated to missing Commonwealth soldiers, more than 72,000 officers and men in the Somme area alone.[2] A staggering total when written in numbers, but impossible to grasp. Dedications from schools, associations, and families lay swathed with poppies at the stone altar in the centre arch. The walls are smothered by soldier's names, each one 1" (2.5cm) high that travel row upon

Thiepval Memorial, July 2016 (Author's Collection).

row, column upon column. They wind around the entire memorial as far as the eye can see, but there are some gaps in this sad roster.

Over the years some of the lost have been found, identified, and reburied in a Commonwealth War Graves Commission cemetery, and so their names have been removed from the memorial, leaving an ironic blank space where once an undiscovered man was commemorated.

Joint Casualty and Compassionate Centre (JCCC)

Since the end of the First World War, towns and villages that follow the old front line in France and Belgium have grown, often expanding across battlefields. More recently, centenary commemorations have seen roads widened, visitor centres built, museums reconfigured, and battle sites made more user friendly. Many of these activities have resulted in discoveries of the missing. Their numbers are greater than is generally realised, for example, 30 bodies were found in 2016 alone. Today, when this occurs, it is the Commemorative (Historic) casework team within the Joint Casualty and Compassionate Centre whose responsibility it is to try and identify the remains.

The JCCC is part of the Ministry of Defence, and offers worldwide casualty reporting 24 hours a day, 365 days a year, for major incidents, post death administration, compassionate and commemorative caseworks for serving members of the armed forces.[3] Recent news footage of RAF C-5 Galaxy planes repatriating casualties home from Afghanistan showed the care and support it gives affected families. The organisation is not well known beyond service families, for whom it offers the certainty of repatriation from anywhere in the world.

It also has responsibility for identifying human remains from the First and Second World Wars. When remains are found, local authorities are contacted, and if they are believed to be British the nearest British Consulate is informed, who in turn contact the JCCC. Local representatives of the Commonwealth War Graves Commission or Defence Attaché take custody along with any accompanying items and note the precise location. Overall, the procedure in such circumstances is a joint effort between the CWGC, the regiment(s) involved and any historical services, personnel records, and the country involved; this can be supplemented where appropriate by the 'forensic and physical analysis of remains or any articles recovered from the site'.[4]

Today, as in the past, it is the location of the body and identification of the uniform which can give a basic identification as to the regiment, thus narrowing down the search. If details concerning rank are retrieved then this can be enough to give the full identity. When these traditional methods narrow down the list to four or five potential individuals then recent advances in DNA profiling

Even the smallest fragments of uniform / personal kit can help identify an individual (By kind permission of the Joint Casualty and Compassionate Centre (Commemorative (Historic) Section) - Author's Collection).

Rank chevrons clearly identify the individual as belonging to a Sergeant (By kind permission of the Joint Casualty and Compassionate Centre (Commemorative (Historic) Section) - Author's Collection).

comes into its own. This needs great sensitivity, as contact should be made with descendants to request comparative DNA in full knowledge that there may be no family connection.

***Lance Corporal John Morrison, 1ˢᵗ Battalion The Black Watch (Royal
Highland Regiment)*** - An example of the Joint Casualty and Compassionate
Centre's work concerning the First World War is the case of Lance Corporal John
Morrison of the 1ˢᵗ Battalion The Black Watch (Royal Highland Regiment). In
January 1915 at Cuinchy, France, John's battalion was put into the line to defend
and hold against an enemy attack. The fighting was intense and John, along with
59 other soldiers, was killed. His last moments were seen by a comrade who
later wrote to his parents 'The attack was fierce, and John got a bullet in the leg.
Nevertheless, he crawled to the assistance of his officer, also wounded, and was
in the act of helping him to remove his pack when he was fatally shot'.[5]

This area of France was fought over for another three years and John remained
there until 2014, when he was discovered by a farmer. Among the several objects
retrieved was John's spoon which would have been tucked into his puttee. As was
widespread practice, John had scratched his service number on his spoon, in this
case 5181, and it was this 'trench art' inscription[6] that led to his military records,
which in turn helped trace his family, whose agreement to a DNA test confirmed
his identity. Working in conjunction with the Commonwealth War Graves
Commission, Lance Corporal Morrison was buried with full military honours

*Lance Corporal Morrison's reburial service on 27 July 2016, Woburn Abbey
Cemetery, Cuinchy, France (Author's Collection).*

on 27 July 2016 at 11.00am in Woburn Abbey Cemetery, Cuinchy, France. His descendants, members of The Black Watch Regiment, the Royal British Legion, the CWGC, and the JCCC were all present. A sign of the times was that the ceremony was announced on the CWGC's website welcoming members of the public to attend. Social media plays a key role in these events today, and this is how my husband and I came to be present at Lance Corporal Morrison's reburial.

Recalling the day, it was warm, breezy but overcast, and on entering the cemetery we were greeted by a representative from the JCCC who handed us an order of service. We were not the only ones there, approximately a hundred people had gathered to witness the event. Hymns were sung and readings given by family members. Shots from the firing party cracked in the air and the Last Post sounded before a piper began the Lament, slowly walking out of the cemetery with the notes fading on the breeze. Morrison's family were thanked by the local Mayor for the sacrifice John had made in defending France. It was at that moment I realised that most people in the cemetery were local, and had taken time out of their day to pay their respects. The ceremony was sad, yet unexpectedly uplifting, and then suddenly the faintest notes of 'Amazing Grace' were hanging in the air.

For me Lance Corporal Morrison's identification based on the recovered artefacts and inscribed spoon was the culmination of four years of research into the story of uniform. I have realised that I am lucky in being able to have found out about George. I know how his death affected my grandmother, but she could visit him. Seeing John Morrison's family made me realise just what it must have been like for families to continue living without any knowledge of where their loved one died, let alone where they were buried. The discovery of John Morrison and many like him is often purely by chance. Archaeological excavations on the Western Front come across human remains while investigating old trench systems and dugouts for several decades now. A very different development occurred in 2009 however, when a ground-breaking archaeological investigation in northern France took place with the forensic purpose of finding and identifying the missing.

Excavating the Missing at Fromelles, France - The use of DNA in archaeology is a comparatively recent development, but has transformed the potential for identifying human remains particularly of twentieth-century wars. It had always long been known that a large number of Allied soldiers had been buried by the Germans in two mass graves after the disastrous Battle of Fromelles[7] in 1916. Until the start of large-scale professional archaeological excavations in 2009, however, the exact locations were unknown.[8]

It was a joint venture involving the French, British, and Australians, whose combined resources funded a scientific laboratory constructed adjacent to the graves at Pheasant Wood. As work progressed it became apparent that

Excavations at Fromelles, France 2009 (By kind permission of the Commonwealth War Graves Commission – Copyright Commonwealth War Graves Commission).

uniforms and kit were relatively well preserved due to the conditions in the soil and thus such items would be valuable evidence for identification.[9] Historical records suggested that most of the buried were likely to be Australians, and the findings of brass cap badges and shoulder titles confirmed this. Australian SD jacket buckles were distinctly different from British ones, and items found in pockets, such as a return train ticket from 'Fremantle to Perth'[10] also indicated an Australian origin. Nevertheless, individual identification depended on DNA studies. In Australia, a search began for family members of soldiers recorded as missing at Fromelles. As a result, from the 250 men found at Pheasant Wood, 144 were identified, with a further 106 still unknown as of 2014.[11] Their remains were laid to rest in the first new CWGC cemetery built in 50 years.[12]

A new museum was built next to the cemetery to tell the story of the Battle of Fromelles, the scientific investigation, the construction of the cemetery, and of the reburials and the families of the men recovered. My own visit to the cemetery and museum in 2015 to investigate the role of uniforms in the identification process was particularly moving, especially the accounts of how much the discoveries and reburials meant to the families. At one end of the Fromelles museum are photographs of Australian soldiers who never made it home, with brief descriptions of who they were. And here I discovered an extraordinary coincidence. Private Simpson was wounded during the Battle of Fromelles and sent back home through the chain of evacuation. He eventually

Ceremony of the last soldier to be buried at New Pheasant Wood Cemetery, Fromelles, France (By kind permission of the Commonwealth War Graves Commission – Copyright Commonwealth War Graves Commission).

arrived in Bristol, where he succumbed to his wounds. He is buried in Soldier's Corner, Arnos Vale Cemetery, just six graves away from George.

Uniforms, Textiles and Salvage Today

The British Army uniform changed little until another major redesign during the 1930s. Service Dress jacket and trousers worn by First World War soldiers were modified slightly in 1922 (1922 Pattern SD), however the basic construction and shape stayed the same. Shoulder patches and the pleats from the chest pockets were removed, just as they had been for the early war emergency pattern. This was replaced in 1937 when the Battle Dress jacket and Trouser emerged (1937 Pattern Battle Dress), and this instantly distinguished the soldier of the Second World War. This design continued to evolve throughout the war years with an austerity pattern (1940 Pattern), and then through to the National Service Years of the late 1940s and 1950s (1949 Pattern). Despite redesigns, surplus stock of the obsolete 1922 Pattern Service Dress remained in depots and regimental stores. Barry Baxter, a veteran of the Royal Electrical and Mechanical Engineers, who joined the army aged 16 in the early 1950s as an apprentice wore a uniform drawn from the surplus 1922 stock.[13] After completing his apprenticeship aged 18 he was issued the 1949 Pattern Battledress jacket and trousers.[14]

Barry Baxter, on the left, with pals wearing 1922 pattern SD (By kind permission of Barry Baxter – Copyright Barry Baxter).

With the end of National Service in 1961, the British Army looked for a new uniform. Developing lightweight combat clothing based on that used during the Korean War, battledress was replaced in the early 1960s by the 1960 Pattern Combat Dress, before adopting the 1960 Pattern DPM (Disruptive Pattern Material) camouflage uniform in 1968. With several variants of the DPM uniform seen in the 1970s[15] and 1990s, since 2010 the British Army has worn the new MTP (Multi-Terrain Pattern) uniform.

The shortened 4ft (1.2m) puttee was re-introduced in the 1960s when the uniform changed from Battle Dress to the 1960 Pattern Combat jacket and trousers.[16] With the soldier's footwear changing from leather to a Direct Moulded Sole (DMS) ankle boot during the early 1960s, and from then onwards, the puttee was worn around the ankle over the DMS boot. The Falklands conflict highlighted how ineffective DMS boots were in cold wet weather. If a soldier did not wear the issued inner sole made of nylon, the rubber outer sole would make their feet sweat. In the cold wet weather of the Falklands, the boot stayed saturated with water. The old condition of trench foot raised its ugly head.[17] The boot was therefore redesigned to the Combat High Leg as worn today, which prevented dirt and mud from entering the top of the boot. The puttee was now obsolete.

The First World War was a time of boom or bust for the textile industry. An easy assumption to make is that the war years gave an economic boost for all business and industry and although this was true for some, for others it was the opposite. With no government contract, a shrinking civilian trade, lack of raw materials, debts due to other bankrupt businesses, insufficient manpower, and a generally exhausted labour force, the climate for growth and investment just did not exist. For some businesses that had been able to hold on, the decades that followed would prove untenable. With other countries such as Japan expanding their own textile trade after the war, Britain was now competing for cheaper fabrics from around the world, and so when the Great Depression of the late 1920s/30s hit and international trade suffered, British textile production fell to a low ebb. This was not the land 'fit for heroes'[18] which so many had expected.

Just as the country began to recover, the boom and bust of war appeared again in 1939, and firms that may had been struggling were awarded new War Office contracts, although for some it only delayed the inevitable. Another six years fighting proved too much for the industry, and after the war ended textile trade continued its decline.

One of the commercial survivors from the First World War is Hainsworth,[19] a company which has been in existence for 230 years, and which today has ten separate divisions. The Parade Wear division still supplies specialist woollen and worsted fabric for ceremonial military uniforms which includes the traditional scarlet cloth for the Guards Regiment and ceremonial tartans for the Scottish regiments. Part of this is their True Heritage range of cloths that consist of serge's, baratheas and flannels made in the same way as they were a hundred years ago.[20] Ideal for the construction of historically correct uniforms and clothing, for dressmakers like myself it is as close to authentic as possible. Hainsworth cloth still follows the same manufacturing process that its work force 200 years ago would recognise, the only difference is that computers run the machinery. But even in this, there is nothing new. In the late eighteenth century looms producing jacquard fabrics with delicate patterns woven through them were created using punch cards that told the loom when to lift the relevant heddle frame[21] - in essence an early computerised system.[22] Despite depression, recession, strikes, and the boom and bust phenomena, Hainsworth survives as a leading textile manufacturer.

Entrance to Hainsworth Mill, Pudsey, West Yorkshire (Author's Collection).

Foxes of Somerset is another to have weathered the stormy twentieth century, continuing to produce top quality cloth sold around the world. During the First World War, and up to the early 1980s, they made puttees for the Ministry of Defence at their factory in Wellington. Decades after this section had ceased production and been mothballed, the doors were unlocked, a time capsule discovered. The order book had been left open at the last date of entry, machinery stood abandoned, and there were yards and yards of puttees. When the original mill in Cullompton, Devon, became the heritage museum for Foxes, the puttees, their story, and associated machinery were placed on display. The surplus stock is now sold through the museum shop, re-packaged in replica early twentieth century period printed labels, and with the 4ft lengths (1.2m) now joined together to re-produce the original 8ft puttee (2.4m).[23]

Gieves and Hawkes were formed in 1974 from two earlier companies with a long tradition in military tailoring. Their flagship store today is at No 1 Saville Row, London. As a business, staying true to their bespoke tailoring roots, Gieves and Hawkes have diversified,[24] branching out into the quality 'ready to wear' markets.[25] Military uniforms however are still their specialism and

Old puttee machinery on display with surplus puttees at Coldharbour Mill Museum, Cullompton, Devon (By kind permission of Coldharbour Mill Museum - Author's Collection).

they continue to supply and maintain officer uniforms for the three branches of Britain's armed services.

We think of salvaging items for reuse as a relative new phenomenon, however 'Make do and Mend', recycling and upcycling are all terms which describe the age-old practice of making new articles of clothing from old. All my sewing life[26] I have done this keenly aware that my mum was never wasteful, and used her sewing skills to great effect. Likewise, my grandmother was adept at 'make do and mend', learned as a necessity during the Second World War. Together with my grandfather she bred rabbits, encouraged by the Ministry of Food to help supplement meagre wartime food rations. The two of them were inventive too, as nothing was wasted - the meat for stews, the bones for stock and the fur sent to a tanner, after which grandmother made gloves, capes, hats, and children shoes which she sold or traded with neighbours. Fashions and attitudes are constantly changing. In my experience of commercial dressmaking and teaching, since the 'credit crunch' of 2008 there has been a notable increase in the number of women, men, and children I have taught who had never touched a sewing machine before.[27] Maintaining and repairing clothes ensures they last longer.

All these hands-on practical skills, whether for hobby or out of necessity, can be done at home, negating the need to spend hard-earned money. We are taught to learn from history, so maybe we should take a backward glance and be inspired by how and what our ancestors salved, combine it with modern technology, and allow history to show us a recycled future.

Finding George - My Journey

In 2014, the *'Blood Swept Lands and Seas of Red'*[28] art installation at the Tower of London became a powerful visual and physical symbol of the human sacrifice made by servicemen and women from Britain and the commonwealth during the First World War. The transformation of a green grassy moat to a river of scarlet and the daily reading of names of Commonwealth soldiers killed saw the 888,246 specially-commissioned poppies[29] take centre stage in public remembrance around the world. Significantly, the poppies at The Tower moved and touched younger generations far removed from that place in history. Inspiring many to learn more about the First World War, moreover, it moved people to research their own family connections to the 'War to end all wars'.[30]

When my grandmother Alice was 89 she had a short spell in hospital. When I visited her she looked dejected and sad. To cheer her up I asked how she wanted to celebrate her 90th birthday in a few months' time, to which she replied, 'God may have taken me by then', and adding that she prayed to God every night to 'take her away'. When I responded that 'well not much good that's doing cause he ain't bloody listening', she laughed and took my hand and looking me direct in the eye said 'you're right, but I am tired and I want to see your grandad again. I miss my daddy so much. I just want God to take me so I can see him again'.[31] For that brief moment, I wasn't looking at an old lady with white hair, but a young girl who had just lost her dad in 1918.

This conversation has haunted me for 20 years. George's death deeply affected my grandmother, changing her

Alice (my grandma) as I had always known her, taken on her 85th Birthday in 1993 (Author's Collection).

life and ultimately impacting on my mother's life as well. This is a personal legacy of the First World War - the impact death, injury and mental trauma had on ordinary men, women and their families, and that has lasted down the generations. In earlier conversations with Alice about George, she passed on the only memories she had of her father. This was the only time she had let down her guard to me, perhaps knowing that I would need to find out all I could about George and his war service.

My research and travels have uncovered much about George's life as well as the uniform that he and millions of other men wore. I now understand his possible rationale for joining up in 1915; I know where he served on the Western Front, and what happened during the last months of his life. I now understand the effect his death had upon my family, and can better comprehend my grandmother, mother and ultimately myself. Seeking out the places George served in France and Belgium, I thought I would find my first visit to a CWGC cemetry depressing. But while occasionally sad, when I now visit a cemetery it is full of peace and comfort.[32] This personal journey has led me to not only understand George, but also the picture we have of him, stood proud in a muddy uniform. My fascination with the uniform and its manufacture ultimately led to this book. I now know how George received his uniform, who made it and how the khaki cloth was produced.

Through researching George I have gained a new perspective on life and found my place in this world, essentially, George and I have come home. I have discovered new places, made new friends in Britain, Belgium, and France. My husband and I have now become one of the many wardens of Talbot House, Poperinghe, a place George probably visited when out of the line. Every step of the way, the uniform was not just something a soldier wore, it defined him, and united him with others, it protected him yet could hurt him too. For many men, the uniform was something to be forgotten, for others it was something that allowed them to be re-discovered.

The only physical reminder I have of George is the much-copied family photograph and the two silk postcards he sent home to Alice. Once touched by George and sent with eternal love, these postcards and their delicate filaments of textile were all his ten-year-old daughter had left of her daddy in 1918. Treasured items of a father she last saw in 1915 and now, a hundred years later, cherished family heirlooms. This is the true 'material culture' of war.

'No longer separated by time, George now seems near'. A commissioned picture from Soren Hawkes entitled 'I'm here love' (By kind permission of Soren Hawkes - Author's Collection).

Appendices

Appendix A

Cloth Manufacture

Scouring (Cleaning)

Fleece had to be washed and bleached to remove dirt, impurities and excess lanoline, a naturally occurring oil which gives wool water repellent qualities. Too much lanoline makes dyeing of the wool difficult, though as the oil had a softening effect on the skin, surplus oil was sold to soap manufacturers. Once processed, the fleece was fed into a machine called a 'willey' to open the wool and detangle the fibres, turning the fibres into the 'top' – the long fibre delivered by the wool comb.[1]

Scribbling and Carding

In need of straightening the 'tops' ready for carding, the 'sliver' – a continuous loose rope or ribbon of fibre[2] - is then passed through a 'scribbling' machine that teased the rough fibres into strands, before being passed through the 'carding' machine. Separating the fibres without twisting them using a series of rollers with wire hooks embedded into it, carding ensured the fibres all ran in the same direction, giving the woollen cloth its distinctive 'nap' – the raised surface on cloth. Once processed, the resulting woollen strands are longer, even-length 'tops',[3] and / or lightly twisted 'roving'[4] or 'slubbing' as it was termed in Yorkshire.[5]

Spinning

Whilst the lightly twisted tops and roving strands are soft and fine, they hold little intrinsic strength so is useless to weave. To create strength, the strands were twisted and wound onto a bobbin to generate yarn. This process had evolved from a drop spindle that used gravity to draw the roving and twist it into yarn, with the need for a spinner to continually twist the spindle by hand, later to be replaced by the spinning wheel.

Operated by hand or foot, the spinning wheel, whilst allowing the spinner to work quicker, could nevertheless still only spin yarn onto one spindle at a time. The mid-eighteenth century would see this process revolutionised, with the invention by James Hargreaves of 'The Spinning Jenny' and Sir Richard Arkwright's Water Frame in the 1760s. Later in the 1770s, Samuel Compton combined elements from both these machines to create the 'Spinning Mule' which enabled yarn to be spun onto around 1000 bobbins at once (compared to the eight on the earlier machines).[6] Originally these new spinning machines had been made for the cotton industry, but small adaptations made them ideal for the woollen and worsted industry. Eight of these machines were installed in Armley Mills, Leeds, and could spin yarn onto 600 bobbins 24 hours a day, six days a week.[7]

The number of twists in the yarn depended on whether it was used for cloth or knitting. Yarn for cloth usually contained one twist (1 ply), yarn for knitting contained two or more twists (2, 3, or 4 ply), with worsted spun yarn stronger than a woollen yarn as it contained more twists.[8] Once roving had been spun and wound onto bobbins it was classed as 'yarn'.

Warping

Passing the yarn through a machine to keep it separate, it was then wound onto a large rotating drum called the 'warping beam' until approximately two inches deep, equating to 4,000 yards (3657m) in total.[9]

A series of pegs on the drum kept the yarn tangle free and determined the weaving width of the cloth.[10] A finished width for woollen cloth was 54 to 60 inches (1.3-1.5m), so to allow for shrinkage in the finishing process, the cloth had to be woven at 90 inches (2.28m). In comparison, worsted cloth with a 56-inch (1.42m) finished width was woven at 76 inches (1.93m). After the beams were filled with yarns they were taken to the weaving floors or sheds.[11]

Weaving

The warping beam was fixed at the back, usually below the main body of the loom. Before weaving commenced, the warps were threaded through eyelets that sat in the 'heels or heddles' frames and continued through the 'reed', which separated the warp threads and 'batted' down the weft threads to create the cloth. The ends of the warps were brought over the front of the loom and attached to a 'cloth beam' on which the woven cloth was slowly wound.[12]

'Twill', the strongest weave, has a distinctive diagonal pattern that runs across the fabric and was traditionally used for serge cloth and uniforms. A 'flying shuttle' that held the weft thread flew from side to side across the front of the loom. To create the weave one of the heddles was raised which created a 'shed' (gap) between the warp threads so the shuttle could fly between them. Once the shuttle had passed, the reed batted down the weft towards the front of the loom. Another heddle raised a different set of warp threads when the shuttle was flung back. The number of heddles and the order they were raised and lowered created the different weaves in the cloth. For a plain weave, two heddles were raised alternately. This resulted in the weft being woven over one warp and under the next across the width.[13]

Prior to mechanisation, the weaver raised and lowered the heddles by pressing the relevant foot peddle and hand weave the shuttle through the warp. After mechanisation, a single weaver could look after multiple looms, as the heddles were raised and lowered automatically and the shuttle was shot from a metal arm. Travelling at approximately 60 miles an hour, the shuttle passed in a blink of an eye, although the speed was reduced if the finished cloth was very wide, delicate, soft or fine.[14] Different classes of cloth could be made and this was denoted by a higher thread count, approximately 20 weft threads per inch could be found in coarse woollens and over 200 in the finest worsted.[15] Regardless of various adaptations for weaving cotton, silk, woollen or worsted cloth the basic methodology had not changed from the earliest hand looms to the power looms of modern day.[16]

Fulling

Worsted, woollen and flannel needed to be washed and shrunk, and was achieved by 'fulling'. Tightening the weave and thickening the warp and weft to create a thick felted appearance to the cloth,[17] fulling was achieved by repeatedly pounding the cloth whilst in water and added an alkali substance.

In the bowels of mill buildings sat 'fulling stocks', large pits with huge wooden hammers and troughs in the base that held the cloth, water and alkali. Fullers Earth, a natural clay absorbent and cleaner, was perfect for this and the hills around Stroud were full of it, helping to propel the wool industries in the south-west for centuries.[18] Fulling stocks were connected by a gearing system that enabled the hammers to be raised and dropped, one after the other, continuously pounding the cloth which caused it to shrink.

During the First World War, some mills were still using this method but the majority had moved to 'milling' machines which were more efficient by forcing the width of the cloth through a small passage and, combined with heat, alkali, and pressure, caused the fabric to shrink.[19] Once 'fulled', the cloth was washed again and stretched out to dry, originally from 'tenter hooks' attached to wooden posts (hence the saying 'on tenter hooks!'). By 1914, however, this was replaced by a frame with hooks on either side that stretched the cloth so it would retain its width as it dried.

Finishing

Once dry, the fabric needed the 'nap' raised, and the traditional method was by using 'teasels,' a tall spiny flowering plant grown in marshes[20] secured into large wooden drums, over which the fabric was passed.[21] Allowing the hooks on the teasel to rough and fluff the fabric, creating the nap,[22] the cloth was then machine 'cropped' (cut) to give the nap an even and smooth appearance. Before the advent of the cropping machine, highly skilled men with hand shears made from iron and wood measuring approximately 4ft (1.21m) in length carried out the work.[23]

Mending and Burling

Before the cloth could leave the mill or specialist finisher it had to be inspected for flaws, mistakes or knots that occurred during weaving. Any imperfections were corrected by hand, after which it was pressed and folded ready to be delivered.[24]

Dyeing

Along with spinning and weaving, dyeing cloth is an ancient practice with early examples found in ancient Egyptian tombs. Up until the middle of the nineteenth century and the advent of the synthetic dye, all dyes were made from natural sources.[25] Although rich in colour and depth, natural dyes faded and were affected by wear, washing, and bleaching by daylight.

The solution to this was discovered by C. J. Fritzsche in 1841[26] when, by distilling indigo and caustic potash, he obtained analine. Known as 'mordants', these chemicals could be added to natural dyes to 'fix' (stabilise) the colour, though it was Henry Perkins, in 1856, who created the first synthetic dye. Cloth can be dyed at various stages in its production which created a variety of colour and appearance to the finished fabric. Warp and weft could be dyed before weaving commenced in either the same colour or in contrast, or when after weaving when the cloth was finished. Roving was dyed before spinning and this was called 'dyed in the wool' and was used in the production of khaki serge.[27]

Director's responsibilities within Quartermaster General

Director of Ordnance	Provision and administration of ammunition, equipment, clothing, and all stores of all kinds other than medical and veterinary stores. Provision of technical vehicles or artillery, engineer units as well as the provision and administration of workshops on L. of C. for the repair of all kinds.
Director of Transport	Provision, administration, and distribution of all transport (except technical vehicles), excluding railway and sea transport but including inland water transport.
Director of Railway Transport	Provision and administration of railway transport. Controls the construction, working and maintenance of all railways. Provision of telegraph operators for railway circuits. Controls the working of telephone and telegraphs allotted to the railway service.
Director of Works	Provision, construction and maintenance of buildings, offices, stores, camping grounds, roads, etc. on the L. of C. The provision of water supply, gas, electric lighting, or other technical plant needed for military purposes on L. of C. and not provided by other services.
Director of Remounts	Provision, administration, training, and distribution of all animals.
Director of Veterinary Services	Care of sick animals. Provision and administration of veterinary hospitals and advice to their distribution. Provision of veterinary stores. Inspections and recommendations regarding health and efficiency of the animals of the forces.
Director of Postal Services	Provision and administration of all postal communications.
Paymaster in Chief	Supervision and control of all pay and cashier's offices. Responsibility for bringing to account all monies payable and received on public service.

Appendix C
Corps / Division Compositions

II Corps	V Corps	VI Corps
12th Division	3rd Division	6th Division
28th Division	17th Division	14th Division
50th Division	46th Division	49th Division
1st Canadian Division		

Useful Websites / Information[1]

British Army Campaign Medal Cards (Rolls Index)

Comprising of approximately 4.8 million records, the rolls index can be searched for free at The National Archives, Kew, Surrey (www.nationalarchives.gov.uk), as well as genealogy websites Ancestry (www.ancestry.co.uk), and Find My Past (www.findmypast.co.uk).

Created by the Army Medal Office (AMO) near the end of the war, the Medal Index Cards collection is the most complete listing of individuals who served in the British Army in the First World War - approximately 90% of soldiers' names. The women's Medal cards are at present held at the Imperial War Museum, London (www.iwm.org).

Naval Medal and Award Rolls

Listing over 1.5 million officers, ratings and individuals entitled to medals and awards with the Royal Navy and Royal Marines, the Naval Medal and Award Rolls can be searched for free at The National Archives, Kew, Surrey (ADM 171, 202 rolls), as well as the genealogy websites Ancestry and Find My Past.

British Army Service Records

Known as the 'Burnt Documents',[2] the British Army Service Records contain the surviving service records of non-commissioned officers and other ranks who served during the First World War. Microfilmed by The National Archives, all surviving service and pension records are available to view for free at The National Archives (War Office records - WO363), Kew, Surrey, or for a fee at the genealogy websites Ancestry or Find My Past.

British Army Pension Records

Holding the surviving service records of non-commissioned officers and other ranks who served during the First World War, the Pension Records are War Office records (WO364). Known as the 'Unburnt collection', they can be viewed for free at The National Archives, Kew, Surrey, or for a fee at the genealogy websites Ancestry and Find My Past.

Silver War Badge Records

Authorised by King George V in September 1916, the Silver War Badge (SWB) was created to recognise all military personnel who had served since 4th August 1914, and had been medically discharged. With applications to wear the SWB topping almost 1 million (including those who left service before the award was instituted in 1916), the records are sometimes the only evidence of a person's war service and can be viewed for free at The National Archives, Kew, Surrey (WO 329, 2958–3255), or via the genealogy website Ancestry for a fee.

Commonwealth War Graves Commission

Established in 1917 to record the graves of the men and women of the British Commonwealth who died in the First World War, the Commonwealth War Graves Commission (CWGC) (www.cwgc.org) hold a register of where a member of the Armed Forces (Army, Navy, Air Force, Merchant Navy) and Civilians from the United Kingdom, Australia, Canada, India, New Zealand and South Africa are buried/commemorated around the world.[3]

Soldiers and Officers Died in the Great War

Compiled by the War Office and published by His Majesty's Stationery Office (HMSO) in 1921 within 80 volumes are approximately 660,000 names of British soldiers (other ranks) who died in the First World War. A similar list of approximately 42,000 officers who died was published in one volume in 1919.

The listings for 'Soldiers Died in the Great War 1914-1918' can be consulted at the Imperial War Museum London (Department of Printed Books) (www. iwm.org), The National Archives, Kew, Surrey (www.nationalarchives.gov. uk), most city and county central libraries, as well as the genealogy websites Ancestry (www.ancestry.co.uk), Find My Past (www.findmypast.co.uk), and Forces War Records (www.forces-war-records.co.uk).

'Cross of Sacrifice' Volumes

The 'Cross of Sacrifice' volumes are records of all officers of all services who died during the First World War whilst serving with the British, Commonwealth and Colonial regiments and Corps. Published in 1993 as an alphabetical record by S D and D B Jarvis, the volumes can be viewed at the Imperial War Museum London and The National Archives, Kew, Surrey.

Royal Navy and Royal Marines War Graves Roll

Free to view at The National Archives, Kew, Surrey, the Roll is also available for a fee at the genealogy websites Ancestry, and has the names of Royal Navy and Royal Marine Officers and ratings who died on active service in the First World War.

Royal Naval Division Casualties of the Great War

Raised by the Admiralty to serve in the role as Infantrymen on the Western Front, the Roll has been corrected and revised from earlier listings of Royal Naval Division casualties and is available for a fee from genealogy websites Ancestry.

Royal Flying Corps and Royal Air Force Casualties

Giving details of the casualty, aircraft involved and (sometimes) the next of kin, RFC and RAF Casualty cards are available at the RAF Museum Hendon, north London (www.rafmuseum.org.uk). In addition, there are records held at The National Archives, Kew, Surrey which relate to RFC and RAF casualties, records of squadrons, officers reported missing and messages from the Germans about missing pilots.

Merchant Navy

The yearly 'Registers of Deceased Seamen' for 1914 to 1918 are held at The National Archives, Kew, Surrey.

'De Ruvigny's' Roll of Honour 1914-1924

Available to search at the genealogy websites Ancestry, Find My Past, and Forces War Records, the six volumes hold a biographical record of approximately 26,000 casualties who fell in the First World War.

Compiled by the 9th Marquis of Ruvigny and Raineval, and published by the Standard Art Book Company, London, this is not a complete list of casualties who died, with most of the recorded names dating only from the early years of the war.

National Roll of the Great War

A national roll of those who fought in the First World War, the 14 volumes produced by the National Publishing Company list approximately 100,000 participants of the war and is arranged into regions. Able to be viewed for a fee at the genealogy websites Ancestry and Find My Past, it is worth noting that the roll does not cover all the country, especially the south-west.

Ireland, Casualties of the First World War Roll of Honour

Compiled by the Irish National War Memorial, eight volumes contain the name, rank and regimental number of approximately 49,000 personnel, and can be found via the genealogy websites Ancestry (www.ancestry.co.uk), and Find My Past (www.findmypast.co.uk).

Town War Memorials

Most towns and villages in the United Kingdom have a war memorial or plaque listing the names of those who died serving their country in the First World War. In many cases the names of those killed during the Second World War have been added to the memorial.

Those villages whose men all returned safely and therefore do not have a memorial are known as a 'Thankful Village' (also known as Blessed Village). To date, 54 civil parishes in England and Wales have been found as having all their soldiers return from war. There are no settlements in Scotland or Ireland that did not lose a member of the community in the First World War.

Established in 1989 as a project to locate all the war memorials in Britain and to record the names on them, the UK National Inventory of War Memorials (UKNIWM) can be consulted via the IWM, London website (www.ukniwm. org.uk), War Memorials Online (www.warmemorialsonline.org.uk), and War Memorials Trust (www.warmemorials.org).

Newspapers

The British Library in London (www.bl.uk) hold collections of the national newspapers to view, while various main libraries hold microfiche copies of local newspapers that can be viewed for free. Alternatively for a fee 'The Times Archives' (www.store3.thetimes.co.uk) and 'The British Newspaper Archive' (www.britishnewspaperarchive.co.uk) lists over 400 newspaper titles that can be viewed online.

Awards and citations listed in 'The London Gazette' are available to view at The National Archives, Kew, Surrey or at The Gazette (www.thegazette.co.uk).

British Soldiers' Wills

Thousands of wills made by British soldiers who lost their lives in the First World War have been published online by the British Government (www.gov.uk/probate-search), and are available to download for a small fee.

Other Useful Links

Australian First World War Military Service Records

Archived in the Australian National Archives are the Service Records of men and women who served in the Australian Imperial Force (AIF) during the First World War. All digitised, the records are available in the series B2455 and can be downloaded for free (www.naa.gov.au).

Canadian First World War Military Service Records

Held by the Library and Archives Canada, the Service Records for approximately 619,000 Canadians who served with the Canadian Expeditionary Force during the First World War are available to search online (www.collectionscanada.gc.ca).

New Zealand First World War Military Service Records

The War Service Records for the New Zealand forces are held by the Archives New Zealand, and can be searched via www.archives.govt.nz.

US First World War Military Service Records

Approximately 80% of the Service Records dating from the First World War were destroyed by fire in 1973. The surviving records, some 6.5 million records, were put in a "B" File (Burned File) area and later the reconstructed files were named the "R" Files (Reconstructed Files). US Navy / Marine Corps Service Records were not affected by the fire (www.archives.gov).

Places to Visit

Textile Heritage Today

Dean Clough Mills, Halifax

Gigantic industrial buildings that once bellowed smoke like giant dragons have become quiet, standing as a visual reminder of what had been. Old derelict mills are finding new uses such as Dean Clough. A colossal complex of buildings that was once a carpet mill in Halifax, West Yorkshire, it has now been redeveloped into offices, shops, restaurants, and a Travelodge. A perfect place for me to stay whilst researching this book, Dean Clough Mills provides an excellent base to explore the textile heritage of Halifax, Bradford, Leeds, Huddersfield, and Colne Valley for yourselves.

Armley Mills, Leeds

Now housing the Industrial Museum, Armley Mills tells the story of not just cloth manufacture, but the wholesale garment industry for which Leeds became famous, and still is today. Exploring the manufacturing process from start to finish, the exhibition in the depths of this mill show how Britain is still today the world leaders in quality produced fabric and articles (www.leeds.gov.uk/museumsandgalleries/Pages/armleymills.aspx).

Manchester's City Art Gallery

One of the largest British assemblages of fashion, clothing and documentary archives spanning six centuries, the collections can be found at their Gallery of Costume, Platt Hall, Rusholme, Manchester (www.manchesterartgallery.org/visit/gallery-of-costume/).

Coldharbour Mill Museum, Cullompton

Originally owned by Fox Brothers, Coldharbour Mill is one of the oldest woollen mills in Britain to have been in continuous production since 1797, and is a rare surviving example of Georgian architecture, industry, and enterprise. Taking fleece from all over the world, the mill transformed it into yarn, cloth, textiles, and the world famous 'puttee', the iconic leg binding of the First World War 'Tommy' Atkins (www.coldharbourmill.org.uk).

Dunkirk Mill, Nailsworth

Situated in the Stroud valley of Gloucestershire, Dunkirk Mill has been beautifully restored into homes, but check out the Stroudwater Textile Trust webpage for open days throughout the year, as housed deep in the bowels of this magnificent building is the waterwheel that originally powered the mill above. In this small space, there are several pieces of machinery still in working condition where members from the Stroudwater Textile Trust will take you on textile journey of discovery (www.stroud-textile.org.uk/mills/dunkirk-mill/).

Imperial War Museum (IWM)

The most well-known of museums which focus on the military aspect of textiles and heritage, the IWM's sound archives bring the individual to life, ensuring their war is never forgotten. Sited in London, Manchester and Cambridgeshire, the archive collections can be accessed via their website (www.iwm.org.uk).

National Army Museum, London

Telling the story of the British Army from its inception through to modern day, the National Army Museum has an extensive archive that features many original uniforms, documents, and artefacts useful to research (www.nam.ac.uk).

Gloucestershire Regiment & Royal Engineers Museums

Situated in the historic Gloucester docks and Gillingham, Medway respectively, the Soldiers of Gloucestershire and Royal Engineers museums tell the story of the regiments / corps foundation to the present day. An excellent resource for exploration, check the internet for the regimental / corps museum you are interested in, as when undertaking research, the regimental museum is an ideal starting place to explore a soldier's wartime service (www.soldiersofglos.com) (www.re-museum.co.uk/).

Poperinghe Centre, Belgium

Approximately 50-minute drive from Dunkirk ferry port, France and still affectionately known to many as 'Pop', Poperinghe was the gateway to the front as nearly everything in the Ypres salient travelled through it at some point in time. The market place today is full of restaurants including De Ranke, once known as '*La Poupée*', a favourite with soldiers due to the waitress, Ginger, the pretty daughter of the owner. Despite the relaxation Poperinghe had to offer it was also the place where several arrested British soldiers were 'shot at dawn' - the cells still exist behind the Town Hall. Wander up *Gasthuisstraat* and there you will find the 'Every Man's Club', Talbot House (www.poperinge.be/).

Talbot House, Poperinghe

During the First World War, 'Toc H' witnessed thousands of British soldiers pass through its doors, with everyone receiving a welcoming cup of tea in the process. Today it is a living museum and when you enter the house a welcoming cup of tea is still on offer to every visitor. Following on the ethos from its inception in 1915, Talbot House still offers accommodation for anyone wishing to explore the Ypres Salient. The house is the museum and the moment you walk in it feels like home (www.talbothouse.be/en/museum/home).

Behind the Lines Museum 1914-1918, Krombeke (Poperinghe)

This is a small hidden gem of a place and is located in the attic of a café bar situated on the main road from Proven. A privately-run museum and collection, the artefacts were rescued by the current owner's father in the decades following the war. Housing one of the largest sections of relief trench map rescued from Château La Lovie which had been the Headquarters of the Second Army in Belgium, the owner is also an expert on René Matton photographs. Check the website for times of opening, it is also an excellent place for food (www.hetjagershof.be/Home/Museum).

Ypres (Ieper) Centre, Belgium

Drive, walk or cycle 12km east of Poperinghe and you will find this legendry market town and the iconic rebuilt Cloth Hall. There are numerous restaurants, one of my favourites being T'Ganzeke, situated behind the Cloth Hall (www.ieper.be).

In Flanders' Field Museum, Ypres

Situated within the Cloth Hall, the museum was renamed in the late 1990s the 'In Flanders' Fields' Museum after the famous poem by Canadian John McCrae. Telling the story of the First World War in the West Flanders region, the museum is an engaging place and shows the aspect of war from the Belgium perspective as well as the British (www.inflandersfields.be).

Menin Gate, Ypres

No trip to the Salient would be complete without a visit to the Menin Gate and the 'Last Post Ceremony'. Undertaken every evening at 8 o'clock sharp, the Last Post has been played under the Menin Gate Memorial since 1928, and is the traditional salute to the memory of the British and Commonwealth soldiers, sailors and airmen who died in the Ypres Salient during the First World War and have no known grave (www.lastpost.be/en/home).

Commonwealth War Graves Cemeteries

A short drive from Ypres is Tyne Cot cemetery, the largest CWGC cemetery in the world. It has an excellent visitor centre explaining the history of the cemetery and its creation. Tyne Cot takes your breath away by its sheer size, but as you travel along the front, there are numerous small cemeteries including Railway Wood, where George fought much of his war. These small cemeteries are usually situated in small woods, or in the middle of farmer's fields but are worthy of a visit. But importantly, there are CWGC graves and cemeteries here in Britain, you don't need to visit the Western Front to pay your respects. There are c.23,000 sites in 154 countries around the world, 13,000 of which can be found here in Britain, consisting of either a single grave in churchyards to the 5,000 graves in Brocklewood Cemetery, Surrey. George is buried in Soldier's Corner, Arnos Vale, Bristol which is maintained by the CWGC (www.cwgc.org).

Memorial Museum Passchendaele 1917, Zonnebeke, Belgium

A short drive from Tyne Cot is the Memorial Museum Passchendaele 1917 that details the Third Battle of Ypres (Passchendaele). Located at Zonnebeke, the museum features examples of British, French, and German trenches and includes a surviving 'flat pack' house that was sent by America after Armistice as temporary houses for Belgium civilians (www.passchendaele.be/en).

Bibliography

Anon. (1914) *The Cutter's Practical Guide to British Military Service Uniforms*. London: The John Williamson Company Limited.

Anon Editorials. (1914 – 1917) *The Tailor and Cutter Journal Issues: 6 August 1914, 27 August 1914, 17 September 1914, 29 October 1914, 5 November 1914, 10 December 1914, January 1915, 4 February 1915, 11 February 1915, 1 April 1915, May 1915, 17 June 1915, 14 October 1915, 4 November 1915, 9 December 1915, 8 June 1916, 13 July 1916, 10 August 1916, 19 October 1916, 4 November 1916, 11 October 1917.* Manchester City Galleries: Gallery of Costume, Platt Hall.

Anon. (1915) *12th (Service) Battalion Gloucestershire Regiment "Bristol's Own" Souvenir.* Bristol: The Colston Publishing Limited.

Anon. (1920) *Bristol's Own at Home and Abroad. Reminiscences by an Original Member.* Bristol: Western Daily Press.

Anon. (2014) *Groote Beweging – Spoorlijnen en Hoofdwegen in Kaart Gebracht.* Poperinge: Stad Poperinge.

Anon. (2015) *From Tradition to Protection – British Military Headgear in the First World War*. Ypres: Philippe Oosterlinck Collection - In Flanders Field Museum.

Anon. (2016) *Work of the Joint Casualty and Compassionate Centre*. Gloucester: Unpublished J.C.C.C Promotional Leaflet.

Anon. (2016) *Order of Service–Lance Corporal John Morrison, Cuinchy France 26th July 2016.* Gloucester: Unpublished J.C.C.C Publication.

Arthur, M. (2003) *Forgotten Voices of the Great War: A New History of WW1 in the Words of the Men and Women Who Were There*. London: Edbury Press.

Barton, P. and Vandewalle, J. (2007) *Beneath Flanders Fields. The Tunnellers War 1914 -1918*. Staplehurst: Spellmount.

Binney, M. and Crompton, S. (2014) *One Saville Row: The Invention of the English Gentleman. Gieves and Hawkes*. Paris: Flammarion.

Bown, D. (1996) *The Complete Book of Sewing: A Practical Step by Step Guide to Sewing Techniques*. London: Dorling Kindersley Publishing.

Bradshaw, G. (1913 Reprinted 2012) *Bradshaw's Continental Railway guide book of 1913*. Newton Abbot: Old House Books.

Bridger, G. (2013) *The Great War Handbook-A Guide for Family Historians and Students of the Conflict*. Barnsley: Pen & Sword Books.

Brown, M. (1999) *Tommy Goes to War*. Stroud: Tempus Publishing Limited.

Brown, M. and Osgood, R. (2009) *Digging up Plugstreet: The Archaeology of a Great War Battlefield*. Yeovil: Haynes Publishing.

Bull, S. (ed.) (2008*) An Officer's Manual of the Western Front 1914-1918*. London: Conway.

Burns, M G. (1992) *British Combat Dress since 1945*. London: Arms and Armour Press.

Butler, R. (1999) *Richborough Port*. Ramsgate: Ramsgate Maritime Museum/ East Kent Maritime Trust.

Carbery, A D. (1924) *The New Zealand Medical Service in the Great War 1914 – 1918*. Auckland: Whitcombe and Tombs Limited.

Chapman, P. (2001) *In the Shadow of Hell: Ypres Sector 1914–1918. Cameos of the Western Front*. Barnsley: Pen and Sword Military.

Cornwell, B. (1994) *Sharpe's Regiment*. London: Penguin Books.

Crane, D. (2013) *Empires of the Dead-How One Man's Vision Led to the Creation of WW1's War Graves*. Glasgow: William Collins (Kindle Edition).

Dearle, N B. (1929) *An Economic Chronicle of the Great War for Great Britain and Ireland 1914–1919*. London: Humphrey Milford/Oxford University Press.

Doyle, P. (2008) *Introducing Tommy's War. British Military Memorabilia 1914-1918*. Marlborough: The Crowood Press.

Edmonds, J. (1932) *History of the Great War Based on Official Documents. Military Operations France and Belgium 1914*. London: His Majesty's Stationery Office.

Edmonds, J. (1932) *History of the Great War Based on Official Documents. Military Operations France and Belgium 1916*. London: MacMillan and Co Limited.

Edmonds, J. and Wynne, G. (1927) *History of the Great War Based on Official Documents. Military Operations France and Belgium 1915. Vol.1 Winter 1914-15 Battle of Neuve Chapelle: Battle of Ypres*. London: His Majesty's Stationery Office.

Forbes, A. (1929) *A History of the Army Ordnance Services. Volume III The Great War*. London: The Medici Society Limited.

Gavaghan, M. (2006) *The Story British Unknown Warrior*. Le Touquet: M & L Publications.

George, D L. (1938) *War Memoirs of David Lloyd George Volume 2*. London: Odhams Press.

Godley, A. (1997) The Development of the Clothing Industry: Technology and Fashion. *Textile History 28* Vol. 1: 3–10.

Grieve, G., and Newman, B. (1936 Reprinted 2006) *The Story of the Tunnelling Companies, Royal Engineers, during the World War*. Uckfield: Naval & Military Press.

Halsey, F W. (1919) *The Literary Digest History of the World War Volume V*. New York: Funk & Wagnalls Company.

Hammerton, J A. (Editor) (1915) *The War Illustrated Album de Luxe – Volume III The Spring Campaign - 1915*. London: The Amalgamated Press Limited.

Hammerton, J A. (Editor) (1917) *The War Illustrated Album de Luxe – Volume VII The Autumn Campaign of 1916*. London: The Amalgamated Press Limited.

Hammerton, J A. (1918) *A Popular History of the Great War. Volume V. The Year of Victory*. London: Fleetway House.

Henniker, A M. (1937*) Official History of the Great War. Transportation on the Western Front 1914–1918.* London: His Majesty's Stationery Office.

Hooper, C. (2014) *Railways of the Great War with Michael Portillo*. London: Bantam Press.

Hunter, J A. (1922) *From the Raw Material to the Finished Product*. London: Sir Isaac pitman & Sons Limited.

Imperial War Museum Image Library - *IWM Q29383, IWM Q29394 & IWM Q29392*. Licenced by kind permission of The Imperial War Museum Archives. © Crown Copyright. IWM.

James, E A. (1924) *A Record of the Battles and Engagements of the British Armies in France and Flanders 1914–1918*. Aldershot: Gale & Polden Limited.

John, R K. (2015) B*attle Beneath the Trenches. The Cornish Miners of 251 Tunnelling Company RE*. Barnsley: Pen and Sword Military.

Kenyon, F. (1918) *War Graves: How the Cemeteries Abroad will be Designed / Report to the Imperial War Graves Commission*. London: His Majesty's Stationery Office.

Leeman, J. (1962) The Body Snatchers-Unpublished Manuscript. In Summers, J. (2007) *Remembered – The History of the Commonwealth War Graves Commission*. London: Merrell Publishers Limited.

Lloyd, E M H. (1924) *Experiments in State Control at the War Office and the Ministry of Food*. London: Humphrey Milford.

Loe, L., Barker, C., Brady, K., Cox, M., and Webb, H. (2014) *Remember Me To All – The archaeological recovery and identification of soldiers who fought and died in the Battle of Fromelles 1916*. Oxford: Oxford Archaeology Monograph No.23.

Louagie, J. (2015) *A Touch of Paradise in Hell. Talbot House, Poperinge - Every-Man's Sanctuary from the Trenches*. Solihull: Helion & Co.

Lowe, T A. (1920) *The Western Battlefields: A Guide to the British Line*. London: Gale and Polden.

Marks, D. (2011) *"Bristol's Own" The 12th Battalion Gloucestershire Regiment 1914–1918*. Thatcham: DolmanScott Books.

McHenry, I. (2015) *Subterranean Sappers – A History of 177th Tunnelling Company RE From 1915 to 1919*. London: Uniform Press Limited.

Messenger, C. (2006) *Call-To-Arms: The British Army 1914 – 18*. London: Cassell Military Paperbacks.

Miles, S T. (2016) *The Western Front: Landscape, Tourism and Heritage*. Barnsley: Pen and Sword Books Limited.

Nicholls, T B. (1937) *Organisation, Strategy and Tactics of The Army Medical Services in War*. Baltimore: William Wood and Company.

Novello, I., and Weatherly, F E. (1914) *Bravo Bristol!* London: Boosey & Company.

Palmer, M., and Neaverson, P. (2005) *The Textile Industry of South West England: A Social Archaeology*. Stroud: The History Press.

Patch, H., with Van Emden, R. (2008) *The Last Fighting Tommy – The Life of Harry Patch, the Only Surviving Veteran of the Trenches*. London: Bloomsbury Publishing PLC.

Pegler, M., and Chappell, M. (1996) *British Tommy 1914–18*. Oxford: Osprey Publishing.

Pollendine, C. (2013) *Campaign 1914–Volume 1*. Hitchin: Military Mode Publishing.

Pollendine, C. (2015) Campaign 1915–Volume 2. Hitchin: Military Mode Publishing.

Poole, B W. (1920) *The Clothing Trades Industry*. London: Sir Isaac Pitman & Sons Limited.

Pressinger, S H. (2000) *Khaki Uniform First Introduction (1848) and Hodson's Memorial*. London: Sandilands Press.

Rawson, A. (2014) *The British Army 1914–1918*. Stroud: The History Press.

Roberts, D. (1996) *Minds at War: The Poetry and Experience of the First World War*. Burgess Hill: Saxon Books.

Royal Logistics Corps Museum Archives. (2015) *Miscellaneous Papers-Army Ordnance Corps and Army Service Corps Archives*. Aldershot.

Royal Logistics Corps Museum Archives. (2015) Postcard Sent to Lord Kitchener 1914. In *Miscellaneous Papers-Army Ordnance Corps and Army Service Corps Archives*. Aldershot.

Royal Logistics Corps Museum Archives. (2015) *Miscellaneous Papers-Plans for Central Delousing and Bathing Stations*. Aldershot.

Royal Logistics Corps Museum Archives. (2015) *Memorandums by Captain Alec E Balfour, The Gordon Highlanders (Attached to A.O.D. Pimlico) 1915-1918*. Aldershot.

Royal Logistics Corps Museum Archives. (2015) *Lecture of the Army Ordnance Department-It's Organisation and Duties at Home and in the Field. Lieutenant Colonel T.B.A. Leaky. Army Ordnance Department. Revised 30*[th] *September 1916*. Aldershot.

Royal Logistics Corps Museum Archives. (2015) *Synopsis of Lectures given by Lieutenant. Col. F K Puckle. Assistant Quartermaster General of the British Army January 1918*. Aldershot.

Royal Logistics Corps Museum Archives. (2015) *Miscellaneous Papers-Inspectorate of Laundries.* Aldershot.

Royal Logistics Corps Museum Archives. (2015) *Miscellaneous Papers-Proposed Army Laundry.* Aldershot.

Royal Logistics Corps Museum Archives. (2015) *Miscellaneous Papers-Fifth Army Laundry–Abbeville Instruction to Formations.* Aldershot.

Royal Logistics Corps Museum Archives. (2015) *Miscellaneous Papers-Statistics of Fifth Army Laundry.* Aldershot.

Royal Logistics Corps Museum Archives. (2015) *Miscellaneous Papers-Officer in Charge and Statistics of Fifth Army Laundry.* Aldershot.

Royal Army Logistics Museum Archives. (2015) *General Scheme of Supply of a Division from the Bases to the Trenches.* Aldershot.

Royal Logistics Corps Museum Archives. (2015) *The Directorate of Clothing and Textiles by Brigadier M B Page 1976.* Aldershot.

Roynon, G. (ed.) (2006) *Home Fires Burning: The Great War Diaries of Georgina Lee.* Stroud: The History Press.

Saunders, N J. (2000) Bodies of Metal, Shells of Memory: 'Trench Art' and the Great War Re-cycled. *Journal of Material Culture.* Vol. 5 (1): 34-67.

Saunders, N.J. (2001*) Trench Art.* Barnsley: Leo Cooper.

Saunders, N J. (2010) *Killing Time: Archaeology And The First World War.* Stroud: The History Press.

Smith, D. (1977) *The British Army 1965-80.* Oxford: Osprey Publishing.

Stedman, M. (1998) *Guillemont. Somme. Battleground Europe.* Barnsley: Pen and Sword Military.

Stockwin, A. (ed.) (2005) *Thirty Odd Feet Below Belgium. An Affair of Letters in the Great War 1915–1916.* Tunbridge Wells: ParaPress Limited.

Stone, G F., and Wells, C. (1920) *Bristol And the Great War 1914-1919.* Bristol: JW Arrowsmith.

Strong, R. (2006) *The Hainsworth Story: Seven Generations of Textile Manufacturing.* Huddersfield: Jeremy Mills Publishing Limited.

Summers, J. (2007) *Remembered–The History of the Commonwealth War Graves Commission.* London: Merrell Publishers Limited.

The National Archives. CAB 39/2: *Cabinet and War Cabinet: War Trade Advisory Committee Minutes and Memoranda.*

The National Archives. HO 144/1558/230842: *WAR: Departmental action to be taken in time of War.*

The National Archives. MUN 4/4680: *Shell Manufacture: Shell and Components Manufacture Executive Committee: Minutes of meetings.*

The National Archives. MUN 4/6467: *War Office: Department of Surveyor General of Supplies: Miscellaneous Papers Mainly Concerning Supply of Army Food and Equipment.*

The National Archives. MUN 4/6523: *War Office: Department of Surveyor General of Supplies: Miscellaneous papers relating to Contracts Department organisation and to Army contracts.*

The National Archives. MUN 7/499: *Purchase of Icelandic Wool Clip: 1916 Sept 29–1917 Apr 13.*

The National Archives. WO 33/1076: *Director of Army Contracts: Report.*

The National Archives. WO 95/82: *War Office: First World War and Army of Occupation War Diaries, Part I: France, Belgium, and Germany: General Headquarters: Branches and Services: Controller of Salvage: 1917 Jul–1918 Dec.*

The National Archives. WO 95/291/2: *War Office: First World War and Army of Occupation War Diaries, Part I: France, Belgium, and Germany: Second Army: Headquarters Branches and Services: Deputy Assistant Director Transport.*

The National Archives. WO 95/404: *War Office: First World War and Army of Occupation War Diaries, Part I: France, Belgium, and Germany: Third Army: Army Troops. No. 177th Tunnelling Company Royal Engineers.*

The National Archives. WO 95/498/5: *War Office: First World War and Army of Occupation War Diaries, Part I: France, Belgium, and Germany: Fourth Army: Army Troops:12 Casualty Clearing Station.*

The National Archives. WO 95/753/3: *War Office: First World War and Army of Occupation War Diaries, Part I: France, Belgium, and Germany: 5th Corps: Headquarters Branches and Services: Adjutant and Quarter-Master General.*

The National Archives. WO 95/1016/2: *War Office: First World War and Army of Occupation War Diaries, Part I: France, Belgium, and Germany: 1st Australia and New Zealand Corps: Corps Troops: Corps Baths and Laundry.*

The National Archives. WO 95/1079: *War Office: Canadian Corps. Corps Troops. Canadian War Graves Detachment.*

The National Archives. WO 95/1197/4: *War Office: First World War and Army of Occupation War Diaries, Part I: France, Belgium, and Germany: Headquarters Branches and Services: Adjutant and Quarter-Master General: 17th Divisional Train. Army Service Corps War Diary.*

The National Archives. WO 95/1603/1: *War Office: First World War and Army of Occupation War Diaries, Part I: France, Belgium, and Germany: Divisional Troops,18 Field Ambulance.*

The National Archives. WO 95/1879: *War Office: First World War and Army of Occupation War Diaries, Part I: France, Belgium, and Germany: Headquarters Branches and Services: Adjutant and Quarter-Master General.*

The National Archives. WO 95/2002: *War Office: First World War and Army of Occupation War Diaries, Part I: France, Belgium, and Germany: 17th Division: 50th Infantry Brigade: 7th Battalion East Yorkshire Regiment.*

The National Archives. WO 95/2166: *War Office: First World War and Army of Occupation War Diaries, Part I: France, Belgium, and Germany: Baths and Laundry 5th October 1915. War Diary of the Assistant Director Medical Services. 22nd Division.*

The National Archives. WO 95/2926/1: *War Office: First World War and Army of Occupation War Diaries, Part I: France, Belgium, and Germany.165th Infantry Brigade. 1/5 Battalion King's Liverpool Regiment. 1916 Jan – 1919 Apr.*

The National Archives. WO 95/4020/1: *War Office: First World War and Army of Occupation War Diaries, Part I: France, Belgium, and Germany: Lines of Communication. Calais Base: Chief Ordnance Officer: 1915 Apr–1915 Aug.*

The National Archives. WO 95/4020/3: *War Office: First World War and Army of Occupation War Diaries, Part I: France, Belgium, and Germany: Lines of Communication. Calais Base: Chief Ordnance Officer: 1915 Nov-1915 Dec.*

The National Archives. WO 95/4020/5: *War Office: First World War and Army of Occupation War Diaries, Part I: France, Belgium, and Germany: Lines of Communication. Calais Base: Chief Ordnance Officer: 1916 Apr–1916 Jun.*

The National Archives. WO 95/4020/6: *War Office: First World War and Army of Occupation War Diaries, Part I: France, Belgium, and Germany: Lines of Communication. Calais Base: Chief Ordnance Officer: 1916 Jul–1916 Aug.*

The National Archives. WO 95/4020/7: *War Office: First World War and Army of Occupation War Diaries, Part I: France, Belgium, and Germany: Lines of Communication. Calais Base: Chief Ordnance Officer: 1916 Sept–1916 Dec.*

The National Archives. WO 95/4041: *War Office: First World War and Army of Occupation War Diaries, Part I: France, Belgium, and Germany: Lines of Communication. Nantes Area; Nancy Area; and Paris Area.*

The National Archives. WO 95/4041/8: *War Office: First World War and Army of Occupation War Diaries, Part I: France, Belgium, and Germany: Lines of Communication. Paris Area: Chief Ordnance Officer.*

The National Archives. WO 95/4046/2: *War Office: First World War and Army of Occupation War Diaries, Part I: France, Belgium, and Germany: Lines of Communication. Rouen Base: Chief Ordnance Officer: 1916 May–1916 Jul.*

The National Archives. WO 95/4046/3: *War Office: First World War and Army of Occupation War Diaries, Part I: France, Belgium, and Germany: Lines of Communication. Rouen Base: Chief Ordnance Officer: 1916 Aug–1917 Dec.*

The National Archives. WO 107/71: *Office of the Commander in Chief and War Office: Quartermaster General's Department: Correspondence and Papers: Salvage Directorate: Notes on Salvage.*

The National Archives. WO 107/72: *Office of the Commander in Chief and War Office: Quartermaster General's Department: Correspondence and*

Papers: History of the Organisation and Development of the Quartermaster General's Services (British Armies in France). Salvage.

The National Archives. WO 123/58: *Army Circulars, Memoranda, Orders and Regulations. War Office: Army Orders 204 of 1916 (Published 6th July 1916) / Army Council Instruction No:1637 of 22nd August 1916 (Refined by Army Council Instruction No:2075 of 3rd November 1916).*

The National Archives. WO 123/59: *Army Circulars, Memoranda, Orders and Regulations. War Office: Army Orders 4 of 1918 (Published 20th December 1917).*

The National Archives. WO 188/146: *War Office: Chemical Defence Research Department and Chemical Defence Experimental Establishment, later Chemical and Biological Defence Establishment, Porton: Correspondence and Papers. Treatment of clothing with antiseptic substances in relation to wound infection.*

The National Archives. WO 359/15: *War Office: Army Clothing Department: Register of Changes (15).*

The National Archives. WO 377/44: *War Office: Historical Memoranda etc., on Army Clothing with a list of source material in WO classes in PRO.*

Tomczyszyn, P. (2004) A Material Link between War and Peace: First World War Silk Postcards. In Saunders, N J. (Ed.) *Matters of Conflict: Material Culture, Memory and the First World War*. London: Routledge:123-133.

Turner, Steve. (2002) *Amazing Grace: The Story of America's Most Beloved Song*. New York: Harper Collins.

Tynan, J. (2013) *British Army Uniform and the First World War–Men in Khaki*. London: Palgrave Macmillan.

Van Emden, R. (ed.) (2009) *Sapper Martin. The Secret Great War Diary of Jack Martin*. London: Bloomsbury Publishing PLC.

War Office. (1915) *War Organisation. Field Service Regulations Part II. Organisation and Administration 1909 (Reprinted, with Amendments to October 1914)*. London: His Majesty's Stationery Office.

War Office. (1917) *War Establishments. Field Service Pocket Book 1914 (Reprinted Amendments in 1916 and 1917)*. London: His Majesty's Stationery Office.

War Office. (1922) *Statistics of the Military Effort of the British Empire During the Great War 1914–1920*. London: His Majesty's Stationery Office.

Westlake, R. (1988) *Regulations for the clothing of the Army Part I Regular Forces 1914 (excluding the Special reserve)-Clothing Regulations 1914*. Chippenham: Anthony Rowe.

Whitehorne, A C. (1936) 'Khaki and Service Dress'. *Journal of the Society for Army Historical Research*. Vol. 15: 181 – 182.

Yarwood, D. (1986) *The Encyclopaedia of World Costume*. London: MacMillan Publishing Company.

Websites (In Chronological Order of Access):

George H Ball, Sergeant MM 16795 / 102818 Service Records. (Courtesy of TNA) (2014) - www.ancestry.co.uk.
A – Z of British Sewing Manufacturers. (2015) - www.sewmuse.co.uk/britishsmm.htm.
Allen, T. *Real Photographic Postcards from WW1.* (2015) - www.worldwar1postcards.com/real-photographic-ww1-postcards.php.
Grave Registration Report Form for Bristol Arnos Vale Cemetery–G H Ball. (2015) –www.cwgc.org.
Frister & Rossmann. (2015) - www.sewalot.com/frister_rossmann.htm.
Medal Rolls Honours Book. (Courtesy of TNA) (2015) - www.ancestry.co.uk.
Respirators for Troops, Protection Against Poisonous Gas, War Office Announcement. Wednesday 28th April 1915. Liverpool Daily Post. (2015) - www.britishnewspaperarchive.co.uk.
Respirators – War Office Require No More At Present. Friday 30th April 1915. Western Daily Press. (2015) - www.britishnewspaperarchive.co.uk.
Respirators (Improved). Friday 4th June 1915. Portsmouth Evening News. (2015) -www.britishnewspaperarchive.co.uk.
Askaroff, A. *Singer Sewing Machines Through the Ages 1850 – 1940.* (2015) - www.sewalot.com/singer_through_the_ages.htm.
The Long, Long Trail. (2015) - www.1914-1918.net.
The Great War – 1914 – 1918 A Guide to WW1 Battlefields and History of the First World War (2015) - www.greatwar.co.uk.
1911 Census. (2016) – www.ancestry.co.uk.
Australian War Memorial: PR05609 – Collection relating to Private Henry George Whiting. (2016) – www.awm.gov.au.
Body Lice. (2016) - www.firstworldwar.com/atoz/bodylice.htm.
Buttons. (2016) - www.firminhouse.com/international/buttons.htm.
Commonwealth War Graves Commission-Pheasant Wood Cemetery. (2016) – www.cwgc.org.
Encyclopædia Britannica – Explosive Chemical Product. (2016) – www.britannica.com/technology/explosive/Other-explosives#ref624977.
Health & Safety Executive-Dust. (2016) - www.hse.gov.uk/textiles/dust.htm.
History of viscose. (2016) - www.viscose.us.
Imperial War Museum Collection - Boots, ankle length DMS (UNI 6492). (2016) – www.iwm.org.uk.
Imperial War Museum Collection - Cap, 1915 pattern Winter Trench Cap (UNI 12591). (2016) – www.iwm.org.uk.
Imperial War Museum Collection - Webbing, 1908 Pattern (set) (UNI EQU 3941). (2016) – www.iwm.org.uk.

Imperial War Museum Collection - Photograph of Men of 2nd Battalion Cameroonians (Scottish Rifles), washing themselves in a ruined house in Lievin. 16th May 1918. (UNI Q6620) (2016) - www.iwm.org.uk.

Money - Lance Corporal Lockwood Diary Entry "drawing 10 frcs – 8/4d." (2016) - www.1914-1918.invisionzone.com/forums.

Sapper Alfred Jones 102816 Service Records. (Courtesy of TNA) (2016) - www.ancestry.co.uk.

The Cloth Hall (Lakenhalle) in Ieper / Ypres. (2016) - www.greatwar.co.uk.

The Gloucestershire Regiment in The Great War. (2016) - www.remembering.org.uk/glosregtofficers.

The History of the Zipper. (2016) - www.thomasnet.com/articles/hardware/zipper-history.

The Second Battle of Ypres. (2016) - www.greatwar.co.uk/battles/second-ypres-1915.

The Western Front Today - Hellfire Corner. (2016) - www.firstworldwar.com/today/hellfirecorner.htm.

Trench Fever. (2016) - www.firstworldwar.com/atoz/trenchfever.htm.

Connelly, M. *The First Generation of Pilgrims to the Western Front.* (2016) – www.gatewaysfww.org.uk

Currency Converter 1915 to 2005 The National Archives / 2005 to 2017 This is Money. (2017) - www.nationalarchives.gov.uk/currency/results.asp#mid / www.thisismoney.co.uk/money/bills/article-1633409/Historic-inflation-calculator-value-money-changed-1900.html.

Gas Gangrene in the First World War by Grace E.F. Holmes, MD, Professor of Paediatrics and of Preventive Medicine Emerita, University of Kansas School of Medicine. (2017) – http://www.kumc.edu/wwi/index-of-essays/gas-gangrene.html.

Hansard 1803 – 2005 Defence of the Realm Act (No 2) Bill – Commons 27th August 1914. (2017) - Hansard.millbankssystems.com.

Hansard 1803 – 2005 Soldiers' Sock – Commons 17th November 1914. (2017) - Hansard.millbankssystems.com.

Hansard 1803 – 2005 Asphyxiating Gases (Respirators and Helmets) – Commons 6th May 1915. (2017) - Hansard.millbankssystems.com.

Hansard 1803 – 2005 Relief of Unemployment – Commons 7th November 1921. (2017) – Hansard.millbankssystems.com.

Life on Board – Clothing. (2017) – www.maryrose.org.

Military Service Act 1916. (2017) – www.parliament.uk.

Sir Anthony Bowlby Consulting Surgeon to the B.E.F. (2017) - www.nam.ac.uk/whats-on/lunchtime-lectures/videoarchive/warsurgery-1914-1918.

South London and Maudsley NHS Trust. (2017) - www.slam.nhs.uk/about-us/art-and-history/our-history/1900-2000.

Symptoms of Gas Gangrene. (2017) - www.healthline.com.

The Jacquard mechanism, Paisley Museum. (2017) – https://www.youtube.com/
    watch?v=OlJns3fPItE.
*Third Battle Ypres 1917 WW1 Footage Hell Fire Corner Menin Road Then and
    Now.* (2017) – www.youtube.com/watch?v=CKTRk7lrm7c.
UCL Petrie Museum's Tarkhan Dress: World's Oldest Woven Garment. (2017) –
    www.ucl.ac.uk.
Picture Postcards from the Great War 1914 -1918. (2017) - www.
    worldwar1postcards.com.

Personal Communication (In Chronological Order):

Alice Hilda Wedlock (nee Ball) (1990s).
Nicholas Fear, 'Nick In Time' (2009).
Dominiek Dendooven, In-Flanders Field Museum, Ypres, Belgium (2015).
Armley Mills Industrial Museum Tour – Leeds Museums and Galleries (2015).
Coldharbour Mill Museum, Cullompton, Devon (2015).
*Peter Tilley, Curator - Gieves and Hawkes Archives, No.1 Savile Row, London
    W1* (2015).
Charles Booth, Soldiers Corner Historian Arnos Vale Cemetery, Bristol (2015).
The Stroudwater Textile Trust Open Day - Dunkirk Mill, Stroud (2015).
*Veterans Affairs Canada: Tunic / Information board re Subaltern George Hicks -
    Visitor Centre at Beaumont-Hamel Newfoundland Memorial, France* (2015).
Bertin Deniverier. Trustee of Talbot House, Poperinghe, Belgium (2016).
Christine Pécourt, L'Amartinierre Courcelles-au-Bois, France (2016).
Guy Depootr. Behind the Lines Museum 1914-1918, Belgium (2016).
Information board Ypres Ramparts, Ypres, Belgium (2016).
Johan Regheere. Local Historian, Belgium (2016).
Otterburn Mill, Northumberland (2017).

End Notes

Introduction

1 Anon Editorials. The Tailor and Cutter Journal. *Making Khaki Cloth.* 14 October 1915. Manchester City Galleries: Gallery of Costume, Platt Hall.

2 Tynan, J. (2013) *British Army Uniform and the First World War–Men in Khaki.* London: Palgrave Macmillan:17.

3 War Office. (1922) *Statistics of the Military Effort of the British Empire During the Great War 1914–1920.* London: His Majesty's Stationery Office:739.

4 Tynan, J. (2013) *British Army Uniform and the First World War–Men in Khaki.* London: Palgrave Macmillan:9.

5 *Ibid*: 869.

6 5,399,563 - War Office. (1922) *Statistics of the Military Effort of the British Empire During the Great War 1914–1920.* London: His Majesty's Stationery Office:739.

7 The precursor to the Royal Air Force (RAF).

8 Identified as being an Australian by the collar badges and shoulder titles, one of which was in his small pack on his back – a practice not uncommon amongst the Infantry as the carrying of webbing often resulted in the shoulder titles becoming detached (Brown, M. and Osgood, R. (2009) *Digging up Plugstreet: The Archaeology of a Great War Battlefield.* Yeovil: Haynes Publishing:135-152).

9 Loe, L., Barker, C., Brady, K., Cox, M., and Webb, H. (2014) *Remember Me To All – The archaeological recovery and identification of soldiers who fought and died in the Battle of Fromelles 1916.* Oxford: Oxford Archaeology Monograph No.23:1,194,210.

10 DNA – Deoxyribonucleic Acid.

11 Historical garments belonging to great families or Royalty have been preserved such as the Norman Hartnell Coronation dress brought out to commemorate the sixtieth anniversary of HM The Queen's Coronation in 2013.

12 *UCL Petrie Museum's Tarkhan Dress: World's Oldest Woven Garment.* (2017) – www.ucl. ac.uk.

13 *Life on Board – Clothing.* (2017) - www.maryrose.org.

14 Saunders, N J. (2000) Bodies of Metal, Shells of Memory: 'Trench Art' and the Great War Re-cycled. *Journal of Material Culture.* Vol. 5 (1):34–67.

15 Henry and Elizabeth Jones were later guardians of Alice Ball.

16 Rawson, A. (2014) *The British Army 1914–1918.* Stroud: The History Press:24–25.

17 *Ibid*:30.

18 *Ibid*:30.

19 Divided into categories A, B and D, men with overseas service primarily made up category A and was limited to *c.*6,000. The rest were placed in B category and could transfer into A if a vacancy appeared. Category D men who had extend their reserve service for a further

four years could be called up if category B were exhausted of men. On declaration of war, category A and B were sent to Regular battalions and many category D men reenlisted during the recruitment campaigns (Rawson, A. (2014) *The British Army 1914–1918.* Stroud: The History Press:19).

20 War Office (1922) *Statistics of the Military Effort of the British Empire During the Great War 1914 – 1920.* London: His Majesty's Stationery Office:30.

21 Rawson, A. (2014) *The British Army 1914–1918.* Stroud: The History Press:19.

22 Bridger, G. (2013) *The Great War Handbook-A Guide for Family Historians and Students of the Conflict.* Barnsley: Pen & Sword Books:63.

23 *Ibid*:57.

24 Lord Kitchener was appointed Secretary State of War on 5 August 1914, and believed the war would last several years and not with the popular notion that it would be over by Christmas. Recognising the BEF would need additional men, a new army, Parliament passed an Act on 6 August 1914 to increase the British Army by 500,000 between the ages of 19 and 30 and on 8 August Kitchener made his first appeal for an initial 100,000 volunteers (Dearle, N B. (1929) *An Economic Chronicle of the Great War for Great Britain and Ireland 1914–1919.* London: Humphrey Milford / Oxford University Press:2-4). Men would serve for three years or for the duration of war whichever lasted longer and could choose which regiments to serve with. Within days' men from across the country formed queues outside recruiting offices and enlisted into this Third Army, one that would be separate from the Regulars and Territorials, and which would very quickly become known as 'Kitchener's New Army'; *The Gloucestershire Regiment in The Great War* - www.remembering.org.uk/ glosregtofficers.

25 This second force would have more than 500 new battalions and would contain the word Imperial 'Service' in brackets after their number to distinguish them from the Regular and Territorial Army, such as 7th (Imperial Service) Battalion, Gloucestershire Regiment. These battalions would form three new armies referred to as K1, K2, K3 and later K4 (October 1914 – April 1915). *Ibid.*

26 Touring the country Lord Derby encouraged enlistment, stating in a speech he gave on 28 August 1914 that 'this should be a battalion of pals…' to a groups of office workers in Liverpool. Bridger, G. (2013) *The Great War Handbook-A Guide for Family Historians and Students of the Conflict.* Barnsley: Pen & Sword Books:64.

27 Marks, D. (2011) *"Bristol's Own" The 12th Battalion Gloucestershire Regiment 1914–1918.* Thatcham: DolmanScott Books.

28 Renamed Fourth New Army (K4) in April 1915.

29 Unknown. (1915) *12th (Service) Battalion Gloucestershire Regiment "Bristol's Own" Souvenir.* Bristol: The Colston Publishing Limited.

30 *Ibid.*

31 *Ibid.*

32 Private F B Vaughan, 12th Battalion Yorkshire and Lancashire wrote: 'I said to the boss, 'I want to join the Army, I want to be released from my job', so he said to me, 'Here in the steelworks you are doing just as much for your country, just as much for the nation, as though you were in the Army.' Well I couldn't see myself catching the 8.40 to Brightside every morning and leaving for home in the afternoon, doing little jobs in the evening, and all the time my pals were suffering – probably dying somewhere – they were serving their country, I couldn't see myself carrying on in that particular way, so I said 'I'm awfully sorry

but I have made my mind up, I must go' (Arthur, M. (2003) *Forgotten Voices of the Great War: A New History of WW1 in the Words of the Men and Women Who Were There*. London: Edbury Press:16-18).

33 Rawson, A. (2014) *The British Army 1914–1918*. Stroud: The History Press:24–25.

34 Undersized (less than 5ft 2") but physically fit men were put into Bantam battalions.

35 *Currency Converter 1915 to 2005 The National Archives / 2005 to 2017 This is Money* (2017) - www.nationalarchives.gov.uk/currency/results.asp#mid / www.thisismoney.co.uk/money/bills/article-1633409/Historic-inflation-calculator-value-money-changed-1900.html.

36 Lloyd, E M H. (1924) *Experiments in State Control at the War Office and the Ministry of Food*. London: Humphrey Milford.

Chapter 1

1 Whitehorne, A C. (1936) 'Khaki and Service Dress'. *Journal of the Society for Army Historical Research*. Vol. 15:181–182 - As Cited by Tynan (2013):2.

2 Pressinger, S H. (2000) *Khaki Uniform First Introduction (1848) and Hodson's Memorial*. London: Sandilands Press: 5 – As Cited by Tynan (2013):2.

3 Whitehorne, A C. (1936) 'Khaki and Service Dress'. *Journal of the Society for Army Historical Research*. Vol. 15: 181 – 182 - As Cited by Tynan (2013):2.

4 Approved by the War Office, an example of the clothing would be deposited, signed, sealed, and certified as being the `Sealed Pattern`.

5 Often abbreviated to 1902 PSD (ORs).

6 1907 PSD (ORs).

7 Pollendine, C. (2013) *Campaign 1914–Volume 1*. Hitchin: Military Mode Publishing.

8 The National Archives. WO 123/58: *Army Circulars, Memoranda, Orders, and Regulations. War Office: Army Orders 204 of 1916 (Published 6th July 1916) / Army Council Instruction No:1637 of 22nd August 1916 (Refined by Army Council Instruction No:2075 of 3rd November 1916)*.

9 Anon Editorials. The Tailor and Cutter Journal. *Distinction for the Wounded*. 13 July 1916. Manchester City Galleries: Gallery of Costume, Platt Hall.

10 The National Archives. WO 123/59: *Army Circulars, Memoranda, Orders, and Regulations. War Office: Army Orders 4 of 1918 (Published 20th December 1917)*.

11 Depending on the soldier's height they were often either too long or too short.

12 Anon. (2015) *From Tradition to Protection – British Military Headgear in the First World War*. Ypres: Philippe Oosterlinck Collection - In Flanders Field Museum.

13 *Imperial War Museum Collection - Cap, 1915 pattern Winter Trench Cap (UNI 12591)*. (2016) – www.iwm.org.uk.

14 Royal Army Clothing Pattern Numbers 8706 and 9066 of 1916 – Dated 11th March 1916.

15 Anon. (2015) *From Tradition to Protection – British Military Headgear in the First World War*. Ypres: Philippe Oosterlinck Collection - In Flanders Field Museum.

16 In the case of the Royal Naval Division, the battalion i.e. Anson, Hood, Drake Battalion etc.

17 'Grandad' collar - collarless shirt.

18 Originally issued in brown leather which was polished black when behind the lines and 'dubbed' with brown dubbing when in the line, the colour of the boot eventually changed from brown to black mid-way through the war.

19 Pegler, M., and Chappell, M. (1996) *British Tommy 1914–18*. Oxford: Osprey Publishing:12-13.

20 *Ibid*:13.
21 *Imperial War Museum Collection - Webbing, 1908 Pattern (set) (UNI EQU 3941).* (2016) – www.iwm.org.uk.
22 Pegler, M., and Chappell, M. (1996) *British Tommy 1914–18*. Oxford: Osprey Publishing:13.
23 Pollendine, C. (2013) *Campaign 1914–Volume 1*. Hitchin: Military Mode Publishing:126.
24 First developed in 1855 by George Audemars, his methodologies were however impractical for commercial use. Similarly, 'chardonney silk,' patented in 1884 by Hilaire de Charbonnet, was found to be too unsafe for use as it was highly flammable. Finally, in 1894, Charles Cross, Edward Bevan and Clayton Beadle found a way to commercially and safely produce a practical artificial silk. Patenting the product 'viscose,' in its simple form it is derived from wood pulp using chemical solution to create a fibre that can be spun. Around 1905 an American firm began producing their own version – *History of viscose*. (2016) - www.viscose.us.
25 *Veterans Affairs Canada: Tunic / Information board re Subaltern George Hicks* - Visitor Centre at Beaumont-Hamel Newfoundland Memorial, France (2015).
26 Anon Editorials. The Tailor and Cutter Journal. 11 February 1915. Manchester City Galleries: Gallery of Costume, Platt Hall.
27 Pollendine, C. (2013) *Campaign 1914–Volume 1*. Hitchin: Military Mode Publishing:132.
28 Anon. (2015) *From Tradition to Protection – British Military Headgear in the First World War*. Ypres: Philippe Oosterlinck Collection - In Flanders Field Museum.
29 Pollendine, C. (2013) *Campaign 1914–Volume 1*. Hitchin: Military Mode Publishing:137-138.
30 Royal Logistics Corps Museum Archives. (2015) Postcard Sent to Lord Kitchener 1914. In *Miscellaneous Papers-Army Ordnance Corps and Army Service Corps Archives*. Aldershot.
31 Anon. (1920) *Bristol's Own at Home and Abroad. Reminiscences by an Original Member.* Bristol: Western Daily Press:7
32 Messenger, C. (2006) *Call-To-Arms: The British Army 1914 – 18*. London: Cassell Military Paperbacks:116.
33 Anon Editorials. The Tailor and Cutter Journal. 5 November 1914. Manchester City Galleries: Gallery of Costume, Platt Hall.
34 Novello, I., and Weatherly, F E. (1914) *Bravo Bristol!* London: Boosey & Company.
35 Anon. (1915) *12th (Service) Battalion Gloucestershire Regiment "Bristol's Own" Souvenir.* Bristol: The Colston Publishing Limited:20.
36 Pers.Comm – *Nicholas Fear, Nick In Time*.
37 A theme used by Bernard Cornwell in his novel 'Sharpe's Regiment' - Cornwell, B. (1994) *Sharpe's Regiment*. London: Penguin Books.
38 Royal Logistics Corps Museum Archives. (2015) *The Directorate of Clothing and Textiles by Brigadier M B Page 1976*. Aldershot.
39 Lloyd, E M H. (1924) *Experiments in State Control at the War Office and the Ministry of Food*. London: Humphrey Milford:11.
40 Royal Logistics Corps Museum Archives. (2015) *The Directorate of Clothing and Textiles by Brigadier M B Page 1976*. Aldershot.
41 Lloyd, E M H. (1924) *Experiments in State Control at the War Office and the Ministry of Food*. London: Humphrey Milford:14.
42 Royal Logistics Corps Museum Archives. (2015) *The Directorate of Clothing and Textiles by Brigadier M B Page 1976*. Aldershot.
43 *Ibid*.

44 *Ibid.*
45 In July 1914, the Contracts Department employed fifty-six officials and clerks. Lloyd, E M H. (1924) *Experiments in State Control at the War Office and the Ministry of Food*. London: Humphrey Milford:14.
46 *Ibid*:14.
47 *Ibid*:15.
48 *Ibid*:15.
49 The National Archives. WO 33/1076: *Director of Army Contracts: Report.*
50 *Ibid.*
51 *Ibid.*
52 Anon Editorials. The Tailor and Cutter Journal. *Visit to the Royal Army Clothing Factory.* 6 August 1914. Manchester City Galleries: Gallery of Costume, Platt Hall.
53 Including British Executive staff of *c.* 350 civil servants from the Board of Trade. Lloyd, E M H. (1924) *Experiments in State Control at the War Office and the Ministry of Food.* London: Humphrey Milford:15.
54 The National Archives. MUN 4/6467: *War Office: Department of Surveyor General of Supplies: Miscellaneous Papers Mainly Concerning Supply of Army Food and Equipment.*
55 To ease pressure many of these uniforms were produced in the USA and Canada, as well as the UK. Messenger, C. (2006) *Call-To-Arms: The British Army 1914 – 18.* London: Cassell Military Paperbacks:116.
56 Pollendine, C. (2015) *Campaign 1915–Volume 2.* Hitchin: Military Mode Publishing: 8-26.
57 'Date after which.'
58 Anon Editorials. The Tailor and Cutter Journal. *Lord Kitchener's Appeal to Tailors.* 10 December 1914. Manchester City Galleries: Gallery of Costume, Platt Hall.
59 Lloyd, E M H. (1924) *Experiments in State Control at the War Office and the Ministry of Food.* London: Humphrey Milford:33-34.
60 Gunner J W Palmer, Royal Field Artillery in Arthur, M. (2003) *Forgotten Voices of the Great War: A New History of WW1 in the Words of the Men and Women Who Were There.* London: Edbury Press:31.
61 Anon Editorials. The Tailor and Cutter Journal. 4 February 1915. Manchester City Galleries: Gallery of Costume, Platt Hall.
62 Finished uniform / clothing was Inspected by QMG [branch] 9.
63 George, D L. (1938) *War Memoirs of David Lloyd George Volume 2.* London: Odhams Press.
64 Royal Logistics Corps Museum Archives. (2015) *Memorandums by Captain Alec E Balfour, The Gordon Highlanders (Attached to A.O.D. Pimlico) 1915-1918.* Aldershot.
65 *Ibid.*
66 The National Archives. WO 377/44: *War Office: Historical Memoranda etc., on Army Clothing with a list of source material in WO classes in PRO.*
67 *Ibid.*
68 The National Archives. MUN 4/4680: *Shell Manufacture: Shell and Components Manufacture Executive Committee: Minutes of meetings.*
69 Royal Logistics Corps Museum Archives. (2015) *Memorandums by Captain Alec E Balfour, The Gordon Highlanders (Attached to A.O.D. Pimlico) 1915-1918.* Aldershot.
70 A short close-fitting leather sleeveless jacket worn over the SD Jacket.
71 Dearle, N B. (1929) *An Economic Chronicle of the Great War for Great Britain and Ireland 1914–1919.* London: Humphrey Milford/Oxford University Press:107.

72 The National Archives. MUN 4/6523: *War Office: Department of Surveyor General of Supplies: Miscellaneous papers relating to Contracts Department organisation and to Army contracts.*

73 *Currency Converter 1915 to 2005 The National Archives / 2005 to 2017 This is Money (2017)* - www.nationalarchives.gov.uk/currency/results.asp#mid / www.thisismoney.co.uk/money/bills/article-1633409/Historic-inflation-calculator-value-money-changed-1900.html.

74 *Ibid*:152-154.

75 War Office. (1922) *Statistics of the Military Effort of the British Empire During the Great War 1914–1920*. London: His Majesty's Stationery Office:541.

76 Pers.Comm - *Peter Tilley, Curator, Gieves & Hawkes Archives.*

77 The very same people that the Bristol's Own recruitment poster was aimed at.

78 Anon Editorials. The Tailor and Cutter Journal. 27 August 1914. Manchester City Galleries: Gallery of Costume, Platt Hall.

79 Anon Editorials. The Tailor and Cutter Journal. 17 September 1914. Manchester City Galleries: Gallery of Costume, Platt Hall.

80 Anon Editorials. The Tailor and Cutter Journal. 29 October 1914. Manchester City Galleries: Gallery of Costume, Platt Hall.

81 Royal Logistics Corps Museum Archives. (2015) *Memorandums by Captain Alec E Balfour, The Gordon Highlanders (Attached to A.O.D. Pimlico) 1915-1918.* Aldershot.

82 'Poperinghe' was the First War spelling for the modern Belgian town of Poperinge. For continuity throughout the book I have used the wartime spelling.

83 McHenry, I. (2015) Subterranean Sappers – A History of 177th Tunnelling Company RE From 1915 to 1919. London: Uniform Press Limited:26.

84 Government agents negotiating direct with Russian Jute farmers and having the power to oversee the transportation to Archangel with the permission of the Russian Government in exchange for a line of credit in London to buy supplies. Lloyd, E M H. (1924) *Experiments in State Control at the War Office and the Ministry of Food*. London: Humphrey Milford:67-71

85 The National Archives. CAB 39/2: *Cabinet and War Cabinet: War Trade Advisory Committee Minutes and Memoranda* / MUN 7/499: *Purchase of Icelandic Wool Clip: 1916 Sept 29–1917 Apr 13.*

86 *Hansard 1803 – 2005 Defence of the Realm Act (No 2) Bill – Commons 27th August 1914* - Hansard.millbankssystems.com.

Chapter 2

1 Twain, M. (1905) The Czar's Soliloquy. *The North American Review*. Vol.180 (3):321-322.

2 Palmer, M., and Neaverson, P. (2005) *The Textile Industry of South West England: A Social Archaeology.* Stroud: The History Press.

3 Hunter, J A. (1922) *From the Raw Material to the Finished Product*. London: Sir Isaac Pitman & Sons Limited:22-23.

4 *Ibid*:8.

5 *Ibid*:6-7.

6 *Ibid*:20.

7 Anon Editorials. The Tailor and Cutter Journal. *New Khaki Cloth Contracts.* 9 December 1915. Manchester City Galleries: Gallery of Costume, Platt Hall.

8   Bown, D. (1996) *The Complete Book of Sewing: A Practical Step by Step Guide to Sewing Techniques*. London: Dorling Kindersley Publishing: 48.

9   Based on the order and succession of the manufacturing process as cited by Hunter, J A. (1922) *From the Raw Material to the Finished Product*. London: Sir Isaac Pitman & Sons Limited:57.

10 Pers.Comm – *Otterburn Mill, Northumberland* (2017).

11 Hunter, J A. (1922) *From the Raw Material to the Finished Product*. London: Sir Isaac Pitman & Sons Limited:46-53; The long fibre delivered by the wool comb. *Ibid*:119.

12 *Ibid*:43-52, 118.

13 Pers.Comm - *Armley Mills Industrial Museum* – Leeds Museums and Galleries (2015).

14 Yarwood, D. (1986) *The Encyclopaedia of World Costume*. London: MacMillan Publishing Company:432.

15 *Ibid*: 436.

16 Yarwood, D. (1986) *The Encyclopaedia of World Costume*. London: MacMillan Publishing Company:408.

17 Hunter, J A. (1922) *From the Raw Material to the Finished Product*. London: Sir Isaac Pitman & Sons Limited: 66.

18 The best teasels came from the lowlands of France and Germany.

19 Pers.Comm - *Armley Mills Industrial Museum* – Leeds Museums and Galleries (2015).

20 Pers.Comm - *The Stroudwater Textile Trust* (2015).

21 Pers.Comm - *Armley Mills Industrial Museum* – Leeds Museums and Galleries (2015).

22 *Ibid*.

23 Tynan, J. (2013) *British Army Uniform and the First World War–Men in Khaki*. London: Palgrave Macmillan: 9.

24 Dearle, N B. (1929) *An Economic Chronicle of the Great War for Great Britain and Ireland 1914–1919*. London: Humphrey Milford/Oxford University Press:34.

25 Anon Editorials. The Tailor and Cutter Journal. 14 October 1915. Manchester City Galleries: Gallery of Costume, Platt Hall.

26 Pers.Comm - *Armley Mills Industrial Museum* – Leeds Museums and Galleries (2015).

27 Anon Editorials. The Tailor and Cutter Journal. May 1915. Manchester City Galleries: Gallery of Costume, Platt Hall.

28 *Ibid*.

29 *Currency Converter 1915 to 2005 The National Archives / 2005 to 2017 This is Money (2017)* - www.nationalarchives.gov.uk/currency/results.asp#mid / www.thisismoney.co.uk/money/bills/article-1633409/Historic-inflation-calculator-value-money-changed-1900.html.

30 The circumference of Earth at the equator is c.40,030km.

31 Strong, R. (2006) *The Hainsworth Story: Seven Generations of Textile Manufacturing*. Huddersfield: Jeremy Mills Publishing Limited:67.

32 Dearle, N B. (1929) *An Economic Chronicle of the Great War for Great Britain and Ireland 1914–1919*. London: Humphrey Milford/Oxford University Press:92.

33 56" (1.42m) wide.

34 The close weave of worsted fabrics took longer to produce.

35 Strong, R. (2006) *The Hainsworth Story: Seven Generations of Textile Manufacturing*. Huddersfield: Jeremy Mills Publishing Limited: 67.

36 *Ibid*: 51-67.

37 Anon Editorials. The Tailor and Cutter Journal. *Clothing Companies of the War*. January 1915. Manchester City Galleries: Gallery of Costume, Platt Hall.

38 Logged next to a job number.

39 Godley, A. (1997) The Development of the Clothing Industry: Technology and Fashion. *Textile History 28* Vol. 1: 3–10.

40 Anon Editorials. The Tailor and Cutter Journal. *Visit to the Royal Army Clothing Factory*. 6 August 1914. Manchester City Galleries: Gallery of Costume, Platt Hall.

41 *Ibid.*

42 This was done using a 'Marsdon' Process Marker.

43 Developed in 1840 by John Barren, an early Leeds clothing manufacturer, and inspired by a woodworking machine, the 'band knife' was first constructed by the Leeds engineering firm Grentley and Batley and held in position by a large cast iron frame on a metal table. It was situated so the knife could pass through a hole in the centre (Pers.Comm - *Armley Mills Industrial Museum* – Leeds Museums and Galleries (2015).

44 Anon Editorials. The Tailor and Cutter Journal. *Visit to the Royal Army Clothing Factory*. 6 August 1914. Manchester City Galleries: Gallery of Costume, Platt Hall.

45 Often described as the man that did for sewing machines what Ford did for the cars, Singer is one of the most iconic and easily recognisable brands in the world, symbolising the sewing machine as much as Hoover does the vacuum cleaner. Singer was not however the first to design the machine. The first machine recognisable as a sewing machine was designed and patented, complete with a description of workings, in 1790 by Thomas Saint. But it appears he never invented it (Yarwood, D. (1986) *The Encyclopaedia of World Costume*. London: MacMillan Publishing Company:362). In 1830, the French tailor Barthelemy Thimmonier created a single thread that made a stitch which 'chained' together. Using the eighty machines he had built for the manufacture of uniform for the French Army, the machines however were destroyed by workers who were worried about the threat on their livelihood. Between 1830 to 1860, three men, one of whom was Isaac Singer, developed their own versions of Thimmonier's machine and in 1851 Singer's first machine was patented and manufactured (Askaroff, A. *Singer Sewing Machines Through the Ages 1850 – 1940*. (2015) (www.sewalot.com/singer_through_the_ages.htm). Initially designing his two thread 'lock stitch' machine for the domestic marketplace, Singer later branched into the industrial market, while the British firm Bradbury designed, patented, and produced first an industrial sewing machine, before branching in to the domestic market. A growing marketplace, by 1910 Leeds had fourteen separate sewing machine manufacturers.

46 The sewing machine had to be 'timed' correctly so that the needle holding the top thread would pass through the fabric and loop the underneath thread, pulling it tight to form a stitch.

47 *A – Z of British Sewing Manufacturers*. (2015) - www.sewmuse.co.uk/britishsmm.htm.

48 *Frister & Rossmann*. (2015) - www.sewalot.com/frister_rossmann.htm.

49 Anon Editorials. The Tailor and Cutter Journal. *Modern Labour Saving Machines*. 19 October 1916. Manchester City Galleries: Gallery of Costume, Platt Hall.

50 *Ibid.*

51 *Ibid.*

52 Scotland manufactured the majority of sandbags needed for the Western Front, the quantity of which grew to staggering proportions when entrenching became the norm.

53 Dearle, N B. (1929) *An Economic Chronicle of the Great War for Great Britain and Ireland 1914–1919*. London: Humphrey Milford/Oxford University Press:120.

54 Lloyd, E M H. (1924) *Experiments in State Control at the War Office and the Ministry of Food*. London: Humphrey Milford.

55 Although the first zip was invented in 1851, it was not until 1913 that what would be recognised as a modern zip was invented. That said, it would take until the 1930s before zips were used in the clothing industry (http://www.thomasnet.com/articles/hardware/zipper-history). A zip could break and would be difficult for the average 'Tommy' to fix in the field, a button however was easily to replace.

56 War Office. (1922) *Statistics of the Military Effort of the British Empire During the Great War 1914–1920*. London: His Majesty's Stationery Office: 869.

57 Anon Editorials. The Tailor and Cutter Journal. *Visit to the Royal Army Clothing Factory*. 6 August 1914. Manchester City Galleries: Gallery of Costume, Platt Hall.

58 In 1974, Gieves Ltd acquired Hawkes & Co.

59 Ypres is the French, and Ieper the Dutch spelling of the Belgian town found in the province of West Flanders. Known as 'Wipers' (pronounced 'Y'-Pers) by the British Imperial forces during the First War, for continuity I have used the French spelling throughout the book.

60 Binney, M. and Crompton, S. (2014) *One Saville Row: The Invention of the English Gentleman. Gieves and Hawkes*. Paris: Flammarion: 142.

61 Anon Editorials. The Tailor and Cutter Journal. *A Word Picture*. 4 November 1915. Manchester City Galleries: Gallery of Costume, Platt Hall.

62 Traditionally, pressing was carried out with a cast iron that was placed on special fuel stoves which kept the iron constantly hot.

63 Anon Editorials. The Tailor and Cutter Journal. *More about Khaki Contracts*. 1 April 1915. Manchester City Galleries: Gallery of Costume, Platt Hall.

64 Holding position above the tailor, everyone in the workroom answered to the Cutter who could hire or fire.

65 Anon Editorials. The Tailor and Cutter Journal. *More about Khaki Contracts*. 1 April 1915. Manchester City Galleries: Gallery of Costume, Platt Hall.

66 Poole, B W. (1920) *The Clothing Trades Industry*. London: Sir Isaac Pitman & Sons Limited:6-7.

67 A trimmer would collect and return customers blocks to where they were stored, cut, and prepare all required trims and could, if allowed, cut the cloth once the cutter had marked the pattern out.

68 Poole, B W. (1920) *The Clothing Trades Industry*. London: Sir Isaac Pitman & Sons Limited:9.

69 A shoulder can slope lower than another, a leg can be longer than another, differences that may only be small but could affect the way a garment hung.

70 Poole, B W. (1920) *The Clothing Trades Industry*. London: Sir Isaac Pitman & Sons Limited:6-7.

71 Pers.Comm - *Peter Tilley, Curator - Gieves and Hawkes Archives, Bath* (2015).

72 It took years to train to be a cutter as well as judgment and talent to do the job.

73 And still is!

74 The front pattern pieces had chalk lines transferred to the right side of the cloth and basting (temporary stitch) secured the inlays (underlining) to the front.

75 The more common method the tailor used.

76 A tailor adopted the traditional position of sitting cross legged on workroom tables to complete the sewing.

77 Atmospheric gas mixed with compressed air travelled through tube connected to the iron which was very heavy. Pressing machines applied c.260lbs of pressure to a seam and was operated by foot pedal using unskilled labour, boys and girls entering the trade at 14 often started here (Poole, B W. (1920) *The Clothing Trades Industry*. London: Sir Isaac Pitman & Sons Limited:77-90).

78 P Binney, M. and Crompton, S. (2014) *One Saville Row: The Invention of the English Gentleman. Gieves and Hawkes.* Paris: Flammarion:142.

79 Anon Editorials. The Tailor and Cutter Journal. 4 November 1916. Manchester City Galleries: Gallery of Costume, Platt Hall.

80 *Military Service Act 1916.* (2017) – www.parliament.uk.

81 Dearle, N B. (1929) *An Economic Chronicle of the Great War for Great Britain and Ireland 1914–1919.* London: Humphrey Milford/Oxford University Press:324.

82 *Ibid*:25-27, 48, 196.

83 *Ibid*:52.

84 *Ibid*:141.

85 Anon Editorials. The Tailor and Cutter Journal. *Standard Khaki.* 11 October 1917. Manchester City Galleries: Gallery of Costume, Platt Hall.

86 Dearle, N B. (1929) *An Economic Chronicle of the Great War for Great Britain and Ireland 1914–1919.* London: Humphrey Milford/Oxford University Press:160,198.

87 *Ibid*:215.

88 Pers.Comm - *Armley Mills Industrial Museum* – Leeds Museums and Galleries (2015).

89 Strong, R. (2006) *The Hainsworth Story: Seven Generations of Textile Manufacturing.* Huddersfield: Jeremy Mills Publishing Limited:67.

90 Dearle, N B. (1929) *An Economic Chronicle of the Great War for Great Britain and Ireland 1914–1919.* London: Humphrey Milford/Oxford University Press:31.

91 *Ibid*:51.

92 *Ibid*:62.

93 Anon Editorials. The Tailor and Cutter Journal. *Making Khaki Cloth.* 14 October 1915. Manchester City Galleries: Gallery of Costume, Platt Hall.

94 Dearle, N B. (1929) *An Economic Chronicle of the Great War for Great Britain and Ireland 1914–1919.* London: Humphrey Milford/Oxford University Press:92, 180.

95 *The Second Battle of Ypres.* (2016) - www.greatwar.co.uk/battles/second-ypres-1915.

96 Hansard 1803 – 2005 Asphyxiating Gases (Respirators and Helmets) – Commons 6th May 1915 - Hansard.millbankssystems.com.

97 Edmonds, J. and Wynne, G. (1927) History of the Great War Based on Official Documents. Military Operations France and Belgium 1915. Vol.1 Winter 1914-15 Battle of Neuve Chapelle: Battle of Ypres. London: His Majesty's Stationery Office.

98 *Respirators for Troops, Protection Against Poisonous Gas, War Office Announcement. Wednesday 28th April 1915. Liverpool Daily Post.* (2015) - www.britishnewspaperarchive.co.uk.

99 Roynon, G. (ed.) (2006) *Home Fires Burning: The Great War Diaries of Georgina Lee.* Stroud: The History Press.

100 *Respirators – War Office Require No More At Present. Friday 30th April 1915. Western Press.* (2015) - www.britishnewspaperarchive.co.uk.

101 Edmonds, J. and Wynne, G. (1927) History of the Great War Based on Official Documents. Military Operations France and Belgium 1915. Vol.1 Winter 1914-15 Battle of Neuve Chapelle: Battle of Ypres. London: His Majesty's Stationery Office.

102 Rawson, A. (2014) *The British Army 1914–1918*. Stroud: The History Press.

103 *Respirators (Improved). Friday 4ᵗʰ June 1915. Portsmouth Evening News.* (2015) -www. britishnewspaperarchive.co.uk.

104 The National Archives. WO 359/15: *War Office: Army Clothing Department: Register of Changes* (15).

105 Forbes, A. (1929) *A History of the Army Ordnance Services. Volume III The Great War.* London: The Medici Society Limited:110.

106 Rawson, A. (2014) *The British Army 1914–1918*. Stroud: The History Press.

107 The National Archives. WO 359/15: *War Office: Army Clothing Department: Register of Changes* (15).

108 Rawson, A. (2014) *The British Army 1914–1918*. Stroud: The History Press.

109 *Ibid.*

110 Small pockets in the temple allowed for them to be wiped clear.

111 Rawson, A. (2014) *The British Army 1914–1918*. Stroud: The History Press.

112 Anon. (2015) *From Tradition to Protection – British Military Headgear in the First World War.* Ypres: Philippe Oosterlinck Collection - In Flanders Field Museum.

113 Roynon, G. (ed.) (2006) *Home Fires Burning: The Great War Diaries of Georgina Lee.* Stroud: The History Press.

114 *Ibid.*

115 Van Emden, R. (ed.) (2009) *Sapper Martin. The Secret Great War Diary of Jack Martin.* London: Bloomsbury Publishing PLC:62.

116 Hansard 1803 – 2005 Soldiers' Sock – Commons 17ᵗʰ November 1914 - Hansard. millbankssystems.com.

117 War Office. (1922) Statistics of the Military Effort of the British Empire During the Great War 1914–1920. London: His Majesty's Stationery Office.

Chapter 3

1 *Sapper Alfred Jones 102816 Service Records.* (Courtesy of TNA) (2016) - www.ancestry.co.uk.

2 Less than 1% of the battalion strength.

3 *1911 Census.* (2016) – www.ancestry.co.uk.

4 *George H Ball, Sergeant MM 16795 / 102818 Service Records.* (Courtesy of TNA) (2014) - www.ancestry.co.uk / *Sapper Alfred Jones 102816 Service Records.* (Courtesy of TNA) (2016) - www.ancestry.co.uk.

5 *George H Ball, Sergeant MM 16795 / 102818 Service Records.* (Courtesy of TNA) (2014) - www.ancestry.co.uk.

6 War Office. (1915) *War Organisation. Field Service Regulations Part II. Organisation and Administration 1909 (Reprinted, with Amendments to October 1914).* London: His Majesty's Stationery Office:25.

7 Whilst units were mobilised prior to the outbreak of war, the full might of Britain's war machine was not set in motion until the deadline was passed.

8 When the orders went out for the army to mobilise, the Railway European Committee took over the railway network with immediate effect; The National Archives. HO 144/1558/230842: *WAR: Departmental action to be taken in time of War.*

9 Royal Logistics Corps Museum Archives. (2015) *Synopsis of Lectures given by Lieutenant. Col. F K Puckle. Assistant quartermaster General of the British Army January 1918.* Aldershot.

10 Such as Pimlico and Woolwich.

11 As well as conducting inspections, Q.M.G. 9 also arranged and provided the transport required for the stores, with the exception of the Royal Navy's ships. For this, Q.M.G. 9 informed the Admiralty of the supplies, men, horses, and transport vehicles that needed shipping overseas. Ordnance staff of this branch were attached to Embarkation Commandants at home ports to assist in the supervision of loading ships and duties included the preparation of 'bills of landing' that accompanied each consignment sent.

12 A covered railway goods wagon.

13 Stone, G F., and Wells, C. (1920) *Bristol And the Great War 1914-1919.* Bristol: JW Arrowsmith.

14 Edmonds, J. (1932) *History of the Great War Based on Official Documents. Military Operations France and Belgium 1914.* London: His Majesty's Stationery Office:30.

15 Alterations had to be made to Littlehampton to receive 'empties' from Calais, as smaller vessels could only dock at Littlehampton.

16 Hooper, C. (2014) *Railways of the Great War with Michael Portillo.* London: Bantam Press:53-55.

17 The National Archives. WO 95/4020/3: *War Office: First World War and Army of Occupation War Diaries, Part I: France, Belgium, and Germany: Lines of Communication. Calais Base: Chief Ordnance Officer: 1915 Nov-1915 Dec.*

18 Butler, R. (1999) *Richborough Port. Ramsgate*: Ramsgate Maritime Museum/East Kent Maritime Trust:6.

19 *Ibid*:18.

20 War Office. (1915) *War Organisation. Field Service Regulations Part II. Organisation and Administration 1909 (Reprinted, with Amendments to October 1914).* London: His Majesty's Stationery Office:90.

21 War Office. (1917) *War Establishments. Field Service Pocket Book 1914 (Reprinted Amendments in 1916 and 1917).* London: His Majesty's Stationery Office:136.

22 *Ibid*:155.

23 Dearle, N B. (1929) *An Economic Chronicle of the Great War for Great Britain and Ireland 1914–1919.* London: Humphrey Milford/Oxford University Press:121.

24 The National Archives. WO 95/4020/3: *War Office: First World War and Army of Occupation War Diaries, Part I: France, Belgium, and Germany: Lines of Communication. Calais Base: Chief Ordnance Officer: 1915 Nov-1915 Dec.*

25 France and Belgium.

26 War Office. (1917) *War Establishments. Field Service Pocket Book 1914 (Reprinted Amendments in 1916 and 1917).* London: His Majesty's Stationery Office:24.

27 The extensive canal network in Belgium and France was ideal to assist the conveyance of goods, one which the British Army used to profound effect. The Royal Engineers Inland Water Transport Section was formed in December 1914, and made effective use of the French barges and canals to relieve pressure on the railways.

28 War Office. (1917) *War Establishments. Field Service Pocket Book 1914 (Reprinted Amendments in 1916 and 1917). London: His Majesty's Stationery Office*:25-26.

29 *Ibid*:12.

30 A fighting unit, of which Bristol's Own belonged had its own horse and wagon transport that was used to carry soldier's baggage to new billets, as well as provided all food, ammunition, and stores (including clothing) to the unit whilst at the front.

31 'Trains' also referred to transport vehicles at divisional and brigade level.

32 The National Archives. WO 95/291/2: *War Office: First World War and Army of Occupation War Diaries, Part I: France, Belgium, and Germany: Second Army: Headquarters Branches and Services: Deputy Assistant Director Transport.*

    The 177th Tunnelling Company was assigned on its formation at Terdgehem, Belgium four lorries from G.H.Q on 25th May 1915. It of interest to note that in June 1916 the lorries were inspected but without a favourable outcome, as Captain Rendell (M.T. Inspection Branch) reported on 15th June 1916, regarding the Peerless lorries of 177th Tunnelling Company 'These lorries were found to be in a very poor condition; many of the parts were loose and petrol was dripping …. Conditions of the vehicles point to the fact that they are not inspected frequently. Brought the matter to the notice of XIV. Corps.' (The National Archives. WO 95/291/2: *War Office: First World War and Army of Occupation War Diaries, Part I: France, Belgium, and Germany: Second Army: Headquarters Branches and Services: Deputy Assistant Director Transport*). This speaks volumes about conditions at the front

33 Garages and workshops existed on the Line of Communication to repair motor vehicles. Without frequent inspection within the units, small repairs that could be fixed easily quickly turned into large repairs that took time and required more parts.

34 The National Archives. WO 95/291/2: War Office: *First World War and Army of Occupation War Diaries, Part I: France, Belgium, and Germany: Second Army: Headquarters Branches and Services: Deputy Assistant Director Transport.*

35 Belgian locomotives and rolling stock were also transported south into France to ensure they didn't fall into German hands.

36 The National Archives. WO 95/4046/2: *War Office: First World War and Army of Occupation War Diaries, Part I: France, Belgium, and Germany: Lines of Communication. Rouen Base: Chief Ordnance Officer: 1916 May–1916 Jul.*

37 The National Archives. WO 95/4020/1: *War Office: First World War and Army of Occupation War Diaries, Part I: France, Belgium, and Germany: Lines of Communication. Calais Base: Chief Ordnance Officer: 1915 Apr–1915 Aug.*

38 The insatiable appetite of the British Army for uniform would see the Line of Communication network expand to such enormous proportions that, by the end of the war, it met with an ever-expanding trench system to resemble spreading tree roots.

39 War Office. (1915) *War Organisation. Field Service Regulations Part II. Organisation and Administration 1909 (Reprinted, with Amendments to October 1914). London: His Majesty's Stationery Office*:36.

40 Royal Logistics Corps Museum Archives. (2015) *Miscellaneous Papers-Army Ordnance Corps and Army Service Corps Archives*. Aldershot.

41 The National Archives. WO 95/404: *War Office: First World War and Army of Occupation War Diaries, Part I: France, Belgium, and Germany: Third Army: Army Troops. No. 177th Tunnelling Company Royal Engineers.*

42 Royal Logistics Corps Museum Archives. (2015) *Lecture of the Army Ordnance Department-It's Organisation and Duties at Home and in the Field. Lieutenant Colonel T.B.A. Leaky. Army Ordnance Department. Revised 30th September 1916.* Aldershot.

43 Royal Logistics Corps Museum Archives. (2015) *Miscellaneous Papers-Army Ordnance Corps and Army Service Corps Archives.* Aldershot.

44 The National Archives. WO 95/4020/5: *War Office: First World War and Army of Occupation War Diaries, Part I: France, Belgium, and Germany: Lines of Communication. Calais Base: Chief Ordnance Officer: 1916 Apr–1916 Jun.*

45 The National Archives. WO 95/4020/1: *War Office: First World War and Army of Occupation War Diaries, Part I: France, Belgium, and Germany: Lines of Communication. Calais Base: Chief Ordnance Officer: 1915 Apr–1915 Aug.*

46 This number did not include men that worked on the Line of Communication or medical personnel.

47 Royal Army Logistics Museum Archives. (2015) *General Scheme of Supply of a Division from the Bases to the Trenches.* Aldershot.

48 Bull, S. (ed.) (2008) *An Officer's Manual of the Western Front 1914-1918.* London: Conway:56; War Office. (1917) *War Establishments. Field Service Pocket Book 1914 (Reprinted Amendments in 1916 and 1917).* London: His Majesty's Stationery Office:121.

49 Henniker, A M. (1937) *Official History of the Great War. Transportation on the Western Front 1914–1918.* London: His Majesty's Stationery Office.

50 Bradshaw, G. (1913 Reprinted 2012) *Bradshaw's Continental Railway guide book of 1913.* Newton Abbot: Old House Books.

51 Hooper, C. (2014) *Railways of the Great War with Michael Portillo.* London: Bantam Press:19-50.

52 Henniker, A M. (1937) *Official History of the Great War. Transportation on the Western Front 1914–1918.* London: His Majesty's Stationery Office:49.

53 *Ibid*:55.

54 The National Archives. WO 95/4020/3: *War Office: First World War and Army of Occupation War Diaries, Part I: France, Belgium, and Germany: Lines of Communication. Calais Base: Chief Ordnance Officer: 1915 Nov-1915 Dec.*

55 The National Archives. WO 95/4020/5: *War Office: First World War and Army of Occupation War Diaries, Part I: France, Belgium, and Germany: Lines of Communication. Calais Base: Chief Ordnance Officer: 1916 Apr–1916 Jun.*

56 If sited close enough to the base port, then motor transport could be used in lieu of railways. In the case of St Omer Advance Supply Depot, it had all three modes of transport available to it – rail, water, and motor.

57 The National Archives. WO 95/4020/3: *War Office: First World War and Army of Occupation War Diaries, Part I: France, Belgium, and Germany: Lines of Communication. Calais Base: Chief Ordnance Officer: 1915 Nov-1915 Dec.*

58 Royal Logistics Corps Museum Archives. (2015) *Miscellaneous Papers-Army Ordnance Corps and Army Service Corps Archives.* Aldershot.

59 Henniker, A M. (1937) *Official History of the Great War. Transportation on the Western Front 1914–1918.* London: His Majesty's Stationery Office:1.

60 *Ibid*:49.

61 Divisions and corps moved in and out of sections and could be sent to other Army area, the advantages of which prevented complacently, whilst also relieved the stress and pressure

men endured in dangerous sectors. Fresh recruits and new battalions could be sent to a quiet, safer sector to acclimatise to trench life (Barton, P. and Vandewalle, J. (2007) *Beneath Flanders Fields. The Tunnellers War 1914 -1918*. Staplehurst: Spellmount:67).

62 Grieve, G., and Newman, B. (1936 Reprinted 2006) *The Story of the Tunnelling Companies, Royal Engineers, during the World War*. Uckfield: Naval & Military Press:75.

63 Barton, P. and Vandewalle, J. (2007) *Beneath Flanders Fields. The Tunnellers War 1914 -1918*. Staplehurst: Spellmount.

64 The National Archives. WO 95/404: *War Office: First World War and Army of Occupation War Diaries, Part I: France, Belgium, and Germany: Third Army: Army Troops. No. 177th Tunnelling Company Royal Engineers*.

65 War Office. (1915) *War Organisation. Field Service Regulations Part II. Organisation and Administration 1909 (Reprinted, with Amendments to October 1914)*. London: His Majesty's Stationery Office:36.

66 Royal Army Logistics Museum Archives. (2015) *General Scheme of Supply of a Division from the Bases to the Trenches*. Aldershot:11.

67 McHenry, I. (2015) Subterranean Sappers – A History of 177th Tunnelling Company RE From 1915 to 1919. London: Uniform Press Limited:26; *Third Battle Ypres 1917 WW1 Footage Hell Fire Corner Menin Road Then and Now*. (2017) - www.youtube.com/watch?v=CKTRk7lrm7c.

68 Royal Army Logistics Museum Archives. (2015) *General Scheme of Supply of a Division from the Bases to the Trenches*. Aldershot:10.

69 If the Railhead was large enough, as at Poperinghe and Ypres, lorries were reversed up to the railway wagons, where the stores and supplies were loaded straight from wagon to lorry. If this was not possible then the railway wagon was unloaded and the stores placed in a convenient location, not an efficient or productive method.

70 The National Archives. WO 95/4046/3: *War Office: First World War and Army of Occupation War Diaries, Part I: France, Belgium, and Germany: Lines of Communication. Rouen Base: Chief Ordnance Officer: 1916 Aug–1917 Dec.*

71 Forbes, A. (1929) *A History of the Army Ordnance Services. Volume III The Great War*. London: The Medici Society Limited:46,70.

72 Royal Army Logistics Museum Archives. (2015) *General Scheme of Supply of a Division from the Bases to the Trenches*. Aldershot:11.

73 Royal Army Logistics Museum Archives. (2015) *General Scheme of Supply of a Division from the Bases to the Trenches*. Aldershot:11.

74 During October 1915, the 17th Divisional Train had taken over a camp in fields in BusseBoom, Belgium, where conditions were similar to those in the front line. 'Rain again all day, camp's nothing but a sea of mud now – fortunately the horse standings put down by the 3rd Divl [Divisional] Train are very good and holding out well – most of lines have some sort of wind screen erected and in some cases partially roofed in, so that the horses are doing well…'. Congestion and the state of the roads all had an impact on the movement to goods, which the 17th Divisional Train experienced first-hand when they 'left the dump at 4.30pm, returned to camp 2.30am…'. Passing through a heavily shelled Ypres, the route back was compounded yet further by a convoy of ten wagons, loaded with straw and destined for men in the trenches. Adding further to the congestion, conditions became so bad that on 25th November 1915, a Corps Road Control Scheme was instigated in the Ypres Salient.

75 Issuing a map to show which roads were 'up' and which 'down,' the Corps Road Control
    Scheme created, in effect, a large 'one way' system. Indicating which roads could take
    single or double lines of traffic, one of the most dangerous places the wagons had to
    negotiate when taking goods to the front was an important intersection immediately
    outside Ypres.

    Under constant observation and well within range of German artillery, the road
    intersection known as 'Hell Fire Corner' was to have a canvas screens erected to restrict the
    enemy's visibility of British transport and troop movements. Wagon drivers galloped their
    horses through and motor transport sped up to pass the intersection as rapidly as possible;
    for the same safety reasons, many such movements were carried out at night. Original film
    footage of Hellfire Corner still exists and can be viewed, along with the various modes
    of transport used to pass through a ruined Ypres (including Decauville Light Railway
    tracks) - *The Western Front Today - Hellfire Corner. (2016) -www.firstworldwar.com/today/*
    hellfirecorner.htm; Third Battle Ypres 1917 WW1 Footage Hell Fire Corner Menin Road
    Then and Now. (2017) - www.youtube.com/watch?v=CKTRk7lrm7c.

76 An emotive subject, when horses were wounded, they were sent to veterinary hospital to
    recover and rest, just like a soldier. There were even horse ambulances. Different breeds of
    horses and mules were suited to distinct types of roles. Mules were pack animals and could
    carry heavy loads and were usually used in the final stages of moving food and ammunition
    to the trench dumps, often struggling over duckboards leading to the front line. Nevertheless,
    they had an inherent ability to stay shore footed as they made their way around shell holes
    on-route to the front.

77 War Office. (1917) *War Establishments. Field Service Pocket Book 1914 (Reprinted*
    Amendments in 1916 and 1917). London: His Majesty's Stationery Office:134.

78 *Ibid*:134.

79 *Ibid*:134.

80 Forbes, A. (1929) *A History of the Army Ordnance Services. Volume III The Great War.*
    London: The Medici Society Limited:77.

81 Corps routine Orders Sunday 6th February 1916. The National Archives. WO 95/753/3: *War*
    Office: First World War and Army of Occupation War Diaries, Part I: France, Belgium, and
    Germany: 5th Corps: Headquarters Branches and Services: Adjutant and Quarter-Master
    General.

82 The National Archives. WO 95/4020/5: *War Office: First World War and Army of Occupation*
    War Diaries, Part I: France, Belgium, and Germany: Lines of Communication. Calais Base:
    Chief Ordnance Officer: 1916 Apr–1916 Jun.

83 Corps routine Orders Friday 13th March 1916. The National Archives. WO 95/753/3: *War*
    Office: First World War and Army of Occupation War Diaries, Part I: France, Belgium, and
    Germany: 5th Corps: Headquarters Branches and Services: Adjutant and Quarter-Master
    General.

84 Edmonds, J. (1932) *History of the Great War Based on Official Documents. Military*
    Operations France and Belgium 1916. London: MacMillan and Co Limited:97.

85 The Princess Mary Gift Fund box was an embossed brass box paid for by a public fund
    backed by Princess Mary. Issued as a present Christmas 1914, the box contained a variety of
    items such as tobacco and chocolate.

86 Forbes, A. (1929) *A History of the Army Ordnance Services. Volume III The Great War.*
    London: The Medici Society Limited:87.

Chapter 4

1   The Tailor and Cutter Journal. 17th June 1915. Manchester City Galleries: Gallery of Costume, Platt Hall.

2   Doyle, P. (2008) *Introducing Tommy's War. British Military Memorabilia 1914-1918*. Marlborough: The Crowood Press.

3   Rawson, A. (2014) *The British Army 1914–1918*. Stroud: The History Press.

4   *Ibid.*

5   Doyle, P. (2008) *Introducing Tommy's War. British Military Memorabilia 1914-1918*. Marlborough: The Crowood Press.

6   Brown, M. (1999) *Tommy Goes to War*. Stroud: Tempus Publishing Limited:57.

7   *Ibid*:60.

8   Van Emden, R. (ed.) (2009) *Sapper Martin. The Secret Great War Diary of Jack Martin*. London: Bloomsbury Publishing PLC:93.

9   *Ibid*:95.

10 War Office. (1922) *Statistics of the Military Effort of the British Empire During the Great War 1914–1920*. London: His Majesty's Stationery Office:869.

11 The Tailor and Cutter Journal. 10th August 1916. Manchester City Galleries: Gallery of Costume, Platt Hall.

12 The National Archives. WO 95/4020/3: *War Office: First World War and Army of Occupation War Diaries, Part I: France, Belgium, and Germany: Lines of Communication. Calais Base: Chief Ordnance Officer: 1915 Nov-1915 Dec.*

13 *Johan Regheere. Local Historian, Belgium* (2016)

14 George was most likely quickly elevated to the rank of 'Tunneller' based on his experience as a Coal Face Examiner in civilian life.

15 George H Ball, Sergeant MM 16795 / 102818 Service Records. (Courtesy of TNA) (2014) - www.ancestry.co.uk.

16 John, R K. (2015) *Battle Beneath the Trenches. The Cornish Miners of 251 Tunnelling Company RE*. Barnsley: Pen and Sword Military:23.

17 A term coined from the unique way in which specialist miners dug out the sewers and underground railway tunnels beneath London and Manchester – lying on an angled board and 'kicking' out with both feet the clay spoil with a spade.

18 Barton, P. and Vandewalle, J. (2007) *Beneath Flanders Fields. The Tunnellers War 1914 -1918*. Staplehurst: Spellmount:65; *Currency Converter 1915 to 2005 The National Archives / 2005 to 2017 This is Money (2017)* - www.nationalarchives.gov.uk/currency/results.asp#mid / www.thisismoney.co.uk/money/bills/article-1633409/Historic-inflation-calculator-value-money-changed-1900.html.

19 John, R K. (2015) *Battle Beneath the Trenches. The Cornish Miners of 251 Tunnelling Company RE*. Barnsley: Pen and Sword Military:33.

20 Grieve, G., and Newman, B. (1936 Reprinted 2006) *The Story of the Tunnelling Companies, Royal Engineers, during the World War*. Uckfield: Naval & Military Press.

21 McHenry, I. (2015) *Subterranean Sappers – A History of 177th Tunnelling Company RE From 1915 to 1919*. London: Uniform Press Limited:40.

22 *Ibid.*

23 Guncotton was initially use as the main explosive in the tunnels. Invented in 1845, guncotton was made from cotton dipped in a mixture of acids and was intended to be used

as a propellant for munitions. Waste fibres, dust and rags produced in the manufacturing of textiles are flammable, so combine this with chemicals and the effect proved powerful.

24 Tunnellers packed explosives into the gallery and tamped it with sandbags, left a space and then packed the next set of explosives. This was repeated until the required amount of explosive was set, controlling the direction of the blast. Ammonal was later used as it was more stable than guncotton. Supplied in waterproof bags, calculations were needed to work out the correct number of explosives to use, type of geology, and position and depth of friendly mines, (John, R K. (2015) *Battle Beneath the Trenches. The Cornish Miners of 251 Tunnelling Company RE*. Barnsley: Pen and Sword Military:54-55).

25 Stockwin, A. (ed.) (2005) *Thirty Odd Feet Below Belgium. An Affair of Letters in the Great War 1915–1916*. Tunbridge Wells: ParaPress Limited:39.

26 The camouflet was used underground to destroy galleries. If the enemy was detected, the camouflet could be bored in the direction of the noise and fired to bring the enemy gallery down. Both sides were trying to 'out dig' each other and blow mines to destroy sections of the front, aiding their advancements into no man's land.

27 *1911 Census*. (2016) – www.ancestry.co.uk.

28 Tunnellers worked in constant water regardless of the season and pumps were needed to stop flooding. Oxygen was a big issue, with air pumps operated by hand, whilst gas, the old enemy of a miner, had to be overcome. Pockets of carbon monoxide could be hit whilst digging and lesser amounts could render a man unconscious (John, R K. (2015) *Battle Beneath the Trenches. The Cornish Miners of 251 Tunnelling Company RE*. Barnsley: Pen and Sword Military:38) *Ibid*:50). Despite these conditions and hardships, the rate the Tunneller could dig was extraordinary. During June 1916, the 177th, removed 36ft (11m) of clay from a gallery supported with timber that measured just 4ft 6 x 2ft 3 (1.3 x 0.38m).

29 Overall, Tunnellers and the infantry worked alongside each other without issue. 2nd Lieutenant Boothby 177th Tunnelling Company wrote on 20th March 1916 'The Guards are now in our trench sector. Gad! They're a fine lot of men.... We have several of them attached to us…' (Stockwin, A. (ed.) (2005) *Thirty Odd Feet Below Belgium. An Affair of Letters in the Great War 1915–1916*. Tunbridge Wells: ParaPress Limited:67,69). A Little over a month later however he complains about white hair due to 'stress and worry,' writing 'When in the trenches the real enemy is behind, a horrible *bete noire* which assumed the shape of working parties which are promised (and of course don't turn up), material, cooking, work reports and quarrelling with the infantry company commander of the trench, who is a G'dsman & probably a duke for all I know. Fearful swank to quarrel with duke, what! 'Fraid I am not very tactful with these people…' (*Ibid*:78).

30 *Information board Ypres Ramparts* - Ypres, Belgium (2016).

31 The National Archives. WO 95/404: *War Office: First World War and Army of Occupation War Diaries, Part I: France, Belgium, and Germany: Third Army: Army Troops. No. 177th Tunnelling Company Royal Engineers*; Further extensions and dugouts were constructed within the ramparts throughout the war.

32 Captain Philip Wheeler Bliss – First Officer Commanding, 177th Tunnelling Company RE.

33 *Barton, P. and Vandewalle, J.* (2007) *Beneath Flanders Fields. The Tunnellers War 1914 -1918*. Staplehurst: Spellmount:216.

34 In describing this situation, Lieutenant Sawers wrote 'At that time there was no living accommodation up in the line. Out men had to live in the ramparts at Ypres, and walk up at dusk and come back at dawn. Those were the two shifts...,' adding 'Each man knew which

face he had to be at and when, and so long as he was there at the right time we didn't mind when or how he got up. So, they used to travel up and down in little packs of two or three' (McHenry, I. (2015) *Subterranean Sappers – A History of 177th Tunnelling Company RE From 1915 to 1919*. London: Uniform Press Limited:43).

35 *Sapper Alfred Jones 102816 Service Records*. (Courtesy of TNA) (2016) - www.ancestry.co.uk.

36 Barton, P. and Vandewalle, J. (2007) *Beneath Flanders Fields. The Tunnellers War 1914 -1918*. Staplehurst: Spellmount:217.

37 Van Emden, R. (ed.) (2009) *Sapper Martin. The Secret Great War Diary of Jack Martin*. London: Bloomsbury Publishing PLC:30.

38 Pegler, M., and Chappell, M. (1996) *British Tommy 1914–18*. Oxford: Osprey Publishing.

39 The National Archives. WO 95/2002: *War Office: First World War and Army of Occupation War Diaries, Part I: France, Belgium, and Germany: 17th Division: 50th Infantry Brigade: 7th Battalion East Yorkshire Regiment*.

40 Chapman, P. (2001) *In the Shadow of Hell: Ypres Sector 1914–1918. Cameos of the Western Front*. Barnsley: Pen and Sword Military:24.

41 *Body Lice*. (2016) - www.firstworldwar.com/atoz/bodylice.htm.

42 The National Archives. WO 95/1016/2: *War Office: First World War and Army of Occupation War Diaries, Part I: France, Belgium, and Germany: 1st Australia and New Zealand Corps: Corps Troops: Corps Baths and Laundry*.

43 *Trench Fever*. (2016) - www.firstworldwar.com/atoz/trenchfever.htm.

44 Brown, M. (1999) *Tommy Goes to War*. Stroud: Tempus Publishing Limited:60.

45 *Ibid*:61.

46 Chapman, P. (2001) *In the Shadow of Hell: Ypres Sector 1914–1918. Cameos of the Western Front*. Barnsley: Pen and Sword Military:24.

47 Imperial War Museum Collection - *Photograph of Men of 2nd Battalion Cameroonians (Scottish Rifles), washing themselves in a ruined house in Lievin. 16th May 1918*. (UNI Q6620) (2016) - www.iwm.org.uk.

48 *Ibid*:20-21.

49 Anon. (2014) *Groote Beweging – Spoorlijnen en Hoofdwegen in Kaart Gebracht*. Poperinge: Stad Poperinge.

50 Chapman, P. (2001) *In the Shadow of Hell: Ypres Sector 1914–1918. Cameos of the Western Front*. Barnsley: Pen and Sword Military:20-21.

51 The National Archives. WO 95/2166: *War Office: First World War and Army of Occupation War Diaries, Part I: France, Belgium, and Germany: Baths and Laundry 5th October 1915. War Diary of the Assistant Director Medical Services. 22nd Division*.

52 Royal Logistics Corps Museum Archives. (2015) *Miscellaneous Papers-Plans for Central Delousing and Bathing Stations*. Aldershot.

53 Pers Comm. *Guy Depootr. Behind the Lines Museum, Belgium* (2016).

54 Louagie, J. (2015) *A Touch of Paradise in Hell. Talbot House, Poperinge - Every-Man's Sanctuary from the Trenches*. Solihull: Helion & Co:331.

55 Nicholls, T B. (1937) *Organisation, Strategy and Tactics of The Army Medical Services in War*. Baltimore: William Wood and Company.

56 First Battle of Ypres – 19 October to 22 November 1914.

57 Van Emden, R. (ed.) (2009) *Sapper Martin. The Secret Great War Diary of Jack Martin*. London: Bloomsbury Publishing PLC:62.

58 Carbery, A. D. (1924) *The New Zealand Medical Service in the Great War 1914 – 1918.* Auckland: Whitcombe and Tombs Limited:176-177.

59 Royal Logistics Corps Museum Archives. (2015) *Miscellaneous Papers-Fifth Army Laundry–Abbeville Instruction to Formations.* Aldershot.

60 Royal Logistics Corps Museum Archives. (2015) *Miscellaneous Papers-Inspectorate of Laundries.* Aldershot.

61 Proceedings of Conference on the Lice Problem. Held at 5th Australian Divisional Headquarters, 16th July 1917. The National Archives. WO 95/1016/2: *War Office: First World War and Army of Occupation War Diaries, Part I: France, Belgium, and Germany: 1st Australia and New Zealand Corps: Corps Troops: Corps Baths and Laundr*y.

62 Royal Logistics Corps Museum Archives. (2015) *Miscellaneous Papers-Proposed Army Laundry.* Aldershot.

63 Royal Logistics Corps Museum Archives. (2015) *Miscellaneous Papers-Statistics of Fifth Army Laundry.* Aldershot.

64 Royal Logistics Corps Museum Archives. (2015) *Miscellaneous Papers-Fifth Army Laundry–Abbeville Instruction to Formations.* Aldershot.

65 Royal Logistics Corps Museum Archives. (2015) *Miscellaneous Papers-Inspectorate of Laundries.* Aldershot.

66 Royal Logistics Corps Museum Archives. (2015) *Miscellaneous Papers-Fifth Army Laundry–Abbeville Instruction to Formations.* Aldershot.

67 Royal Logistics Corps Museum Archives. (2015) *Miscellaneous Papers-Statistics of Fifth Army Laundry.* Aldershot.

68 Royal Logistics Corps Museum Archives. (2015) *Miscellaneous Papers-Officer in Charge and Statistics of Fifth Army Laundry.* Aldershot.

69 Royal Logistics Corps Museum Archives. (2015) *Miscellaneous Papers-Statistics of Fifth Army Laundry.* Aldershot.

70 Royal Logistics Corps Museum Archives. (2015) *Miscellaneous Papers-Officer in Charge and Statistics of Fifth Army Laundry.* Aldershot.

71 Royal Logistics Corps Museum Archives. (2015) *Miscellaneous Papers-Statistics of Fifth Army Laundry.* Aldershot.

72 Brown, M. (1999) *Tommy Goes to War. Stroud*: Tempus Publishing Limited:75-77.

73 Chapman, P. (2001) *In the Shadow of Hell: Ypres Sector 1914–1918. Cameos of the Western Front.* Barnsley: Pen and Sword Military:10.

74 Pers Comm: *Bertin Deniverier. Trustee of Talbot House, Poperinge, Belgium* (2016).

75 Tomczyszyn, P. (2004) A Material Link between War and Peace: First World War Silk Postcards. In Saunders, N J. (Ed.) *Matters of Conflict: Material Culture, Memory and the First World War.* London: Routledge:123-133.

76 Doyle, P. (2008) *Introducing Tommy's War. British Military Memorabilia 1914-1918.* Marlborough: The Crowood Press.

77 Private Collection belonging to Mrs Ruth Price. Granddaughter of Sgt George Ball MM.

78 *Allen, T. Real Photographic Postcards from WW1.* (2015) - www.worldwar1postcards.com/ real-photographic-ww1-postcards.php.

79 *George H Ball, Sergeant MM 16795 / 102818 Service Records.* (Courtesy of TNA) (2014) - www.ancestry.co.uk.

80 The National Archives. WO 95/404: *War Office: First World War and Army of Occupation War Diaries, Part I: France, Belgium, and Germany: Third Army: Army Troops. No. 177th Tunnelling Company Royal Engineers.*

81 The National Archives. WO 95/1603/1: *War Office: First World War and Army of Occupation War Diaries, Part I: France, Belgium, and Germany: Divisional Troops, 18 Field Ambulance.*

82 *George H Ball, Sergeant MM 16795 / 102818 Service Records.* (Courtesy of TNA) (2014) - www.ancestry.co.uk.

83 Historical note: Some of the original house in Proven today still bear the faded paint denoting the number of Officers and or men that can be accommodated there. Residents were paid per day depending on accommodation.

84 Pers.Comm - *Guy Depootr.* Expert and collector of René Matton Photographs confirmed the identity of René Matton as the photographer of George (Behind the Lines Museum, Belgium (2016)).

85 - A 'Tommy in Wonderland' by unknown author, 58th Division, September 1917. In Louagie, J. (2015) *A Touch of Paradise in Hell. Talbot House, Poperinge - Every-Man's Sanctuary from the Trenches.* Solihull: Helion & Co:231.

86 Chapman, P. (2001) *In the Shadow of Hell: Ypres Sector 1914–1918. Cameos of the Western Front.* Barnsley: Pen and Sword Military:7.

87 Patch, H., with Van Emden, R. (2008) *The Last Fighting Tommy – The Life of Harry Patch, the Only Surviving Veteran of the Trenches.* London: Bloomsbury Publishing PLC:82-84.

88 Louagie, J. (2015) *A Touch of Paradise in Hell. Talbot House, Poperinge - Every-Man's Sanctuary from the Trenches.* Solihull: Helion & Co:237.

89 *Ibid*:235.

90 Patch, H., with Van Emden, R. (2008) *The Last Fighting Tommy – The Life of Harry Patch, the Only Surviving Veteran of the Trenches.* London: Bloomsbury Publishing PLC:84.

91 In the Talbot House archives, they have visitor's books dating to the First World War, signed by hundreds of soldiers who passed through the doors. Despite a search, no trace of George Ball has, to date, been found. Pers.Comm - *Bertin Deniverier. Trustee of Talbot House, Poperinghe, Belgium* (2016).

92 N.N, 58th Division, September 1917 - Louagie, J. (2015) *A Touch of Paradise in Hell. Talbot House, Poperinge - Every-Man's Sanctuary from the Trenches.* Solihull: Helion & Co:243.

Chapter 5

1 Forbes, A. (1929) *A History of the Army Ordnance Services. Volume III The Great War.* London: The Medici Society Limited:75.

2 The National Archives. WO 107/72: *Office of the Commander in Chief and War Office: Quartermaster General's Department: Correspondence and Papers: History of the Organisation and Development of the Quartermaster General's Services (British Armies in France). Salvage*:8.

3 Forbes, A. (1929) *A History of the Army Ordnance Services. Volume III The Great War.* London: The Medici Society Limited:75.

4 The National Archives. WO 107/72: *Office of the Commander in Chief and War Office: Quartermaster General's Department: Correspondence and Papers: History of the Organisation and Development of the Quartermaster General's Services (British Armies in France). Salvage*:8.

5 *Ibid*:2.

6   *Ibid*:2.

7   Forbes, A. (1929) *A History of the Army Ordnance Services. Volume III The Great War*. London: The Medici Society Limited:75.

8   The National Archives. WO 107/72: *Office of the Commander in Chief and War Office: Quartermaster General's Department: Correspondence and Papers: History of the Organisation and Development of the Quartermaster General's Services (British Armies in France). Salvage*:2.

9   *Ibid*:9.

10 *Ibid*:9.

11 *Ibid*:3.

12 *Ibid*:9.

13 *Ibid*:3.

14 *Ibid*:4.

15 *Ibid*:4.

16 Lance Corporal Roland Mountfort in July 1916 - Brown, M. (1999) *Tommy Goes to War*. Stroud: Tempus Publishing Limited:129.

17 The National Archives. WO 107/72: *Office of the Commander in Chief and War Office: Quartermaster General's Department: Correspondence and Papers: History of the Organisation and Development of the Quartermaster General's Services (British Armies in France). Salvage*:17.

18 *Ibid*:17.

19 *Ibid*:17.

20 The National Archives. WO 107/72: *Office of the Commander in Chief and War Office: Quartermaster General's Department: Correspondence and Papers: History of the Organisation and Development of the Quartermaster General's Services (British Armies in France). Salvage*:18.

21 *Ibid*:18.

22 *Ibid*:18.

23 *Ibid*:21.

24 The National Archives. WO 107/71: *Office of the Commander in Chief and War Office: Quartermaster General's Department: Correspondence and Papers: Salvage Directorate: Notes on Salvage*:1.

25 The National Archives. WO 107/72: *Office of the Commander in Chief and War Office: Quartermaster General's Department: Correspondence and Papers: History of the Organisation and Development of the Quartermaster General's Services (British Armies in France). Salvage*:24.

26 The National Archives. WO 107/71: *Office of the Commander in Chief and War Office: Quartermaster General's Department: Correspondence and Papers: Salvage Directorate: Notes on Salvage*:1.

27 The National Archives. WO 107/71: *Office of the Commander in Chief and War Office: Quartermaster General's Department: Correspondence and Papers: Salvage Directorate: Notes on Salvage*:4.

28 The National Archives (TNA) – WO 107 / 71 Office of the Commander in Chief and War Office: Quartermaster General's Department: Correspondence and Papers: Salvage Directorate: Notes on Salvage.

29 The National Archives. WO 107/72: *Office of the Commander in Chief and War Office: Quartermaster General's Department: Correspondence and Papers: History of the Organisation and Development of the Quartermaster General's Services (British Armies in France). Salvage*:21.

30 The National Archives. WO 107/71: *Office of the Commander in Chief and War Office: Quartermaster General's Department: Correspondence and Papers: Salvage Directorate: Notes on Salvage*:6.

31 Stedman, M. (1998) *Guillemont. Somme. Battleground Europe*. Barnsley: Pen and Sword Military:42.

32 12th July 1917.The National Archives. WO 95/82: *War Office: First World War and Army of Occupation War Diaries, Part I: France, Belgium, and Germany: General Headquarters: Branches and Services: Controller of Salvage: 1917 Jul–1917 Dec.*

33 Stedman, M. (1998) *Guillemont. Somme. Battleground Europe*. Barnsley: Pen and Sword Military:37.

34 The National Archives. WO 95/82: *War Office: First World War and Army of Occupation War Diaries, Part I: France, Belgium, and Germany: General Headquarters: Branches and Services: Controller of Salvage: 1917 Jul–1917 Dec.*

35 *Ibid.*

36 The National Archives. WO 107/71: *Office of the Commander in Chief and War Office: Quartermaster General's Department: Correspondence and Papers: Salvage Directorate: Notes on Salvage*:6.

37 *Ibid*:6.

38 *Ibid*:7.

39 *Ibid*:13.

40 *Ibid*:9-10.

41 The National Archives. WO 107/72: *Office of the Commander in Chief and War Office: Quartermaster General's Department: Correspondence and Papers: History of the Organisation and Development of the Quartermaster General's Services (British Armies in France). Salvage*:3.

42 Appendix 1. *Ibid.*

43 Forbes, A. (1929) *A History of the Army Ordnance Services. Volume III The Great War*. London: The Medici Society Limited:100.

44 30th November 1916. The National Archives. WO 95/4020/7: *War Office: First World War and Army of Occupation War Diaries, Part I: France, Belgium, and Germany: Lines of Communication. Calais Base: Chief Ordnance Officer: 1916 Sept–1916 Dec.*

45 The National Archives. WO 107/72: *Office of the Commander in Chief and War Office: Quartermaster General's Department: Correspondence and Papers: History of the Organisation and Development of the Quartermaster General's Services (British Armies in France). Salvage*:8.

46 Forbes, A. (1929) *A History of the Army Ordnance Services. Volume III The Great War*. London: The Medici Society Limited:100.

47 *Ibid*:107.

48 Ordnance Women. The Daily Mail. 30th September 1915. *Ibid*:100.

49 Salving the Battlefield Wreckage, British Military Thrift, The Times. 15th June 1916. *Ibid*:101.

50 16th December 1916. WO 95/4020/7. The National Archives. WO 95/4020/7: *War Office: First World War and Army of Occupation War Diaries, Part I: France, Belgium, and Germany: Lines of Communication. Calais Base: Chief Ordnance Officer: 1916 Sept–1916 Dec.*

51 Forbes, A. (1929) *A History of the Army Ordnance Services. Volume III The Great War*. London: The Medici Society Limited:110.

52 7,677,000 Helmets were dealt with - Forbes, A. (1929) *A History of the Army Ordnance Services. Volume III The Great War*. London: The Medici Society Limited:111.

53 *Ibid*:111.

54 15th September 1915. The National Archives. WO 95/4020/2: *War Office: First World War and Army of Occupation War Diaries, Part I: France, Belgium, and Germany: Lines of Communication. Calais Base: Chief Ordnance Officer: 1915 Nov-1915 Dec.*

55 Forbes, A. (1929) *A History of the Army Ordnance Services. Volume III The Great War*. London: The Medici Society Limited:110.

56 Forbes, A. (1929) *A History of the Army Ordnance Services. Volume III The Great War*. London: The Medici Society Limited:110.

57 *Medal Rolls Honours Book.* (Courtesy of TNA) (2015) - www.ancestry.co.uk.

58 *Ibid*:109.

59 Hammerton, J A. (1918) *A Popular History of the Great War. Volume V. The Year of Victory*. London: Fleetway House:513.

60 Forbes, A. (1929) *A History of the Army Ordnance Services. Volume III The Great War*. London: The Medici Society Limited:109.

61 16th August 1916. Return of issues to the German Prisoners of War during the month of August 1916. The National Archives. WO 95/4020/6: *War Office: First World War and Army of Occupation War Diaries, Part I: France, Belgium, and Germany: Lines of Communication. Calais Base: Chief Ordnance Officer: 1916 Jul–1916 Aug.*

62 Forbes, A. (1929) *A History of the Army Ordnance Services. Volume III The Great War*. London: The Medici Society Limited:109.

63 *Ibid*:74.

64 Royal Logistics Corps Museum Archives. (2015) *Lecture of the Army Ordnance Department-It's Organisation and Duties at Home and in the Field. Lieutenant Colonel T.B.A. Leaky. Army Ordnance Department. Revised 30th September 1916.* Aldershot.

65 26th August 1916. WO 95/4020/6: War Office: *First World War and Army of Occupation War Diaries, Part I: France, Belgium, and Germany: Lines of Communication. Calais Base: Chief Ordnance Officer: 1916 Jul–1916 Aug.*

66 Memo on Work of the Surveyor General of Supplies. The National Archives. MUN 4/6523: *War Office: Department of Surveyor General of Supplies: Miscellaneous papers relating to Contracts Department organisation and to Army contracts.*

67 Base Routine Orders No.23439 – Boot Repairs. The National Archives. WO 95/4046/3: *War Office: First World War and Army of Occupation War Diaries, Part I: France, Belgium, and Germany: Lines of Communication. Rouen Base: Chief Ordnance Officer: 1916 Aug–1917 Dec.*

68 Forbes, A. (1929) *A History of the Army Ordnance Services. Volume III The Great War*. London: The Medici Society Limited:25.

69 The Tailor and Cutter Journal. *Tailors Making and Repairing Uniforms Behind the Lines. Official Photograph issued for Press Bureau by Topical.* 10th August 1916. Manchester City Galleries: Gallery of Costume, Platt Hall.

70 Forbes, A. (1929) *A History of the Army Ordnance Services. Volume III The Great War*. London: The Medici Society Limited:101-102.

71 21st May 1918. The National Archives. WO 95/82: *War Office: First World War and Army of Occupation War Diaries, Part I: France, Belgium, and Germany: General Headquarters: Branches and Services: Controller of Salvage: 1917 Jul–1918 Dec;* Forbes, A. (1929) *A History of the Army Ordnance Services. Volume III The Great War.* London: The Medici Society Limited:104.

72 Pers.Comm - *Christine Pécourt, L'Amartinierre Courcelles-au-Bois,* France (2016).

73 Forbes, A. (1929) *A History of the Army Ordnance Services. Volume III The Great War.* London: The Medici Society Limited:104.

74 The National Archives. WO 95/4046/2: *War Office: First World War and Army of Occupation War Diaries, Part I: France, Belgium, and Germany: Lines of Communication. Rouen Base: Chief Ordnance Officer: 1916 May–1916 Jul.*

75 12th and 13th August 1916. The National Archives. WO 95/4046/3: War Office: First World War and Army of Occupation War Diaries, Part I: France, Belgium, and Germany: Lines of Communication. Rouen Base: Chief Ordnance Officer: 1916 Aug–1917 Dec.

76 The National Archives. WO 95/4041/8: *War Office: First World War and Army of Occupation War Diaries, Part I: France, Belgium, and Germany: Lines of Communication. Paris Area: Chief Ordnance Officer.*

77 Forbes, A. (1929) *A History of the Army Ordnance Services. Volume III The Great War.* London: The Medici Society Limited:104-105.

78 *Ibid*:105.

79 *Ibid*:106.

80 *Ibid*:110.

81 Base Routine Orders. No 1750. Disposal of Old Clothing as Rags. 13 July 1916. The National Archives. WO 95/4046/2: *War Office: First World War and Army of Occupation War Diaries, Part I: France, Belgium, and Germany: Lines of Communication. Rouen Base: Chief Ordnance Officer: 1916 May–1916 Jul.*

82 The National Archives. WO 95/4020/5: *War Office: First World War and Army of Occupation War Diaries, Part I: France, Belgium, and Germany: Lines of Communication. Calais Base: Chief Ordnance Officer: 1916 Apr–1916 Jun.*

83 The Tailor and Cutter Journal. 29th October 1914. Manchester City Galleries: Gallery of Costume, Platt Hall.

84 Royal Logistics Corps Museum Archives. (2015) *Memorandums by Captain Alec E Balfour, The Gordon Highlanders (Attached to A.O.D. Pimlico) 1915-1918.* Aldershot:5.

85 Memorandum Regarding Unrest Among the Wool Trade Operatives. The National Archives. MUN 4/6467: *War Office: Department of Surveyor General of Supplies: Miscellaneous Papers Mainly Concerning Supply of Army Food and Equipment.*

86 Memorandum on the Work of Contract Department of War Office. The National Archives. MUN 4/6523: *War Office: Department of Surveyor General of Supplies: Miscellaneous papers relating to Contracts Department organisation and to Army contracts.*

87 *Ibid.*

88 *Ibid.*

89 Germany had to, by the end of each month, have completed certain criteria and targets for the Armistice to stay in place. The likelihood of war breaking out again was small, nevertheless it could happen if Germany did not adhere to the terms.

90 The National Archives. WO 107/72: *Office of the Commander in Chief and War Office: Quartermaster General's Department: Correspondence and Papers: History of the Organisation and Development of the Quartermaster General's Services (British Armies in France). Salvage*:13.

91 *Ibid*:13.

92 *Ibid*:5.

93 *Ibid*:6.

94 *Ibid*:7,13.

95 1/7/1917- 174th Tunnelling Company placed at the disposal of Controller of Mines for Salvage. 2/7/1917 – 10 sappers to each Trones and Maricourt dumps. War Diary. The National Archives. WO 95/82: *War Office: First World War and Army of Occupation War Diaries, Part I: France, Belgium, and Germany: General Headquarters: Branches and Services: Controller of Salvage: 1917 Jul–1918 Dec.*

96 The National Archives. WO 107/72: *Office of the Commander in Chief and War Office: Quartermaster General's Department: Correspondence and Papers: History of the Organisation and Development of the Quartermaster General's Services (British Armies in France). Salvage*:14.

97 *Ibid*:14.

98 Forbes, A. (1929) *A History of the Army Ordnance Services. Volume III The Great War*. London: The Medici Society Limited:106.

Chapter 6

1 The National Archives. WO 95/498/5: *War Office: First World War and Army of Occupation War Diaries, Part I: France, Belgium, and Germany: Fourth Army: Army Troops:12 Casualty Clearing Station.*

2 *George H Ball, Sergeant MM 16795 / 102818 Service Records*. (Courtesy of TNA) (2014) - www.ancestry.co.uk.

3 The National Archives. WO 95/404: *War Office: First World War and Army of Occupation War Diaries, Part I: France, Belgium, and Germany: Third Army: Army Troops. No. 177th Tunnelling Company Royal Engineers.*

4 James, E A. (1924) *A Record of the Battles and Engagements of the British Armies in France and Flanders 1914–1918*. Aldershot: Gale & Polden Limited:17-27.

5 *George H Ball, Sergeant MM 16795 / 102818 Service Records*. (Courtesy of TNA) (2014) - www.ancestry.co.uk.

6 War Office (1917) *War Establishments. Field Service Pocket Book 1914 (Reprinted Amendments in 1916 and 1917)* (London) His Majesty's Stationery Office:199.

7 Bridger, G. (2013) *The Great War Handbook - A Guide for Family Historians and Students of the Conflict* (Barnsley) Pen & Sword Books.

8 Nicholls, T B. (1937) *Organisation, Strategy and Tactics of The Army Medical Services in War*. Baltimore: William Wood and Company:80.

9 *Ibid*:103-111.

10 War Office (1917) *War Establishments. Field Service Pocket Book 1914 (Reprinted Amendments in 1916 and 1917)* (London) His Majesty's Stationery Office:6,198.

11 *The Long, Long Trail.* (2015) - www.1914-1918.net.
12 *George H Ball, Sergeant MM 16795 / 102818 Service Records.* (Courtesy of TNA) (2014) - www.ancestry.co.uk.
13 Nicholls, T B. (1937) *Organisation, Strategy and Tactics of The Army Medical Services in War.* Baltimore: William Wood and Company:77-96.
14 *Ibid*:86.
15 Bridger, G. (2013) *The Great War Handbook - A Guide for Family Historians and Students of the Conflict* (Barnsley) Pen & Sword Books:169.
16 Nicholls, T B. (1937) Organisation, Strategy and Tactics of The Army Medical Services in War. Baltimore: William Wood and Company:97-100.
17 *Ibid*:127-142.
18 Elsie Knocker worked largely in the Belgian sector and was engaged in several battlefield rescues of soldiers in no man's land.
19 *Gas Gangrene in the First World War by Grace E.F. Holmes, MD, Professor of Paediatrics and of Preventive Medicine Emerita, University of Kansas School of Medicine.* (2017) – http://www.kumc.edu/wwi/index-of-essays/gas-gangrene.html.
20 *Symptoms of Gas Gangrene* (2017) - www.healthline.com.
21 *Sir Anthony Bowlby Consulting Surgeon to the B.E.F.* (2017) - www.nam.ac.uk/whats-on/lunchtime-lectures/videoarchive/warsurgery-1914-1918.
22 The National Archives. WO 188/146: *War Office: Chemical Defence Research Department and Chemical Defence Experimental Establishment, later Chemical and Biological Defence Establishment, Porton: Correspondence and Papers. Treatment of clothing with antiseptic substances in relation to wound infection.*
23 *Ibid.*
24 South London and Maudsley NHS Trust (2017) - www.slam.nhs.uk/about-us/art-and-history/our-history/1900-2000
25 *George H Ball, Sergeant MM 16795 / 102818 Service Records.* (Courtesy of TNA) (2014) - www.ancestry.co.uk.
26 *The Long, Long Trail.* (2015) - www.1914-1918.net.
27 Several hospitals were enlarged in 1917 to accommodate as many as 2,500 beds.
28 Nicholls, T B. (1937) *Organisation, Strategy and Tactics of The Army Medical Services in War.* Baltimore: William Wood and Company:162-175,190-194.
29 *George H Ball, Sergeant MM 16795 / 102818 Service Records.* (Courtesy of TNA) (2014) - www.ancestry.co.uk.
30 It served during the latter part of the war as a neurological clearing hospital.
31 *George H Ball, Sergeant MM 16795 / 102818 Service Records.* (Courtesy of TNA) (2014) - www.ancestry.co.uk.
32 Stone, G F., and Wells, C. (1920) *Bristol And the Great War 1914-1919.* Bristol: JW Arrowsmith:137.
33 Pers.Comm - Charles Booth, Soldiers Corner Historian Arnos Vale Cemetery.
34 *George H Ball, Sergeant MM 16795 / 102818 Service Records.* (Courtesy of TNA) (2014) - www.ancestry.co.uk.
35 Pers Comm: *Alice Hilda Wedlock (nee Ball)* (1990s).
36 *George H Ball, Sergeant MM 16795 / 102818 Service Records.* (Courtesy of TNA) (2014) - www.ancestry.co.uk.
37 *Grave Registration Report Form for Bristol Arnos Vale Cemetery–G H Ball.* (2015) – www.cwgc.org.

38 Crane, D. (2013) *Empires of the Dead-How One Man's Vision Led to the Creation of WW1's War Graves*. Glasgow: William Collins (Kindle Edition).

39 Kenyon, F. (1918) *War Graves: How the Cemeteries Abroad will be Designed / Report to the Imperial War Graves Commission*. London: His Majesty's Stationery Office:3.

40 Summers, J. (2007) *Remembered–The History of the Commonwealth War Graves Commission*. London: Merrell Publishers Limited.

41 Depicting part of the Somme at Longueval and Delville Wood, on 1 July 1916, the South African Regiment advanced into the wood held by Germany. With heavy and intensive fighting following, the South African Regiment was all but wiped out. Just outside Longueval, Bristol's Own, which had been held in reserve, entered the Battle of the Somme on 29 July 1916. Each blue number equals the total number of soldiers found by the Graves Detachment Units after the war, with the figures indicating where the heaviest fighting took place and where No Man's Land was.

42 Letters from Henry George (Harry) Whiting to Hilda Prowse 17th April 1919 - *Australian War Memorial: PR05609 – Collection relating to Private Henry George Whiting*. (2016) – www.awm.gov.au.

43 Summers, J. (2007) *Remembered–The History of the Commonwealth War Graves Commission*. London: Merrell Publishers Limited.

44 Leeman, J. (1962) *The Body Snatchers-Unpublished Manuscript*. In Summers, J. (2007) *Remembered – The History of the Commonwealth War Graves Commission*. London: Merrell Publishers Limited.

45 Doyle, P. (2008) *Introducing Tommy's War. British Military Memorabilia 1914-1918*. Marlborough: The Crowood Press:82

46 The National Archives. WO 95/4020/6: *War Office: First World War and Army of Occupation War Diaries, Part I: France, Belgium, and Germany: Lines of Communication. Calais Base: Chief Ordnance Officer: 1916 Jul–1916 Aug.*

47 The National Archives. WO 95/4020/7: *War Office: First World War and Army of Occupation War Diaries, Part I: France, Belgium, and Germany: Lines of Communication. Calais Base: Chief Ordnance Officer: 1916 Sept–1916 Dec.*

48 The move from metal to fibreboard Identification discs has also caused problems for archaeologists today due to the fibreboard rots away under some environmental conditions, whilst metal does not.

49 Summers, J. (2007) *Remembered–The History of the Commonwealth War Graves Commission*. London: Merrell Publishers Limited.

50 The National Archives. WO 95/1079: *War Office: Canadian Corps. Corps Troops. Canadian War Graves Detachment.*

51 Gavaghan, M. (2006) *The Story British Unknown Warrior*. Le Touquet: M & L Publications.

52 *Ibid*:15.

53 *Ibid*

54 The very first cenotaph was a wood and plaster structure erected in 1919 as one of several temporary structures erected for London Victory Parade (also known as Peace Day Parade) on 19 July 1919.

55 Gavaghan, M. (2006) *The Story British Unknown Warrior*. Le Touquet: M & L Publications.

56 Connelly, M – The First Generation of Pilgrims to the Western Front (2016) – www.gatewaysfww.org.uk

57 Miles, S T. (2016) The Western Front: Landscape, Tourism, and Heritage (Barnsley) Pen and Sword Books Limited.

58 Lowe, T. A. (1920) The Western Battlefields: A Guide to the British Line (London) Gale and Polden.

59 Connelly, M – The First Generation of Pilgrims to the Western Front (2016) – www.gatewaysfww.org.uk

60 The same can be said today of Battlefield tour coaches that flock to the Western Front every year. Incredibly popular and yet seemingly morbid at the same time. Each tourist has their own reason to visit whether it is an interest in the period, to discover a relative, a need to understand and educate.

61 *The Cloth Hall (Lakenhalle) in Ieper / Ypres.* (2016) - www.greatwar.co.uk.

62 Pers Comm: *Bertin Deniverier. Trustee of Talbot House, Poperinghe, Belgium* (2016).

Chapter 7

1 Major Cockburn, 10th Bn. Royal Rifles Corps Brown, M. (1999) Tommy Goes to War (Stroud) Tempus Publishing Limited:129.

2 Commonwealth War Graves Commission Thiepval Memorial (www.cwgc.org)

3 Within 24 hours the JCCC works quickly and sensitively to gather information and inform the next of kin, with any notification to a next of kin made with a personal visit from the nearest authority if the military unit is unable (for example, overseas). If the person is wounded or sick, the JCCC monitors their condition and current location whilst keeping the family informed. In the more serious of cases, arrangements can be made for the next of kin to be taken to individuals who are in hospitals abroad. If a family member has been injured or killed at home, then the member of armed forces is notified and returned to Great Britain to be with their next of kin. In case of the death of an individual, all repatriations are organised by the JCCC.

4 Anon. (2016) *Work of the Joint Casualty and Compassionate Centre.* Gloucester: Unpublished JCCC Promotional Leaflet.

5 Anon. (2016) *Work of the Joint Casualty and Compassionate Centre: Order of Service –* Lance Corporal John Morrison, Cuinchy France 26th July 2016 (Gloucester) Unpublished JCCC Publication.

6 Parker was identified by a similarly scratched object - Saunders, N J. (2010) *Killing Time: Archaeology And The First World War.* Stroud: The History Press: 173-5.

7 Loe, L *et al* (2014) *Remember Me To All – The archaeological recovery and identification of soldiers who fought and died in the Battle of Fromelles 1916* (Oxford) Oxford Archaeology Monograph No.23.

8 Over the decades, a local historian had pieced together research and narrowed the location of the mass burials to an area called 'Pheasant Wood.' Further research and archaeological geophysical surveys pinpointed the exact location and now the question was how to exhume the remains. Loe, L et al (2014) Remember Me To All – The archaeological recovery and identification of soldiers who fought and died in the Battle of Fromelles 1916 (Oxford) Oxford Archaeology Monograph No.23:1-7.

9 *Ibid*:10.

10 *Ibid*:154,162-163.

11 *Ibid:*210.

12 Commonwealth War Graves Commission (2016) -Pheasant Wood Cemetery – www.cwgc.org.

13 Private collection of Barry Baxter.

14 Pers.Comm - Barry Baxter.

15 Burns, M G. (1992) *British Combat Dress since 1945*. London: Arms and Armour Press.

16 Smith, D (1977) *The British Army 1965-80* (Oxford)Osprey Publishing:12.

17 Imperial War Museum Collection - Boots, ankle length DMS (UNI 6492) (2016) – www. iwm.org.uk.

18 Relief of Unemployment – Commons 7th November 1921 – Hansard.millbankssystems.com

19 The Cue Sports Cloth gave fabric for snooker and pool tables, as well as supplying film, television, and theatres.

20 *Strong, R. (2006) The* Hainsworth Story: Seven Generations of Textile Manufacturing (Huddersfield) Jeremy Mills Publishing Limited.

21 The Jacquard mechanism, first showed in 1801, simplified the way in which complex textiles such as damask were woven. This jacquard loom in action was filmed at Paisley Museum. The Jacquard mechanism, Paisley Museum (2017) - https://www.youtube.com/watch?v=OlJns3fPItE.

22 Pers.Comm - *Armley Mills Industrial Museum* – Leeds Museums and Galleries (2015).

23 Pers.Comm - *Coldharbour Mill Museum, Cullompton* - Devon (2015).

24 One of their more famous designs was a military coat made in the 1980s for Michael Jackson. Pers.Comm - Archivist - Gieves and Hawkes Archives, Bath (2015)

25 Binney, M. and Crompton, S. (2014) One Saville Row: The Invention of the English Gentleman. Gieves and Hawkes (Paris) Flammarion:186.

26 I started when I was 8

27 Initial investment is needed, but invest in a sewing machine and it can give you a wardrobe for years even decades. Arguments are made that it is cheaper to buy than to make, maybe so, but in buying fabric the quality is higher and is easier to buy 100 per cent non-synthetic fabric. The rag trade is a centuries old form of recycling but in other areas we as a modern society who pride ourselves on the ability to 'recycle' are really 'rubbish' at it at the same time. We have all this technology to aid us and yet the Ordnance Department from 110 years ago, would shake their heads at what is continually wasted.

28 *Blood Swept Lands and Seas of Red art installation by Paul Cummins and Tom Piper.* (2016) - www.hrp.org.uk.

29 *Ibid.*

30 A phrase originally coined by H G Wells, American President Woodrow Wilson added the notion that it would end ALL wars.

31 Pers.Comm - *Alice Hilda Wedlock (nee Ball)* (1990s).

32 Occasionally the modern world can be overbearing, and standing in a CWGC cemetery suddenly makes you feel humble and makes some modern problems, not irrelevant, but put into perspective.

Appendix A

1 Hunter, J A. (1922) *From the Raw Material to the Finished Product*. London: Sir Isaac Pitman & Sons Limited:46-53,119.

2 *Ibid*:118.

3 *Ibid*:43-52.

4 *Ibid*:118.

5 Palmer, M., and Neaverson, P. (2005) *The Textile Industry of South West England: A Social Archaeology*. Stroud: The History Press:17-18.
6 Yarwood, D. (1986) *The Encyclopaedia of World Costume*. London: MacMillan Publishing Company:391-392.
7 Pers.Comm - *Armley Mills Industrial Museum* – Leeds Museums and Galleries (2015).
8 *Ibid.*
9 *Ibid.*
10 Yarwood, D. (1986) *The Encyclopaedia of World Costume*. London: MacMillan Publishing Company:435.
11 Hunter, J A. (1922) *From the Raw Material to the Finished Product*. London: Sir Isaac Pitman & Sons Limited:61.
12 Yarwood, D. (1986) *The Encyclopaedia of World Costume*. London: MacMillan Publishing Company:432.
13 *Ibid*: 436.
14 Pers.Comm - *Armley Mills Industrial Museum* – Leeds Museums and Galleries (2015).
15 Hunter, J A. (1922) *From the Raw Material to the Finished Product*. London: Sir Isaac Pitman & Sons Limited:62-63.
16 *Ibid*:60.
17 Yarwood, D. (1986) *The Encyclopaedia of World Costume*. London: MacMillan Publishing Company:408.
18 Pers.Comm - *The Stroudwater Textile Trust* (2015).
19 Hunter, J A. (1922) *From the Raw Material to the Finished Product*. London: Sir Isaac Pitman & Sons Limited: 66.
20 The best teasels came from the lowlands of France and Germany.
21 Pers.Comm - *Armley Mills Industrial Museum* – Leeds Museums and Galleries (2015).
22 Pers.Comm - *The Stroudwater Textile Trust* (2015).
23 Pers.Comm - *Armley Mills Industrial Museum* – Leeds Museums and Galleries (2015).
24 *Ibid.*
25 Yarwood, D. (1986) *The Encyclopaedia of World Costume*. London: MacMillan Publishing Company:136.
26 Yarwood, D. (1986) *The Encyclopaedia of World Costume*. London: MacMillan Publishing Company: 138.
27 Pers.Comm - *Armley Mills Industrial Museum* – Leeds Museums and Galleries (2015).

Family Research

1 Information compiled from The Great War – 1914 – 1918 A Guide to WW1 Battlefields and History of the First World War (www.greatwar.co.uk) and Ancestry (www.ancestry.co.uk).
2 In 1940 during the blitz over London a large part (approximately 60 %) of the 6.5 million records were destroyed by fire and water damage following the bombing raid.
3 They have approximately 2,000 cemeteries in about 150 countries.

Index